Rescuing an Angel

Heel, Mr. Sims, Heal

PEGGY LOVELOCK

WITH

MELVA MICHAELIAN

PAGE PUBLISHING, INC.
New York, NY

First originally published by Page Publishing, Inc. 2019

Cover image by: Marianne Calnen

ISBN 978-1-64462-914-7 (Paperback)
ISBN 978-1-64462-915-4 (Digital)

Printed in the United States of America

Prologue

I found out that loving was well worth the risk,
And that even in losing, you win.

—"I Could Never Outlove the Lord"

Bad accident in crate @5AM. Seemed unaware. To Dr. Crouser @8:30AM. "Sent" for last time @9:17AM, Saturday, April 24, 2010.

This was to be the last entry in the journal that I had been keeping for over four years to monitor Mr. Sims's health.

The visit on Saturday to Dr. Crouser, our longtime veterinarian, was for another injection of Dexamethasone to help ease the inflammation that was ravaging Sim's brain. He had been receiving intravenous injections of this steroid every twelve hours since 8:30 a.m. that Wednesday. Dr. Crouser would do a neurological exam each time to see if there was any improvement. Initially, we thought we were fighting meningitis. However, as the treatments seemed to be doing less and less, it appeared that he was fighting something called GME, a far more aggressive inflammation of the brain that is a combination of mellitus, meningitis, and encephalitis. We were literally trying to spit on a huge inferno to try to put it out. And so this closed the last chapter of a twelve-and-a-half-year love affair between a dog trainer who was just starting out and had a lot to learn and the plucky little Shih Tzu who needed a second chance, who literally became her business partner and mentor.

Sim had a story to tell me. He couldn't tell me with words, but he did with his actions and responses. In order for me to interpret what he was telling me, I had to learn to "peel the onion." I may not have understood everything he was communicating, but I was able to translate a good amount of it. The following account is our story and how we taught each other to understand, love, and respect each other.

Chapter 1

Learn the rules. Then break some.

—*Life's Little Instruction Book*,
H. Jackson Brown Jr.

From the time I was a little girl, I had always loved animals, particularly dogs. I was an only child, and the neighborhood that I lived in had no children my age to play with. I was mainly in the company of adults. I yearned for a dog to be my playmate and companion. Unfortunately, my mother was a bad asthmatic, so the only pet I had as child was a turtle named Myrtle that was kept in a fish bowl. I was about four years old when I got her. At least I think Myrtle was a "her." She lived a good long life for her species, and I had fun taking care of and watching her. However, she didn't fill the need that I felt for a dog.

When I was in either first or second grade, the teacher read us the story of "The Littlest Angel" by Charles Tazewell. It was the story of a little boy who died and went to Heaven. He was only four and a half years old and very unhappy. There was a box that he had left behind under his bed, and he wanted it very badly. An angel was dispatched to get the box and bring it back to him. Even though the story struck me as sad because a little boy had died, the part that always made me cry was when the contents of the box was revealed. Among this child's treasures that he kept in the box was "a limp, tooth-marked leather strap, once worn as a collar by his mongrel dog, which had died as he had lived, in absolute love and infinite devotion." As the single child in my neighborhood, I craved that kind of relationship with a dog of my own.

That day came a couple of months after Frank and I were married. Frank and I had been high school sweethearts. After a seven-year courtship, we were married. Little did we know that very unexpectedly, we would soon be chosen by a puppy rather than the other way around.

The puppy that chose us was given to us by my friend Eva. Eva, whom I met commuting to New York City on the Long Island Railroad, bred her Toy Poodle. The dog had two puppies. One of the puppies was a carbon copy of her mother, both in size and temperament. The other was like the evil twin. She was very fussy about whom she liked and whom she didn't like and was already larger than her mother and sister. From what I was told, whenever someone came to look at the puppies, she made it clear that she didn't like them. Frank and I were visiting Eva one day. Eva had sold the "good" puppy to a family that she felt was acceptable.

Frank and I were sitting on the couch when the puppy climbed up next to me, curled up by my side, and stayed there for the rest of the visit.

"I guess the puppy has decided that she wants to go home with you. She never bothers with anyone. That's why I still have her," Eva said, smiling broadly.

I looked at Frank, wondering if we should take her. We were newly married, living in the top floor of a three-story walk-up apartment just outside of New York City. It was a very small three-room unit that was not air-conditioned, so it was brutally hot in the summer, and the boiler that ran the steam heat and hot water could be less than reliable, and it could become quite frosty in the winter. There were no designated parking spaces, so we usually had a long walk from the car to the apartment. We commuted on the train every day to and from Manhattan and worked long hours. I was an Administrative Assistant at a record company. Frank was the Benefits Manager for a large discount retail chain. Our finances were very tight. With rent, utilities, cost of commuting, and food, we often ran out of money before we ran out of month. Was adding another mouth to feed the smartest thing we could have done? And we drove to Long Island almost every weekend to visit my mother and Frank's family. Should common sense have prevailed? Of course, but being young, foolish, and impulsive, common sense was nowhere to be found, and so we couldn't resist taking the puppy. We named her Topsy. She soon outgrew her "Toy" status and became a good-sized miniature Poodle.

The only regret that I may have about our decision is that we both were uneducated in the ways of raising and training a puppy. I was the type of inexperienced owner that I now refer to as someone who wants to just "add water and stir." I thought if I just put newspaper down in the kitchen and confined the puppy there with food and water all day while we were at work, everything would just fall into place. *Wrong!* We made plenty of mistakes with her.

One of the more colorful mistakes was the day we came home from work and mutually decided that Topsy should have the run of the apartment.

"She's fairly well potty trained, and she just looks so dispirited when we get home," Frank said.

"I know. I think she would enjoy being able to sit on the couch or our bed and look out the window. After all, a puppy needs mental stimulation, right?" I added.

So the die was cast, and the next day, we didn't gate her in the kitchen. When we left, she gave us a somewhat confused look, sitting on the threshold of the kitchen. She probably was wondering why the gate wasn't blocking her. On our way home from work, a less than comfortable commute, we stopped and picked up some groceries, including cans of dog food. Frank packed each paper bag at the store. He fully packed them so that we could carry all of them in one trip to the apartment. Of course, these bags had no handles, so we had to juggle briefcases, my purse, and the heavy bags. As was usually the case, the closest parking spot was about a quarter of a mile away. We trudged up the three flights of stairs, each of us carrying two heavy grocery bags along with our other items. As we reached the second floor, the weight of the dog food cans began to tear the bottom of the bags. I wasn't sure I was going to get to the third floor with everything intact. And my legs were screaming to me to stop and rest. However, I trudged onward and upward. By the time we got to our door, both of us were exhausted. We just wanted to collapse on our couch and catch our breath.

Topsy met us at the front door. A couple of the cans fell out of the torn bottom of my grocery bag, hit the floor with a loud thud, and rolled toward her. It sounded much like thunder rolling across the sky during a storm. This didn't seem to faze Topsy at all. Her tail was wagging, and she couldn't be happier with herself. Her eyes were bright as she bounced up and down, twirling around on her hind legs, waving at us with her front paws. We quickly greeted her, rushing to put the grocery bags in the kitchen before everything we bought landed on the floor.

Once we got our breath back, we began to see what she had done during her first day of freedom. She had grabbed the end of a new roll of toilet paper and redecorated each room of the apartment with it. Paper was on the floor leading from the bathroom. She had then made a left turn and decorated our small bedroom, trailing paper up on the bed and back down again. The paper trail then led to the living room where it was wrapped around the legs of the coffee table, making a path to the dining area where the roll ran out. The rooms looked as if a bunch of errant teenagers had gone wild on Halloween. The exercise she got from doing this must have given her so much physical stimulation that she had left us several small bowel movements scattered throughout her handiwork. And after all of that hard work, she decided to "dig a nest" in one of the cushions on our second-hand, twenty-dollar couch, so that she could rest until we got home, nestling comfortably in the hole where she had exposed the white cotton-like stuffing, some of which was strewn on the carpet. I had no idea that many years later, the very mistakes I made then would become valuable learning experiences that I would refer to over and over again when I began my dog training business.

We moved to Massachusetts in 1976 when Frank accepted a lucrative job offer as a Human Resource Director at a manufacturing company. Once again, we moved into an apartment. However, this one was large, airy, and had central air-conditioning. It took

Topsy little time to adjust because the windows had large sills. They were just the right size to make a perfect perch for her. She would sit on the dining area sill that faced the parking lot and thoroughly enjoyed watching the comings and goings of the complex. She got to be known as the Poodle in the window and amused many.

The breed of dog that had been on my wish list for years was an English Bulldog. From the first time I saw one in the old movie *Since You Went Away*, I knew that I would own one someday. I saw an ad in the local paper for a six-month-old English Bulldog puppy. I called to see if the puppy was still available. The woman who had placed the ad had an English accent and asked me many questions before she agreed that we could come see "Seven Pence." Some of the questions she asked were as follows: Did we ever own a dog? Did we currently have a dog? What did we feed her? Where and how often did we walk her? How big was our apartment? Was someone at home all day with her? I felt as though she was interviewing me to adopt a child, not a dog. I told her that we had Topsy, that she was a six-year-old miniature Poodle, and what I fed her. I also told her that although we lived in an apartment, we had a nice area to walk the dog several times a day. I was not working at this time, so I would be home with the dogs.

As soon as Frank got home from work that evening, I told him that I had found an ad for a six-month-old English Bulldog. The breeder said that we could come look at the pup tonight.

"Did she say how much the puppy cost?" Frank asked me.

"No. Does that make a difference? If we can't afford her, we just won't take her," I said, with my fingers firmly crossed behind my back. Deep down, I knew that you just can't go "look" at puppies if your wallet is in your pocket.

"Let's see what happens when we get there," Frank sighed. For the twenty years Frank had known me and the many different situations we had been through, he knew me well enough to know that when I was that excited about something, there was no point in trying to change my mind.

We talked on the hour-and-a-half ride about what it would be like having two dogs and how well Topsy would accept the puppy. Were we making the right decision?

Needless to say, it was love at first sight. We had definitely made the right decision. The puppy was white with seven brown spots spattered on her body. It almost looked as if someone had shaken a paintbrush and the paint had landed randomly on her. She had the classic pushed-in face and bowed legs. She came to me immediately and pushed her large head into my leg to get my attention. I bent down to pet her and she licked my face. The owner liked us as well and agreed to sell us Seven Pence.

"You will learn that English Bulldogs are very sensitive to your emotions. It is almost as if they know what you are thinking. The breed can be very stubborn. You will know if her feelings are hurt because she will go sulk. And she'll teach you a lot if you just stay open to her moods. You can always call me if you have any questions."

As soon as we got into the car, the puppy curled up on my lap and fell asleep for the journey home. She was just a lovable dog that snored and drooled.

"Isn't she great, Frank?"

"I didn't expect the snoring, but she is really cute and loveable."

"I'm going to change her name to Mugsy. With her personality, Seven Pence seems too stuffy."

Frank agreed with my assessment. She was everything I had hoped for. Loyal, comical, uncoordinated, Mugsy was the opposite of Topsy. Topsy was less than pleased when we got home. She gave us a disgusted look and headed under our bed. Mugsy tried to follow Topsy under the bed. Because of her girth, she was stymied, so she just stayed in a puppy bow position with her rear end up in the air and her head under the bed. I don't know what she communicated to Topsy, but it didn't take too long before they were inseparable buddies. They were quite a striking pair on their walks together: the prim and proper, beautifully groomed Poodle and the lumbering, drooling English Bulldog. And Mugsy desperately wanted to sit next to Topsy on the window sills, but for obvious reasons, this was something they could not enjoy together.

In 1982, we bought our first house. It was a three-bedroom, two-bathroom ranch. The rooms were a nice size, cozy yet not cramped. The yard was one-third of an acre and had been nicely landscaped and well cared for by the previous owner. We had lost Topsy about a year earlier to the complications of diabetes. Mugsy had gone through a grieving period, looking for Topsy around the apartment and on the route that they walked each day. She seemed to be coming out of it just about the time we were getting ready to move. The house we were moving into had a large fenced-in backyard. I couldn't help but think Mugsy would really enjoy this. She would no longer be confined to leash walks and would be able to run around and enjoy the freedom.

One afternoon, on a crisp fall day, the neighborhood boys were playing football in the middle of our quiet street. I went into the backyard to see how Mugsy was enjoying her newfound space and the nice weather. She was nowhere to be found. I called her and looked all over the yard for her. I noticed that one of the gates to the front yard was slightly open. Upon further investigation, I found Mugsy sitting in the middle of the road with each team of football players on either side of her. She was sitting quietly, following the movement of the football as it was thrown back and forth over her head. It was as though she was mesmerized, sitting there, wide-eyed and drooling, as she tracked the path of the football with her eyes, her head moving back and forth. She was thoroughly enjoying it, and the boys thought that she was the greatest dog ever. She became the mascot of both teams. When I recounted the story to Frank, I said, "This is just like the child who you buy an expensive toy for and they have more fun playing with the box it came in. We bought a house with a great yard and the dog would rather sit in the middle of the road!"

Mugsy was everything the breeder told me to expect from her. The longer I had her, the closer we became. And yes, at times I felt as if she was reading my mind. If I was having a bad day, she would stay close by me, placing one of her large front paws on my feet.

When we lost her to a heart condition in 1985, Frank bought me our Chow Chow, whom we named Joi, as a Christmas present.

I was reluctant to get a puppy at this point because my health was failing and no doctor could seem to find out why.

I had done some reading about the breed and felt that I definitely had to take her to obedience classes. She was bred for temperament and was a gentle, loving dog. But anything I read about the breed strongly advised obedience training as soon as possible because the breed can be stubborn and are guard dogs by nature. Joi had a very odd trait as a puppy. She always wanted to be outside. When I would call her, she would hide under a bush and refuse to come to me. I would have to physically pick her up and bring her back into the house. She would be in the house for a short time and then want to go out again. I was confused as to what was going on with her because she was comfortable with us and seemed well adjusted to her new home. Three years later, this mystery would be cleared up. To make a very long story short, the natural gas-powered furnace was faulty, and we were all being exposed to high levels of carbon monoxide. I was left with permanent brain and neurological damage. When I asked the doctor, who was finally able to give me a diagnosis as to why I hadn't been well over the last three years, what could be done for this damage, he said, "You don't seem to understand. This damage is permanent. There is nothing we can do." I promised myself that I would do whatever I had to do to regain as much of my health back as possible. Diet change, as well as retraining my brain by learning new skills, became part of my therapy.

When Joi was a little over three months old, I enrolled her in an obedience class. The dogs in class varied in age from young puppies to one that was three years old. Having never taken an obedience class before, I didn't know what to expect or what I should expect from instructors. I was a little put off at the first lesson. The main instructor went around the room, asking people to introduce themselves and their dogs. He would then mention what the breed of dog was best suited for. When he got to me, I introduced myself and Joi. She was a beautiful bear-looking puppy with a cinnamon-colored coat and black markings around her eyes and muzzle that made her look as though she was wearing a mask. Frank and I used to affectionately call her The Bandit.

"Do you know what Chows were bred for?" he asked me.

I was a little embarrassed being put on the spot, but fortunately, I had done research on the breed.

"They were used as sled dogs," I said tentatively.

"True," the instructor said, "but do you know what else they were bred for?"

I was caught off guard. I could feel the color flushing in my cheeks.

"I'm not sure," I stammered.

"They were used for food. *People ate them!*" he said, greatly amused with the shock value of his statement. I looked down at my beautiful, loving puppy. Maybe I was being too sensitive, but the humor, if there was any in his statement, eluded me.

We went to four of the eight-week classes. The homework for the fourth week was to have the dog do a thirty-minute down stay. Not knowing any better, I took Joi into the living room, turned on the TV, and put her in a down stay. She lasted about a minute and popped up. I placed her down again and again, yet she popped up each time. I could see that she was not at all pleased with this exercise. I placed her down again, and this time, she started gnawing on my fingers. It wasn't done in a vicious manner but, rather, in annoyance with me.

I decided to call the instructor for advice. I was beginning to wonder if the puppy was too young to be expected to do a thirty-minute down stay. When I told the instructor about the problem I was having, he advised me to "don a pair of heavy gloves and hold her down for the thirty minutes." He did not feel that the exercise was too much for the puppy to do. So not knowing any better, I donned a pair of heavy gloves and placed her in a down stay for the fourth time. Now her annoyance escalated to anger. She struggled with me, growled, and nipped at the gloves. At this point, I knew Joi was not up to the task, and I wasn't going to force the issue. I felt that building a good relationship with her was more important than forcing the puppy to do some exercise. Maybe a half hour down stay was appropriate for the older dogs in the class but not my fifteen-week-old puppy. I called the instructor and said I was withdrawing from the class. I told him why, and of course, he strongly disagreed.

At that point, I started buying and reading as many different dog training books as I could find. Some of them made sense to me. Others did not. The books that relied heavily on adverse training methods did not appeal at all to me. It didn't make any sense to me to inflict pain on a dog to get them to do what you wanted them to do and expect to have a trusting relationship with them. So I educated myself with training information and used some of the techniques but let Joi tell me what worked for her and what did not. Luckily for me, she was a loyal, patient dog.

She was very forgiving when I did something that she was opposed to. I learned to read her body language by watching how she held her head, tail, or just her stance and facial expression when she was not comfortable with what I was doing with her. It didn't take very long before she had taught me one of the most important lessons of dog training. To really find out if you are getting your point across to the dog, watch his or her facial expressions, and body language. Learning this is far more important than getting the dog to learn something quickly. Some breeds are faster learners than others. That is not to say that some breeds are smarter than others. It just depends on what they were bred to do. For example, a Labrador Retriever may learn quickly how to pick up a toy and bring it to you. On the other hand, English Bulldogs, with their jowls and pushed-in face, may have a problem being able to execute this task. Thus it will take them longer to learn how to do this.

Chapter 2

What we have here is a failure to communicate.

—Cool Hand Luke, 1967

In April of 1996, my next-door neighbor, Nancy Clarkson, brought home two six-week-old puppies that were littermate sisters from a local rescue group. She proudly brought them over for me to see. They were adorable. Even though they were littermates, they didn't look it. One looked very much like a Soft Coated Wheaten terrier. The other looked like a yellow Lab/Jack Russell mix. I affectionately called them the Clarkson Terriers. Joi stood inside, looking out of the screen door with great interest in the pups.

"Aren't they just the cutest puppies you've ever seen? I couldn't decide which one to take, so I took both of them! School is closed for spring break, and we have the whole week to get them settled."

Nancy had two young teenage daughters, Colleen and Amanda. Her husband, Frank, worked long hours and Nancy was a teacher.

"What are you going to do with the puppies when you and the girls return to school next week and your husband returns to work?" I asked.

I could tell that she didn't appreciate my questions. Her eyebrows arched, and she crossed her arms over her chest. She gave me an icy stare. I knew I had touched a nerve with her.

"I'm sure I'll have them under control by the week's end," she said tersely. Nancy thought she could "just add water and stir."

Without another word, she gathered up the puppies and left. I made a small bet with myself that I would hear from her when the vacation was over.

At the end of the week, I got a call from her, asking me if I would let the puppies out a few times during the day and feed them their lunch. I was more than happy to do it because I could practice what I had learned with Joi. I thought of this new skill as part of my recuperative therapy. I went over to take care of them on Monday. Their names were Jamie and Bailey. They didn't know their names yet, and they hadn't caught on to good toilet habits either. Fortunately, I had lent Nancy a wire crate that I had used for Joi when she was a puppy. It was large enough to hold both Jamie and Bailey for the time being. I was very concerned that once the "puppy cutes" wore off, they just might find themselves back at the rescue. I decided that I would start working with them.

Each day, I worked on teaching them their names. I would hold each puppy in my arms and touch or pet each part of their body. As I touched each part of them, I would use their names, telling them what good puppies they were. This was not only to teach them their names but that the human touch was nothing to be feared. It was to be enjoyed. Once that was accomplished, I started some puppy training. This included teaching them about eliminating outside, things that were appropriate to chew and things that were not, and most importantly, human hands were never to be bitten but only "kissed." They would both give me a rather confused look when I would take them outside on leash to relieve themselves. "Go like good girls," I would tell them cheerfully. At first, I had to keep repeating this over and over again until they each did what they had to do. They would get rewarded with enthusiastic praise and a treat. Eventually, they got the hang of it and understood what my yammering meant.

To teach them that hands were to be "kissed," I would sit on the floor with them, having coated one of my hands with a thin film of peanut butter. I would extend the coated hand saying, "Kisses." Of course, they "kissed" the hand. Peanut butter was irresistible to them. After offering them the coated hand several times, I would place it behind my back and offer them the uncoated hand. If they licked it, they got a treat. If they nibbled at it, I would say, "No bite, kisses," as I offered the coated hand again. I did sustain a few nips with sharp puppy teeth, but considering there were two puppies, barely enough to even mention. It comes with the training territory.

I kept referring to the many books I had used when I trained Joi. As they grew and matured, the training became more intense. I found that the best way to train them was separately. I would give one a special treat and put her in her crate while I worked the other one outside. This not only gave them one-on-one attention; it also taught them that they could be separated and comfortable on their own. They learned their lessons well and could perform all the basic training commands: heel, sit, down, stand, stay, wait, and leave it by the time they were eight months old.

The next step was to work them together. Each would be a distraction to the other, and although they both knew the commands, when they worked together, it became a whole different situation. Eventually, they figured out that I wanted them to obey the commands no matter what was going on. They would look at each other and then comply.

One of the ways I got them to understand this concept was to begin doing the half hour down stay with them. This exercise reinforces with the dog that you are the pack leader. The exercise puts you in charge of space and time. I would go over to Nancy's in the afternoon and put the puppies in a down stay, about six feet away from the couch in her family room, and about three feet from each other. I would then sit on the couch, set a timer, and begin saying my Rosary. I knew that my prayers would take just about half an hour. You can guess that I would always say a prayer that Jamie and Bailey would not break the down stay. If they did, I would have to replace them and start the half hour period all over again. It sometimes made for a very long afternoon. It didn't take them too long to catch on to what I wanted, and soon they would fall asleep for most of the half hour. My prayers were answered.

Once they were used to working together, I began taking them for walks around the neighborhood. They would heel, walking on my left side in perfect unison. I would take them to the park and put them through their paces, having them sit/stay, down/stay, and stand/stay together. At times, I would have one do one type of stay while the other was doing a different one. People began watching all of this. A few struck up a conversation with me.

"These dogs are wonderful. They are so well trained. Where did you take them for training?"

When I told them that I did the training, they asked me if I had my own business. I laughed and would say this was a labor of love.

"You know, you really should start your own dog training business. These dogs are amazing, and a lot of dog owners would give their right arm to have their dogs be this well behaved."

After thinking about it and talking it over with Frank, I decided I was ready to start my own training business. Although my health was far from perfect, I felt that I could do it. The timing was good because Frank had been downsized from his executive position and was trying to start his own consulting business. I was not only skeptical of his decision to consult, I was very worried and afraid. Throughout our marriage, we had faced periods of unemployment. This time, however, we owned a house and had a mortgage to pay every month.

In May of 1997, I started my dog training business and named it *Turn Over a New Leash*. I did not have to finance any large startup costs. Other than buying the office supplies and leashes for training, the costs were minimal. The front lawn of my home provided the space for my training sessions, weather permitting. Another expense that I had was advertising my new business. I placed ads in a small local newspaper that was delivered weekly. There was no charge for this paper, and it had a fairly large circulation. Of course, the advertising was how it made money. I wanted something catchy, so I would make up funny lines such as, "Do you feel like putting your dog in your next yard sale?" Then the following week, my ad would say, "Was the dog the only item *not* sold in your yard sale?" For the Christmas holidays my ad read, "Is your dog naughty or nice?" These lines were always followed by, "Call *Turn Over a New Leash*— personal, one-on-one dog training." If nothing else, these ads drew attention to my business, and people would look for them each week for a laugh.

I felt that there was a place for personal training, as opposed to the usual group training, because of the one-on-one attention that could be given to both the owner and the dog. I did not like the use of heavily aversive methods, nor did I care for all positive (treat) methods. I felt that a foundation of a solid relationship and understanding of what the dog was experiencing was a winning combination.

I developed a temperament test that seemed to fairly accurately sort out a dog's temperament. There were six things that I did to determine the dog's temperament. To see how well the dog was socialized with people and to determine how a particular dog processed a situation, I would happily call the dog to me. After petting and talking to the dog, I would stop the interaction, fold my arms, and look away. I would watch carefully to see what the dog did. Did the dog try to reengage me? Did it look at its owner for guidance? Did it try to amuse itself? Or did it become worried and shut down by obsessively sniffing the area? All these different reactions would tell me whether the dog was an independent thinker, unsure, looking for help from its owner, or so unsure of itself that it became shy and timid. To learn whether the dog was dominant or submissive, I would ask the owner to put the dog on its back. Did the dog readily comply or did it kick, struggle, or strike a protective pose? The remaining four exercises tested the dog for physical sensitivity, noise sensitivity, hand shyness, and food aggression. As I became more experienced, I was able to fine tune my skills to glean even more insight into the dog's personality.

In early spring, Joi became very ill with a serious liver disease. As the spring passed and the summer progressed, my business grew, primarily through recommendations from one person to another as well as the ads I placed in the weekly newspaper. Unfortunately, in August, Joi had become so ill that we had to "send her to the Rainbow Bridge." She was eleven years old, just a couple of months shy of her twelfth birthday. I was devastated. To this day I still have one of her puppy teeth. I made the proclamation to Frank, friends, and even some clients: "No more dogs. I can't have my heart broken again. Because of training I get all the puppy kisses and interactions with dogs that I need." *Famous last words.*

Chapter 3

Does love have a beginning that a meeting's measured by?
Does it happen in a moment like white lightning from the sky?
Can you tell me its dimensions-just this wide and just this high?
When did I start to love you?

—"When Did I Start to Love
You?" Gloria Gaither

In September, I received a call from a woman with a Shih Tzu. She complained that she was having a lot of problems with him. I cringed when she called him a "bad dog." When I asked her for more information, she said that she had four children ages four through eight. The dog's name was Simba and was purchased by her husband for their youngest daughter, Monica.

However, she and her husband were in the midst of a divorce, and she needed help training the dog because "he was awful." Simba was not quite two years old and hadn't been neutered yet. I made an appointment for her and the young dog, and she came in to see me in a few days. When she pulled into my driveway, she got out of the car and was very annoyed because the dog had gotten carsick. "What is wrong with you? Bad dog! You make a mess in the car every time. I'm sick and tired of it!" I asked if this was an unusual occurrence. She said, "No," that he always got car sick.

She transported him in a small blue travel crate. I suggested that she make sure that the crate was facing forward in her van. Sometimes a dog will get car sick riding backward because of the unusual motion. She took him out of the car. He was on the larger side for a Shih Tzu, which also annoyed her. I got the impression that she had wanted to breed him, but he wasn't developing the way she had expected. He also looked as though he had never been groomed in the time she had him. His coat was matted and a nondescript, off-white color.

He came over to me and looked at me with very intelligent, beautiful, wide-set brown eyes. To me, he also somewhat resembled Yoda, the very wise character from Star Wars. My observation of this proved to be more accurate than I knew at the time. I quietly greeted him, and he gave me the signature Shih Tzu swallow. I later learned that the swallow meant "I'm thinking about things and figuring out what's going on here." I listened to all the issues, or rather as she described them, problems that she was having with him. "Simba steals food every chance he gets. His toilet habits also leave much to be desired." She told me that the back bedroom was his place of choice to eliminate. I asked if she was planning to have him neutered, explaining the health and behavior benefits and how it might help the elimination issues. She said she would think about it.

I then proceeded to do the temperament test. He rated very well with Calm/Easygoing/Responsive as his primary personality and Submissive as his underlying trait. The owner told me that one of her boys was in charge of taking care of Simba, feeding and walking him. She also said that the boy had a slight disability that impaired his walking. The dog was always walked to eliminate and the length of the walk depended on the mood of her son. Consequently, Simba sometimes eliminated when he returned home rather than on the walk.

"He's a really nice dog, and I think he will do very well with the training. He just needs some guidance and direction," I told her.

"I don't know about that. He's been a big disappointment to me. I really don't think he's all that smart. But I'll make an appointment for the same time next week."

"That's fine. I'll see you then."

When she returned the following week, I asked her, "How did the training go this week?"

"Not bad and I made an appointment to get the dog neutered."

"Good, especially for the dog's health."

I discreetly suggested that she have the dog groomed before the neutering. The poor little guy was really a mess, and I was concerned. She agreed. We then proceeded with the next lesson. Simba appeared to worship the ground she walked on. However, when she told me of his bad habits, I asked her how she handled the situations.

"He makes me so angry that sometimes I strike him, shake him, or throw him across the room. He just doesn't get the fact that he's supposed to relieve himself outdoors and not try to steal food off the dining table."

It made me very upset, but I kept my thoughts to myself and told her that her method of discipline could harm the dog and would do nothing to build a strong relationship. When the lesson ended, I told her to call me when the vet felt that Simba would be healed enough to resume training.

"He'll be fine. I'll make an appointment for the next week."

"That's only about four days after the dog has the surgery. It might be too soon for the little guy. He may not be up to it."

"I'll see you next week," she said firmly.

I disapproved of how she treated her pet, but just maybe I could educate her.

I called her a few days after Simba had his surgery to see about how he was feeling and about possibly changing her appointment. She was adamant that she would be coming on her usual day. I asked if the vet said it was okay.

"He's fine. He'll be up to it. I want to work on food aggression. He's getting very bad, and no matter how much I discipline him, he still goes after any food that he can steal."

That morning was unusually cold. She had Simba groomed before the neutering, and he had been so matted that all the groomer could do was shave him down. I asked if she had a sweater for him.

She said, "No, of course not, he's a dog."

But I could see him shivering with the cold, so I decided to work with him in the house where he would be warm and comfortable. I made up a "meal" on a paper plate, which consisted of broiled leftover chicken breast, some Swiss cheese, and some bran flakes. I put a twenty-foot leash on him and told her to hold it. I put the plate on the floor and let him approach it and start to eat. I approached him, speaking softly, and took the plate away. I was fully expecting him to respond negatively, but instead, he wagged his tail at me and looked at me with full trust. We repeated the exercise three more times, and I could not get him to elicit so much as a growl. I asked her when he showed aggression regarding food. She said when the kids dropped something on the floor and then tried to get it away from him. I explained to her that to the dog, whatever hit the floor was his and for the kids to be more careful. I also had started working on the "Leave It" command with her. The "Leave It" command teaches the dog to ignore a person, other dog or animal, or object and look at the handler who gave the command. The dog is immediately praised and given a treat. I told her to teach it to the kids so that if Simba went for something, they could tell him "Leave It," and he would divert his attention from the "forbidden object" to them then give him a treat. She still seemed very disgruntled with the dog but said she would give it a try.

Chapter 4

Tell me just how many dates it takes for love to really start?
And just how many kisses will turn "love" into an art?
When does the magic moment come to give away your heart?
When did I start to love you?

—Gloria Gaither

It was now mid-October, 1997. A relative had passed away, and Frank and I were getting ready to travel to Long Island for the funeral the next day. It was about 10:30 p.m. when the phone rang. It was Simba's owner. She said, "Either you take this damn dog or he's going to the pound."

"What happened?" I asked her.

"He tried to bite one of the kids."

Being a trainer, I asked for more details. It seems that the kids were trying to throw him into the bathtub with their toys.

"He's really a bad dog. I've had enough of him," she said angrily.

I told her to calm down. "We've all been there when we've lost all patience with the dog, and five minutes later, we're giving them a kiss and a treat."

She was having none of it. I told her to wait a couple of weeks and call me if she still wanted to give him up. As a professional trainer, I could not readily agree to take the dog. Given the woman's demeanor, I didn't know if she had a hidden agenda. She could, at some point, say that I wanted the dog and talked her into giving him to me. When I got off the phone, I told Frank, "Even though I don't want another dog, Simba is too good to go to the pound. I'll try to place him with someone who I know will take good care of him."

During the ensuing weeks, I asked several people, but there were no takers. Just before Halloween, his owner called me again. I agreed to take him. She said she would drop the kids off at school and then bring the dog to me on October 31.

A friend of mine had sent me a calendar that has a saying for each day of the year. I read the one for that day. It read, "In love there is power. Love can kill fear. Love can tear down walls and build bridges." It stuck in my head because of Simba arriving today and his background. It didn't take too long before I realized how true and pertinent this saying was going to be.

Just after 9:00 a.m. on Halloween morning, the doorbell rang. It was Sim's owner holding the blue travel crate. She launched it across my slate entryway like a bowling ball and said, "I have more out in the car. I'll be right back." I thought she meant that she was going to get the dog, so I moved the crate out of the way. As I picked it up, I could feel something move inside it. I looked in the front opening, and there were those beautiful brown eyes looking at me and then the "swallow." I was appalled at the way he was being treated but held my thoughts while she threw me his toys, wire crate, and food. She wanted the travel kennel back because two weeks earlier, she had gotten another puppy. I could feel the hair bristling on the back of my neck. She asked if the kids could "visit" Simba. I just shrugged and suggested that it was probably best for all involved to make a clean break, but if it was terribly traumatic for the kids to call me and I would agree to set something up. Needless to say, that call never came…thank God.

Chapter 5

Little by little
One step at a time
I'm learning to trust
What you're making of me.

—"Little by Little," Gloria Gaither

First order of business on the day Simba arrived was to change his name, not a major change but enough to give him a new start. His AKC papers listed his sire as Lord of Simba and his dam as Miss Sassy Pants.

This is too easy, I thought. *He's Mr. Sims!* I looked at him and tried out his new name. He looked at me and swallowed with a quizzical look and then began wagging his tail and following me around the house. When he picked up his pace, he had a swagger that always reminded everyone that saw it of the actor Jimmy Cagney. And from that day forward, he and I began the journey of alternating roles of student and teacher.

The next day, November 1, I read my saying for the day. It read, "I am loved, I can risk loving you, for the one that knows me best loves me most." If I had any doubts whether or not I had made the right decision taking Sim, this erased all of them. This saying worked both ways with me, both to Sim and Sim back to me.

I loved to kiss Sim on the top of his forehead, and he seemed to like it as well. He had his own special aroma, and I would breathe in deeply, savoring it. I think that most people are familiar with that new puppy smell that usually enchants all of us. But as the puppy matures, they seem to develop their own special scent. I first became aware of this with Topsy, several years later when we got Mugsy, and then with Joi. They became affectionately known as "the girls." I would brush each one every other day I had them. This is when I first noticed that they each had a slightly different and distinct odor. It was not noticeable until you were very close to them. Each of them were special in their own way, including their scent. Some people may think that I am a bit crazy for noticing this, but this is just one of my observations. I also would notice that if any of them did not feel well, their scent changed, not drastically but enough to alert me to keep an eye on them.

I restarted Sim's pet obedience training. He was a quick study and seemed to enjoy the interaction with me. In those first few days, he got used to the routine of the house. Sim and Frank began structuring their relationship. It was a little odd at first. Sim viewed me as the "pack leader," and although he was respectful to Frank, it appeared that he viewed him as "second in command." If I went to the fridge, Sim would keep a polite distance. However, whenever Frank was eating anything, Sim was right there to see what they could "share."

I set up his wire crate in our bedroom. This is the one that his owner had left with me. It had no mattress. I wasn't sure if this was because he might be a chewer, so I just put a soft towel in it for him. I also noticed that the top of the crate was bowed inward as if either heavy objects had been placed on top of it or that possibly the children had used it as a trampoline. He readily went into it and greatly appreciated the towel.

Next orders of business were to start working on his carsickness problem and make an appointment with our vet for a wellness checkup. I had Sim's records sent to my vet from the vet his former owner took him to. I had to start working on the carsickness first so that when he had his vet visit, the car ride would not overly stress him. I did some research on the problem. I tried a few different ideas, such as having him ride in his crate in the back seat facing forward, using a lavender-based calming spray, and I even tried feeding him a ginger snap before we left the house, but each time, even though he could ride for a longer amount of time, he still became carsick. I never made a big deal of it. I simply stopped the car, cheerfully cleaned up, told him he was a good boy, and started driving again. The odd thing was that every time we practiced this, as soon as we arrived home, Sim would rush under the dining area table and shake. He acted as though he thought I was going to hit him. Something that his former owner did must have established this behavior. Again, I would act cheerful, offer him a treat, which he usually came out for, and tell him he was a good boy. The only way I could keep him from being carsick was by putting a towel on my lap, have Frank drive, and hold Sim, facing forward, on my lap. Little by little, he became better and eventually even enjoyed going for rides. I didn't realize it at the time, but looking back on it, that was one of the ways we bonded and Sim's trust for me continued to grow.

Sim became comfortable enough riding that we were able to take him to a local pet and garden supply store for a picture with Santa Claus. He readily sat on Santa's lap and allowed the photographer to wrap a red, green, and white long knitted scarf around his neck. He and Santa made quite a pair and looked very festive together. When we got the picture back, all I could see was a dog that had an "old" demeanor about him and, of course, those beautiful brown eyes. But they had a sad, soulful look.

Chapter 6

I will take your burden
if you'll let me love you—
Wrap my arms around you—
Give your heart a home.

—Gloria Gaither

According to our vet, Sim was a healthy boy, and his previous records had nothing remarkable in them, just usual vaccinations and the recent neutering. He was so well behaved at the vet's that we took him for a small dish of soft serve vanilla ice cream, which he thoroughly enjoyed. I wasn't happy with the quality of food that he was on, so I changed it to a more nutritious formula. Sim was happy; life was good with us. Every so often, he would become finicky about his food and not eat all of it. I tried changing things around, and it would work for a period. This thought process of mine, trying to figure out Sim's physical problems, became known as "peeling the onion." This means that his major problem may not be the one that it appears to be at first look. The longer I had him, the more "peeling the onion" was done. And just like an onion, sometimes there were many layers to go through before we really got to the heart of his problem.

December 10 was Sim's second birthday. It was the first of many that we would celebrate together. I looked at my calendar and the saying for December 9 was "Gentle as raindrops, Welcome as morning, After the darkness without a warning, Love broke right through, Invading my heart."

How appropriate, I thought. He was destined to be a part of my life. And he invaded my heart and helped to heal it from the loss of Joi. The saying for the tenth was a bit more ominous. "All of us have equal time: twenty-four hours a day. It is with this raw material that we make the statement of our lives. Moments. Life is made up of them." It brought into perspective how we are together for a limited amount of time. We should always make the most and the best of it. And each twenty-four hours that Sim was in my life, our love and respect for each other grew. This continued for twelve-and-a half wonderful years.

The holidays were happy, and one of the many gifts I got for him was a black dog coat with red fleece lining that said "New York Doggie Duds."

Then one day in mid-February, 1998, he would not eat or drink anything. I kept watch over him all day to see if anything would change, but he still refused to eat. I finally took him in through Emergency at the animal hospital. The vet pushed and pressed and exerted pressure on Sim's stomach area with no response. That was until he exerted force, almost like the Heimlich maneuver on the lower stomach. Sim let out a yelp. The vet thought that maybe he had pancreatitis and told me to give him a bland diet for a few days and gave us some medication. I was to call if he got worse. Sim seemed to recover nicely and happily ate up the chicken and rice that I was cooking for him. Here was the first stage of this "peeling the onion" episode.

He was always within eyeshot of me, either watching what I was doing or wanting to engage me in a rollicking game of fetch or hide and seek. One of his favorite games was to steal Ballerina Bear from our bed. Frank had given me a large stuffed toy one Christmas several years ago. She was a very plump bear dressed in a ballerina outfit, including a removable tutu, which is the little skirt that is usually worn in performances. She measured 16" high by 12" wide.

For his size, he had his work cut out for him with her. Sim would sneak down the hall, jump up on our bed and grab Ballerina

Bear. He would then drag her because she was almost as big as Sim, under the bed in the guest bedroom and remove her tutu. He never left a mark or tear on her. The first time I saw him dragging her under the bed, I couldn't help but laugh. His tail was held high, appearing to be very pleased with the theft he had just pulled off. However, as a trainer, I had to teach him the difference between what belonged to him and what belonged to us. I would reach under the bed and take hold of Ballerina Bear. Sim would just look at me, tail wagging, and swallow. Instead of playing with him, I would hold the bear close to me and say, "Mine." I then would hand him one of his favorite toys and say, "Sim, this one is yours. It took several sessions of this training, but eventually he understood. He could then be on the bed with Ballerina Bear and totally ignore her, preferring to curl up with one of his own toys. *He's a real smartie*, I thought. *He has a sense of humor and wants to please me. I'll have to train him carefully because he can figure things out fairly quickly and there's no fooling him. Everything I teach him must be done in a very open and honest fashion.* And Sim the teacher just taught me a very important lesson with this revelation.

I continued his pet obedience training. Pet obedience training is teaching a dog good manners, such as walking nicely on the leash, otherwise known as "heeling." Heeling is when the dog walks along in unison with you on your left side without pulling or trying to run ahead of you. He or she is given the command to "heel." This teaches the dog to walk in that position with you whether you are walking at a normal pace, running, or walking at a snail's pace. The dog also learns the commands to "sit," to "down," to "stand," to "come," to "stay," to "leave it," and to "wait." When the dog is taught to "sit," "down," or "stand," he or she learns to respond the first time the command is given. The "stay" means exactly that. If the dog is commanded to "sit, stay," that means the handler wants the dog to not move from the position or area it was put in, even if the handler walks away. The dog is not to move until the handler returns to the dog and releases the dog from the "stay" position.

"Wait" means "wait for further instruction." An example of this is when the dog is commanded to sit, but the handler is going to call the dog to him or her. Rather than to tell the dog to "stay" when walking away, the dog is told "wait" because within a few seconds the handler is going to tell the dog to "come." This is a very important difference to me. Many dogs get confused if the two words are used interchangeably, and they are not sure whether they are supposed to "wait" or "stay." This confusion can and will make the dogs stay unreliable.

Pet training also teaches the owner how to communicate with the dog in a way that the dog understands what is expected. Dogs are masters of body language. No matter how sweetly you may be talking to the dog, the dog is reading your body language. If your body language is contradicting what your words and tone of voice are saying, the dog will react accordingly. Have you ever noticed that if a person is not particularly comfortable around a dog, the dog will try to win over that person by staying around them? The person doesn't have to say a word. The dog seems to sense their discomfort but does not realize that it is because of them. It seems as though the dog is trying to make the person feel more relaxed. Another example of misinterpreted body language is when a person doesn't want the dog to jump up on them. They step backward with their hands up about chest or shoulder level, possibly saying "No!" or "*Off!*" or "*Don't jump up on me!*" As far as the dog is concerned, the person may as well be saying "*Up, up!*" because that is what the person's body language is saying to the dog. A good trainer will teach you the subtleties and the proper way to interpret your dog's actions and the best way to communicate so that the dog can properly interpret what you are conveying.

Sim and I then had to go on to a very important aspect of pet obedience, which is learning the difference between love and leadership. Sim learned this easily, and we worked well together as a team. Once again, the role of teacher and student was equally divided between us.

Dogs are pack animals. They are born with the instinct to either lead or be led. Many people do not understand how important this aspect of dog ownership is. If we do not take the leadership role with the dog, the dog feels that he or she has to lead us. This is a very stressful situation for the dog. It is impossible for them to do this, either physically or mentally, in a consistent manner. You should educate yourself, either by taking classes or reading books, watching training videos, etc., to learn how to communicate properly with your dog. The saying to memorize is "Properly trained, a man can be dog's best friend," by Cory Ford. There are certain behaviors that a dog exhibits that "train" us. An example of this might be a certain "look" that the dog gives us when it wants to go out, eat, play, or get a treat. The dog gives us the "look," and we respond accordingly. But the dog cannot take a leadership role with us because the dog cannot possibly think, react, and respond to our everyday needs and situations.

Sometimes, when a person allows a dog to do what it pleases or is inconsistent with discipline, the dog becomes confused, sometimes even bossy, and then becomes stressed. When the dog becomes stressed, we begin to see behaviors that we deem inappropriate. The dog may also display some neurotic behaviors because it just doesn't know how to respond, and it continues to try to relieve its stress. The solution to this problem is completely in our hands. The dog should be given "rules" or "boundaries" much as you would give to a young child. You must be a fair leader, and there should be consistency. If something is unacceptable now, it is unacceptable five minutes from now, five days from now, and so on.

One of the worst things that you can do with a dog is to be inconsistent. This adds to their confusion, which adds to their stress. As the leader, you are in charge of all valued rewards. These include, but are not limited to meals, treats, play, petting, toys, walks, and rides. The dog must also learn about saying "please" and "thank you." What this means is that if the dog wants something pleasurable, the dog must first comply with a request from you. For instance, if the dog wants to go out to relieve itself, he or she must "wait," not just barge out of the door. And it doesn't matter whether or not the dog has to be leash walked or if the dog has a fenced-in yard. Of course, you always have to use discretion. If the dog is not feeling well and cannot "hold it," you would not make it "wait" for the usual amount of time. If the dog pesters you while you are watching TV or reading by nudging you with a toy, tell the dog to "wait." After two or three minutes, get up, get a completely different toy and engage the dog in play, telling the dog to "sit" before you begin the game. This is teaching the dog two things. The first one is you will not drop everything and give the dog attention when it wants it. The other thing is that you are in charge of everything, including what games will be played. If the dog doesn't like the game and/or toy that you choose, too bad. The dog will learn that if it wants to play, it will be on your terms.

The love part is easy. Spoil them with toys, games, walks, special treats, petting, talking, a comfortable bed or beds in different areas of the house and, on occasion, allowing them to be on the couch or bed with you but only on your terms. You control when they can be on the couch or bed, for how long, and when they must get off of it. The list goes on and on. Most of us own a dog to love them and for the unconditional love they return to us. The most important thing to remember is that you must always be their "guidance counselor," guiding them in the right direction so that they display the proper behavior. Please note that I don't use the word *alpha*. I don't care for the image that conjures up. As far as I am concerned, only a dog can be the "alpha" to another dog. We are their leaders, stewards, trainers, and counselors.

When I walked Sim, I reinforced his obedience training in different areas, possibly heeling him, doing a down or sit stay, or a recall. This taught him that he could and should respond to my commands no matter where we were and no matter what distraction may be present. I never used harsh methods with him or any of my clients and always rewarded good responses with plenty of affection. Sim's weakest point was his heeling. It seemed as if he always wanted to lag, staying just a few paces behind me. I never knew for sure, but I always felt it had something to do with the way he was handled by the disabled boy who walked Sim in his former life.

As time went on, my business was growing nicely. My client base grew sizably, mainly because of word of mouth. The income from the business was also growing, so I was able to take out an ad in the Yellow Pages. Sim became an active partner, as I would use him as a "demo dog" to show people how a particular exercise should look when done properly. He always readily complied and loved the attention.

Chapter 7

If you don't know where you're going, you
may wind up somewhere else.

—Yogi Berra

Two of my clients and I became training buddies. One had a year-old black pit bull mix named Boomer. Boomer was a big boy with an attitude to match. His owner was Paula, who felt that she needed to get better control over him. I explained that what she should be working toward was more respect from him. Then there was Janet with Abbey. Abbey was a yellow Lab puppy about six months old. Abbey was a very gentle, sensitive girl. Janet wanted basic pet obedience. As the months passed, not only did the women become friends, but the three dogs were like the Three Musketeers. When they were together, they were an odd but striking combination. Boomer was large and athletic-looking, Abbey was a leggy, growing puppy, and then there was short legged, low to the ground Sim.

One day, after the three of us had finished training our dogs in my backyard, we decided to take the leashes off our dogs and let them play. Paula had a large, soft Frisbee in her tote bag. She threw it, and all three dogs went running after it. With Boomer in the lead, Abbey close behind, and Sim bringing up the rear, the three of them disappeared into a row of bushes where the toy had fallen. Boomer came out with the prize in his mouth, his two pals in hot pursuit. Boomer dropped the Frisbee, and Janet picked it up to toss it. We felt that Boomer had an advantage because of his size and because Paula threw it. Janet gave it a good toss, and the three dogs chased after it again. This time, Sim was closer to the other two. Once again, the Frisbee landed in the row of bushes. This time, Abbey came out with the toy. She immediately brought it back to Janet. "Do you want a turn, Peg? Maybe Sim will get it this time."

"No, throw it again, Janet. I think Sim is being a good host and is letting his guests win." Janet tossed it. This time, the three dogs ran as a team. I was amazed that Sim had figured out how to keep up with the other two. The three of them disappeared into the bushes. The one with the prized toy this time was Sim. He ran around the whole yard, his ears flying and his tail held as high as he could possibly hold it. It was as though he was daring the others to get it away from him. "So much for being a good host, girls," I said.

We agreed that the dogs were good buddies but competitive with each other. This got the three of us to talking about getting involved in competitive obedience.

"The dogs are well trained and well behaved," Paula said.

"Abbey is still a little young and is due to be spayed soon. Once she's through that, I'm willing to give it a try," Janet chimed in.

"Well, I guess that settles it. We'll start working seriously toward showing them in obedience." That was the day the competitive bug bit not just us three women but, I believe, the three dogs.

Competitive obedience differs from pet obedience in that all the exercises have to be done with precision. For example, "heeling" that would be acceptable when taking your dog for a walk might not be acceptable enough in the obedience ring to receive a qualifying score for that exercise. According to the AKC obedience rules, perfect heel position is the dog's right ear lined up to the seam of your left pant leg. Hot pants definitely would not be appropriate attire in the obedience ring. There are points assigned to each exercise that the dog has to perform, and you have to receive 50 percent of these points for each exercise to qualify.

My training philosophy never changed. Whether I was working on pet obedience or whether I was training to go into the obedience ring, the handler/dog relationship was the most important element to me. However, there were people participating in competitive obedience who felt that you do whatever you have to do to "win," even if this meant roughly handling your dog and breaking the trust and good relationship.

The more I worked with Sim, the more he taught me how to "read" him. There were days when he worked with great enthusiasm. Then there were the days that for no particular reason I knew of at the time, he was flat and had a pained expression on his face instead of that great enthusiastic "rule the world" look. He had been teaching me at every step of the way, even though I did not realize it at the time.

After about six months of preparing, we all decided to go to a match held at the Westfield Fairgrounds. They were offering the AKC's Canine Good Citizen testing as well as a Pre-Novice obedience class where we could put our dogs through their obedience paces: heeling, stand for examination, recall, and sit and down stays on leash.

The Canine Good Citizen test consisted of ten exercises that the dog had to go through. It was a pass/fail test, meaning you and the dog executed them all correctly or you didn't pass. The point of the test is to show that the dog has had some training, is well-mannered, and is a dog that people would be happy to have in their neighborhood. The ten exercises are: Accept a Friendly Stranger, Sit Politely for Petting, Appearance and Grooming, Out for a Walk (Walking on a Loose Leash), Walk through a Crowd, Sit and Down on Command, Staying in Place, Come When Called, Reaction to Another Dog, Reaction to Distractions, and Supervised Separation. We were extremely nervous, but the dogs were calm and collected. Each one of our dogs took his or her turn, and each passed with flying colors.

On the Supervised Separation, the examiner had people exchange their dog with one of the other people whose dog was being tested. I handed Sim over to a very nice woman named June who was testing her Cairn Terrier named Junior. Sim went readily with her, and Junior happily came with me. We were each put into separate barns. Although the barn I was in was clean, it smelled heavily of cow urine. The evaluator walked past the doorway of each barn several times during the three minutes to see if either dog was anxious, upset, or acting in a manner that would disqualify the dog. One of the rules of any testing is that the dog does not eliminate. Junior was busy sniffing at the bales of hay and then suddenly, without warning, he lifted his leg and peed. I chuckled since I certainly couldn't fault him because of the strong urine smell. He looked up at me. I looked at him and said, "Don't worry, Junior. I won't say anything if you won't either." I swear he winked at me. The evaluator called us out of the barns and asked if everything went all right. June and I both said "yes" just about in unison. Both dogs received their CGC certificate and ribbon.

I realized in that moment that you must never lose sight of the fact that a dog thinks like a dog while we think like humans. Sounds like an obvious statement, but we often expect the dog to think as we do. The lesson here is that we've got to learn how to perceive things as the dog does. This goes a very long way to solidifying a good, trusting relationship with our dog.

We then proceeded to the obedience ring. We took our arm-bands with our entry number on it. Nerves were running very high. Paula was more talkative that usual. Janet's voice had morphed into a very high-pitched tone. As for me, my legs were like Jell-O, and I was sweating profusely. Sim looked at me and gave the "swallow." I looked down at him and realized that he was trying to help me relax. This was my first try at being "judged" in the ring. As a trainer, I felt that I had to at least put on a respectable performance. However, I had no idea what my partner at the other end of the leash was going to do. I was also learning that unlike the Shelties, Border Collies, Golden Retrievers, and Labs, Shih Tzus had no work ethic. *Work* is a four-letter dirty word to them. They were bred to be pampered and revered. Not one ounce of work ethic was included. I did know that Mr. Sims enjoyed the partnership of working with me, so whatever happened, I knew he was giving me his best.

We stepped into the ring. The three of us were competing in the Pre-Novice class. All exercises are done on leash. The judge, a kindly looking woman, smiled at us and showed us where our starting point was to begin heeling. After that, everything became a blur. I remember my hands shaking as I set Sim up for the Stand for Examination. You position the dog in a stand, tell him to stay, and then walk to the end of the six-foot leash, turning to face him. The judge then touches the dog's head and two places on the back, walks away, and says, "Return to your dog." The dog has to stay in the stand position throughout the exam without moving and cannot move until you return to him and the judge says, "Exercise finished." If the dog sits before the end of the exercise, you are disqualified. My heart was in my throat throughout this exercise. Because of my physical disability, my focus was not good and I felt lightheaded, but Sim carried us as a team and pulled it off beautifully.

The last exercise that he had to do by himself was the recall. I set him up in a sit and when the judge said, "Leave your dog," I told him to "wait," walked to the end of the leash, and waited until I heard the judge say, "Call your dog." Sim sat looking intently at me and swallowed. I heard the judge's command, and I called him. He came flying, coming to a stop directly in front of me and sat. The judge then said, "Finish," which means to have your dog return to your left side, which is heel position. I gave him the command, and he promptly walked behind me, moving right to left and finished with a nice sit on my left side. The judge smiled again and said, "See you for sits and downs."

There were a few more dogs that had their turn, and then we all lined up for the one-minute sit/stay and the three-minute down/stay. That minute sit seemed more like an hour because if the dog breaks, he is automatically disqualified. Sim completed both the sit and down stays, and I finally started breathing again.

The judge finished her paperwork and began calling the names of the top four finishers. Sim was fourth! I was speechless, and after all the ribbons he later won, the ribbon he won that day always had a special meaning for me. He proved that with the proper handling and relationship, even a Shih Tzu can and should be shown in obedience. Abbey and Boomer did not fare as well that day but later went on to earn obedience titles.

Later that year, the three of us decided that since our dogs did so well with the CGC test, we would have them tested to see if they could become therapy dogs. The testing was going to be done at a local nursing home with some of the residents watching. The test was very similar to the CGC with the addition of medical equipment, and rather than the accent being on manners, the evaluator was looking more to temperament.

Again the three of us, with nerves running high, met at the site. The three dogs greeted each other in their usual enthusiastic fashion and then proceeded to play. We sat down and wanted the dogs to sit quietly next to us until it was our turn to be evaluated. They sat next to us for a short while and then, one after the other, started horsing around, wrestling, pawing, and verbalizing with each other. We were mortified and tried to have them gather their manners together. They did for a short time and then started in with each other again. At this point, the three of us burst out laughing because our furry friends, even though well trained and behaved, were acting like three little kids playing under the pews at church. However, once again, each dog took its turn, passed with flying colors, and made us proud. The three of us now had certified therapy dogs that could visit hospitals, nursing homes, shut-ins, and anyone else who needed some happiness and comfort.

My aunt, who lived on Long Island, had suffered a serious stroke and was now living in a nursing home. One of the first visits Sim made as a therapy dog was to see her there. We would visit her several times a year. The other residents also looked forward to our visits and enjoyed petting and interacting with Sim. They also were greatly amused when they asked me his name, and I told them it was "Mr. Sims." This seemed to tickle their sense of humor and made him that much more endearing to them.

The stroke that my aunt had suffered damaged her ability to communicate. She could understand what you were saying to her, but when she tried to respond, she would use inappropriate words. For example, she loved to have Sim sit on her lap. She would say how good it felt to have balloons on her lap. She would pet Sim and tell him what a good balloon he was. He just gave me a look and Shih Tzu swallow, and then he would lick her hand. As the conversation continued, her code word would change. *Balloon* might change to *slipper*. It took me a bit of time to decipher this change, but Sim would just go with the flow.

I saw how much Sim enjoyed the therapy work and the attention he received from it. It gave me the idea that I should train Sim for competitive obedience to see how far I could take him. I also felt that would help to diminish the bad memories that he had been exposed to before he came to me. Other than his lagging when heeling, he took to it like a duck to water. I gave him a rest during the winter and again lavished him with gifts during the holidays. He was basically happy and healthy other than occasional small bouts of stomach upset but nothing unusual. What did change was that the longer I had him and took him to be groomed on a regular basis, his coat came back in as white with beautiful golden patches, a far cry from the nondescript coat he came with.

Chapter 8

Our sense of values is revealed by our choices.

—Decision Vision

I received a call from a client who had come to me for basic obedience the year before. She had a Border Collie named Jake. When she first came to me, Jake was not a year old yet, and he was a bit of a handful. He had all the traits that one would want in a good Border Collie. One day, when we were training outside of my house, a car came from one direction, a biker from the other, and my husband was pulling out of the driveway. Jake immediately went into his inbred herding mode and dropped to the ground, watching each movement of the cars and biker. It was as though he was waiting for them to get close together so he could herd them. Fortunately, he was on leash and he was unable to accomplish his "mission." He did well with the training, and so did his owner.

The next time she called me, she was very upset. It seems that Jake had completely "shut down," as though he had a nervous breakdown. She was having her home renovated. She trusted the contractor that she had hired, so she didn't worry that neither she nor her husband would be at home during the day. They had a very nice kennel set up for Jake with a sizeable doghouse that he could go into if the weather got bad. This was the late summer, so there was no real worry about very severe weather. One day, she came home early from work to find twelve of the painters surrounding Jake's kennel, and they were all harassing him. Mary yelled at them to leave the dog alone and that she would talk to the contractor about they had done. She then turned her attention to Jake, who just lay there, staring into space. I told her to call Cashman's School of Veterinary Medicine at Puritan University's behavioral department immediately and make an appointment for Jake to be evaluated. Puritan's is one of the leading veterinary teaching schools and hospitals in the area. After the appointment, she called me. Jake was diagnosed with global fear. This meant that he had become afraid of everything.

The vet she saw at Puritan's gave her a program for Jake that would help to get him over this breakdown. When she told him that she had worked with me on Jake's basic training, the vet said that she should have me work with her and Jake on this regimen. He also asked that after every session that we worked Jake, I should write up the experience and fax it to him so that he could keep check of Jake's progress.

We began slowly with Jake, going over the obedience exercises that he had learned the year before. As each session continued, Jake's confidence seemed to build. I set up the high jump in the backyard and taught Jake how to go over it on command. As the weeks went by and Jake was getting better, we took him to a shopping center that is close by. I had Mary work him, always on leash, of course. I had Mary put Jake in a sit stay, sometimes a down stay. We would do recalls, and then I would take the leash from her and tell her to go into a store to see how confident Jake was without her. At first, I had her stay out of sight for less than a minute. We gradually extended the time until she could stay out of Jake's sight for five minutes without him getting "worried." It probably took us two months to get his confidence to this level.

The next test was to put Jake in a situation where he would not be interacting with other dogs but would be in the same area with them. There was a training class that I had taken Sim to a few times. The trainer that ran the facility was one of the "hard boot" types, but I always worked Sim myself and never let anyone else handle him. Most of the dogs there were well behaved. It was a large training room with a ring set up for people who wanted to learn how to show their dog in breed, which is similar to most of the dog shows that you see on TV. Next to this ring was the obedience ring. We brought Sim, and Frank worked him in obedience while Mary, Jake and I walked the perimeter of the area. Jake was a little anxious, but the more we walked him around, the more relaxed he became. We were both pleased with this outing and planned to return there the following week. Jake seemed to be coming back to his old self.

The following week, the classes were almost full. We walked Jake around the perimeter again and he seemed relaxed. I suggested to Mary that she take Jake into the obedience ring and have him work around the other dogs. If there was a problem, she could just leave the class. Frank was working Sim because I had to sit and take notes of Jake's progress. Janet and Abbey and Paula and Boomer were also in the class. I was sitting next to Janet's husband, Brian. There were several other dogs and handlers taking the class as well. One woman had a young German Shepherd puppy whom she was working. I would say that the puppy was about four months old and was a little young to be working around the older dogs. The dogs did not interact with her, but she seemed rather stressed to me. The trainer running the class gave the command to "down your dogs." Everyone complied except the puppy. I could see that she was afraid to go down. *Down* is a very submissive position for a dog, and if they are not comfortable in their environment, they resist going down. The owner tried several times, but the puppy refused. The trainer walked over and said to the owner in an assertive voice, "Give her to me." It appeared that the owner of the puppy knew the trainer. She handed the trainer the leash. Everyone was watching.

The trainer tightened up on the leash and put his left foot on it up near the puppy's collar. He yelled at the puppy to "Down" as he stomped his foot on the leash. The puppy yelped and kept her hind end up in the air. She was terrified. I saw the expression on the trainer's face and knew that if this were my dog, I would stop the trainer. Instead, the owner giggled. The trainer acted as though the dog was deliberately disobeying him, so to the trainer, it became personal. He continued to stomp on the leash to make the puppy go down. The puppy continued to yelp and jump backward, falling into some folding chairs. The trainer would not let up. Again, he shouted "Down" to the puppy, stomping hard on the leash.

The puppy finally went down from exhaustion. The owner only *then* decided that the puppy had enough and was going to tie her to one of the chairs and work her other dog instead. I couldn't believe what I was seeing, and I could feel the tears rolling down my face. To this day, I don't know exactly what happened, but the puppy got loose from the chair it was tied to, ran over to me, and put her head on my knee. I could almost see tears in her eyes. She looked up at me with a pained expression. I stroked her and said, "I know, girl, you've had a rough day." With that, the owner took the puppy and put her in a crate. Here was a case of an owner who either didn't have a clue as to why her puppy was having a problem with the down exercise or didn't care. The owner also allowed the trainer to abuse her puppy without a word of disapproval. I signaled to Mary and Frank. I was leaving and never coming back. I regret the fact that I didn't speak up at the time, but because it was another trainer's method and venue, I felt the best thing I could do was to leave and lead by example. I knew then and there that I had to find a place to rent where I could run group classes for those who passed my Basic Obedience course and wanted to continue to earn their Canine Good Citizen, learn about becoming a therapy dog, or practice competitive obedience. I knew it was going to be difficult to find a facility, but if it was meant to be, I would find something appropriate.

Chapter 9

There may be no trumpet sound or loud
applause when we make a right decision, just
a calm sense of resolution and peace.

—"Decision Vision"

It was 1999, and two years since its beginning, my business was now growing in leaps and bounds, and I needed to rent an indoor facility so that my business was not at the mercy of the weather either being too hot, too cold, raining, snowing, or too windy. I made arrangements with a groomer to rent space from her for a reasonable fee. However, as we were a one-car family, I had to go shopping for my own set of wheels. I had stopped driving because of never knowing when I might be exposed to carbon monoxide in traffic. When these exposures happened, I became disoriented and could not think clearly. Now with the progress I had made over the last couple of years, I felt more confident and had begun driving again. I found a white Cavalier that I nicknamed The Simsmobile. Because of the business and Sim, I now had my very first car that I solely owned. Even though I purchased it on President's Day, I felt like it was Independence Day for me in more ways than one.

Not only was I training Sim for his Novice title with the AKC, I had also registered him with UKC, United Kennel Club. The Novice class is the first level of competitive obedience. The rules for both clubs are fairly similar. However, on the recall in UKC, the dog has to come over a jump. I worked on this exercise with Sim, and he enjoyed coming over the jump.

Then one evening in February after eating his supper, Sim looked to be in terrible distress, slinking across the kitchen floor then sprawling on his tummy. I immediately went to him to see what was so very wrong. He continued to crawl away from me and ended up under the bed. I sprawled on my belly on the rug trying to reach him, but he was just at arm's length. I spoke softly to him, trying to comfort him. Frank came in from work during this episode. I told him I wasn't sure, but I had the feeling Sim was going to bring up his dinner. Sure enough, I barely got the words out of my mouth when up his meal came. He then seemed relieved but uncomfortable.

As I started to clean up, I said, "I didn't feed the dog a mushroom!" I set aside what looked like a slice of a large mushroom from cap to stem. I rinsed it off and found that it was a piece of latex toy. I scooped Sim up along with the toy and took him to our veterinary hospital's emergency unit. We had to leave him overnight for tests to be sure that he had no more of the foreign object in him. I could show the vet what came up but couldn't tell her what is was. In the sixteen months I had him, he had never destroyed any of his toys, and none of his toys were made of yellow latex.

She called the next day to say he was resting comfortably and there was nothing more in his system. It seems that the piece of toy had been in him since he was a puppy before I got him. She was able to determine this because of the amount of stomach acid that the piece of toy contained. We picked him up, along with some medications, and he seemed to be fine. The theory was that the piece of toy became lodged in the lower portion of his stomach or upper intestines. As he developed, the toy became embedded there. When I started teaching him to jump and was adding oil to his food for his coat, the piece of toy loosened up and came out. This probably also explained the other stomach issues we had seen with him. *Aha*, I thought, *another layer of the onion.*

Chapter 10

I'll spend my winter's springs
Remembering
The heart is a good place
To keep things.

—Hands Across the Seasons

Sim continued training forwardly, but I decided to take some private lessons from a trainer who was also an AKC judge. I felt that I still had a lot to learn and she could help me. There was an obedience trial coming up in September in Maine. As this would be our first real obedience trial, I wanted to give Sim every advantage that I could. This trainer had Shelties herself, so she was rather skeptical about the abilities of a Shih Tzu in the obedience ring because they are not a working breed. She was very competitive with her Shelties, and they usually earned high scores and were in the top four finishers of the classes they competed in.

I made it clear to the trainer that I would not use any harsh corrections on Sim. He had learned to trust me and was doing well without any aversive methods. She was helpful and taught me the ins and outs of the obedience ring. The rules, the things you could do, the things you couldn't. The lesson before we were leaving for Maine, she did a mock trial of the exercises and her last words to me were "Good luck, but he's very green."

We made the trip to Maine without any problem with carsickness. We met the woman with the Goldens, Brenda, and her elderly friend Bev, who was going to show her Pomeranian, Ike. Bev had also shown with great success in obedience with her Pomeranians. Both of their dogs were in the next higher class called "Open." Sim was working in Novice toward a CD or Companion Dog title. Abbey, Sim's Yellow Lab pal, was also in his class. In fact, they were next to each other in order of showing. The others were working in "Open" for a CDX title, which stands for Companion Dog Excellent.

We arrived on Friday evening, and the trials were going to be on Saturday and Sunday. As luck would have it, I had the number one spot for the trials, meaning I was the first one in the ring to start the day. I was very nervous to begin with, and this starting position didn't make me feel any more at ease. We got to the facility, and I walked Sim around to get him acclimated. I then started to lightly work him. Everyone had advice for me. "Do this, don't do that, try to keep his attention on you," which made me even more nervous. However, my teammate wasn't the least bit flustered and just looked at me with those brown eyes, wagged his tail, and swallowed as much as to say, "It's OK. I'll try my best." And best he did.

The Shih Tzu that needed a second chance in life beat many of the big boys, coming in third, receiving a large yellow third-place ribbon and a large green qualifying ribbon. He also received a silver plate for his effort. I was so excited I could hardly sleep that night. Sim had gotten his first leg, the word that is used when a dog gets a qualifying score, the first of three that are needed to earn his CD title. The next morning, we had to do it all over again. As this was his first experience in obedience trials, I didn't know if he would flatten out from stress or fatigue. Again, he just tried his very best and even though he came in fourth this time, the top four finishers were all within a half point of each other, and his score was higher than the day before. *Amazing*, I thought. This time, he got a large white ribbon and another large green qualifying ribbon with a smaller silver plate. My thoughts went to the trainer who said, "He's green."

He sure is, I thought, *and it's just the right shade.*

Sim was the only one that qualified that trip. The more "hard boot" trainers went home empty handed. These same people felt that a dog should be able to perform anywhere, anytime, indoors or out, rain or shine. One person bragged to me that she had shown her dog in a hurricane in Bermuda. *Is it me?* I thought. It didn't sound right or fair to me to ask a dog to perform as if the dog had an "on/off" switch. However, this group kept trying to convince me that this was the way of competitive obedience.

I had tried Sim in a few matches that were held outside. He obviously was very uncomfortable and stressed because of the heat. And the time it started to rain, he started looking for cover. I just couldn't see putting any dog through this.

While we had our pictures taken with the judges in Maine, I asked one of the judges, who had a lot of experience, what her opinion of this situation was. She looked at me earnestly and told me how she and a group she showed with had been in upstate New York in March several years ago. She said it was a cold, misty morning. She showed Toy Poodles and decided that she would not expose them to these conditions. The rest of the group chided her, but she still refused. Two of the other dogs died from the pneumonia they contracted there, and another one became very ill but recovered. She looked into my eyes very intensely and said, "Always remember, *we* are supposed to be the brains of the team. Don't you ever put your dog in jeopardy, no matter what the situation." Her words resounded in my head, and I never forgot her advice.

We had one more leg to go to get the Companion Dog title. There was a trial coming up in November. We worked toward it. Sim was okay but appeared to be bored with the work or possibly tired. He didn't have the same spark as he had earlier. He would go through his paces for me but without the enthusiasm that he usually worked with.

The day of the show came. There was an especially large class, and the day dragged on and on before it was our turn in the obedience ring. The first exercise, Heel on Leash, usually was not a problem. The Heel off Leash was going to be more of an issue because of his lagging. The judge showed us the starting point, asked, "Are you ready?" and off we went. Sim had come alive in the ring for me. He had his jaunty style and wasn't really lagging. We finished the

Heeling portion and then did our Figure 8 portion of Heeling, still on leash. Again, he didn't do badly at all.

After the Figure 8 portion is completed, the leash is removed and handed to a Steward. The rest of the exercises are performed off leash. The next exercise was the Stand for Exam. The judge told me to "Stand your dog, leave when ready." I set Sim and was just ready to tell him to "Stay" when there was a noise that sounded like a bomb went off. It was one of those noises that make the whole room totally quiet for a split second as everyone holds their breath. What happened was a pallet of folding chairs fell, and the sound resounded off the four walls of the gym. Sim looked at me and swallowed hard. The judge said to release and relax him. I took a minute, and then she told me to set him up again. I thought for sure that he would not stand and stay for the exam, and I wouldn't blame him if he didn't. I set him up and told him to stay. I walked about six feet away from him as the judge walked in to examine him. He stayed like a trooper, allowed her to examine him. She said to me, "Return to your dog," and again he stayed until he was released from the exercise. I was amazed. Even a more seasoned obedience dog might not have had the grit to gather himself together and do what he knew I wanted him to do.

We then were guided to the spot to begin the off-leash heeling. Sim was a little tentative but kept going. However, when we approached the spot where he had heard the noise, the judge said "Halt," which means that when I stop, Sim should automatically sit. Well, he wasn't going to sit. It meant that we would just get points off, not a disqualification. The last exercise was the recall, and wouldn't you know it? He had to set up in the exact same place. As I left him to go to the opposite side of the ring, I kept thinking that he might be following me to get away from that spot. Instead, he was sitting like a little soldier, waiting for me to call him. I called, and he came running like the Devil himself was chasing him and sat at my feet. The judge said "Finish," and Sim dutifully came around the back of me to sit at my left side.

Great job, I thought.

The judge smiled broadly and said she'd see us for Sits and Downs. Sim got his Companion Dog title that day, along with special recognition for being the "highest scoring rescue dog." For this accomplishment, he received a beautiful rosewood picture frame. Frank was videotaping us as we worked in the ring. When I later looked at the tape, I could see the stress Sim was experiencing as I left him for the recall. He yawned, licked his lips, and just looked very uncomfortable, but he held on for me. I knew then and there that we had a wonderful bond with each other, but I also knew that it could be very fragile. I must continue to nurture, reinforce, and respect this bond and the trust that he had in me. Sim the Teacher again was teaching me. The initials CD would now be placed after his name. This would precede the initials CGC, which was his Canine Good Citizen Award, and TDI, which was his therapy dog certification. I was very proud of him. I began to think that anything was possible with "Sim, CD, TDI, CGC."

The following January, there was an obedience match being sponsored by the Labrador Retriever Club. Even though Sim had gotten his Companion Dog title, I had not started to teach him the Open exercises yet since I was still working on his United Kennel Club Companion Dog title. I decided to enter him in this match. An obedience match differs from a trial in that even though the teams are scored and ribbons are awarded for the first four finishers, it does not count toward a title. It is used for practice and experience for both the dog and handler. Sim did very well in his solo performance.

When it was time for the "sit" and "down" portion, Sim was first in line, so his place in the ring to execute the exercises was right at the ring gate. We all lined up, and the judge told us to "Sit your dogs." We did and then she told us to "Leave your dogs." I told Sim to stay and walked to the opposite side of the ring. I turned to face him and noticed a little boy, probably about five years old, sitting next to Sim on the other side of the ring gate. He was eating potato chips. I watched as the boy crunched and Sim started to drool. The more the child crunched, the more Sim drooled. I thought for sure that he was going to break the sit. Instead, he continued to stare at me, drooling and swallowing for the whole minute.

"Return to your dogs," the judge said.

When I got to him, I said, "Wow, Sim! What a good boy. I'll give you a special treat as soon as we get through the down exercise." He looked at me and swallowed several times. In the meantime, someone told the child's parent that they should move him back from the ring so that he wouldn't disrupt the dogs in the ring. Sim did just fine with the three-minute down stay and ended up coming in first in the match.

I was so proud of him maintaining himself in the face of potato chips that I couldn't stop giving him treats and kisses. Ask competitors, and they will tell you that this kind of distraction in the ring is their worst nightmare, and if the dog ignores it, it is a handler's happiest dream. Again, he reminded me of the bond that we had together, and it was not to be taken for granted.

Chapter 11

Deep pits are begun with a single shovelful
of dirt, and mountains are
climbed one step at a time.

—Decision Vision

I started teaching Sim some of the Open exercises so he would become familiar with them and not get bored with the Novice work. One of the Open exercises is to retrieve a dumbbell. The dumbbell that is used for this exercise is bright white, made of plastic that is molded, and each end is shaped into a square. When fitted properly, each end of the dumbbell rests snugly next to the dog's cheeks. I measured his mouth by placing a pencil horizontally in it. I then took a pen and marked the pencil at each side of his mouth. I ordered one for him. It was not very large compared to the ones I was used to seeing for the larger dogs that competed. The purpose of this exercise is to show that the dog will retrieve something for you without question. I'm sure Sim would willingly retrieve a prime rib bone, but a white plastic dumbbell is not as enticing. And the downside of using a prime rib bone was the thought of all that meat juice and grease on my light beige rug.

I knew that I first had to teach him the concept of taking this in his mouth and not chewing on it or viewing it as a toy. The "hard boot" trainers advise to use the "ear pinch." This method is to hold the dumbbell in front of the dog's mouth. Then using your fingernails with the dog's ear between your thumb and first two fingers, squeeze the ear until he takes the dumbbell. No way was I going to do that to Mr. Sims. Even if it took me longer to teach him the concept, I knew I had to find a better way. I went back to the trainer that said he was "green" to see what ideas she may have.

I told her up front that I would never do the ear pinch. Between the two of us, we came up with a way to introduce the concept to him. I would sit in a chair and have Sim sit in front of me. I took a pencil and held it with a piece of hotdog behind it. If he wanted the hotdog, he had to put his mouth over the pencil. The first time I offered him the piece of hotdog behind the pencil, he sat and looked at me, swallowed, and gave me that look as if to say, "Huh?"

I continued telling him to "take it" softly and patiently. He finally made a move for it. "Good boy!" I cheered him on. Each night, we would work just a little bit on this. Once he was really comfortable taking the hotdog, I gradually lowered the pencil until it was on the floor with no hotdog behind it. I told him "take it" and he did. I praised him lavishly and gave him a couple of small pieces of hotdog. I knew he was now ready to start working with his dumbbell. It was somewhat stressful for both of us. I was worried that the dumbbell might feel uncomfortable in his mouth and even make it sore. It was stressful for Sim because he wanted to please me but was confused as to what I wanted him to do.

The next part that he had to learn was to pick up the dumbbell and hold it in his mouth until I told him to "give." He was not supposed to either chew or roll it around in his mouth. This concept was a bit tougher for him to understand. Rolling it in his mouth seemed to be a natural instinct. To be "perfect," the dog should just "hold" the dumbbell in his mouth. *That's OK*, I thought. Don't let the search for "perfection" take away the good that is being learned and accomplished. As a Shih Tzu has a somewhat pushed-in face, I was sure that picking a dumbbell off the floor could not be the most comfortable, let alone natural thing to do. "Maybe he's rolling it, trying to make it feel more comfortable in his mouth," I pondered.

The pieces of the exercise were coming together. The final parts are to throw the dumbbell about twenty feet away and send the dog to retrieve it. The dog promptly goes and gets the dumbbell, brings it to the handler, sits at the handler's feet, and waits for the handler to say "give." The handler reaches for the dumbbell, holding each end of it protruding out of the dog's mouth. The dog releases the dumbbell and waits for the handler to signal to "finish." The dog returns to the handler's left side. I started setting Sim up at the end of our hall that was about twenty feet long. I would tell him "wait" and then throw the dumbbell down the hall. He had to wait for me to tell him "take it." Sometimes, he would be so anxious to get it for me that he would get it before I sent him. I'd always laugh and say, "Nice try but not quite. We have to do that again, Sim." And he would come back to the starting point with me with his tail wagging. I knew that if I kept working with him, he would get it.

Again, some of the "hard boot" trainers said that I should be harsher when he goes before I send him. One suggestion was to put a leash on him when working on the exercise. If he went for the dumbbell before he was given the command, I should reach down and sharply pull back on the leash. I refused, and know that many eyes rolled behind my back. But neither of these methods made any sense to me. To me, the "ear pinch" could make the dog afraid of the dumbbell. And giving the dog a hard pull back if he anticipated being sent for the dumbbell, to me, also inflicted unnecessary pain and fear of the very object the dog is supposed to retrieve happily. I was not going to do anything that would break the trust Sim had in me.

With that trust firmly in place, we also continued to work on earning the Companion Dog title with United Kennel Club. He seemed to be having more issues when showing, totally shutting down at times. He would warm up well outside of the ring, but as soon as we entered the ring, he would ignore me, obsessively sniffing the mats, and not responding to the commands I would give him. I thought that it probably had something to do with the experience he had when the chairs fell, and so he was anxious in the ring. I kept working on it with him, but it took him many tries before he got the UKC UCD title, always appearing to be somewhat tentative in the ring. The UKC title is placed in front of the dog's name to define it from AKC titles that the dog may have earned. His full title now was "UCD Mr. Sims, CD, TDI, CGC. I was extremely proud of his accomplishments. I felt that I should continue to train him for the more advanced levels of obedience competition.

Now in Open, the next level of competition after Novice, we are going to ask the dog to "Come, down, come." This, at first, is very confusing for the dog. It takes quite a while and a lot of patience to "explain" this to the dog. The dog will often, at first, ignore the "down" command because it is so used to the straight recall exercise where the dog just does it automatically. This is when a "hard boot" trainer will become physical with the dog, pushing the dog into the "down" and becoming annoyed because the dog "didn't get it" or "didn't drop fast enough." I have been at Obedience Trials where the handler yelled "*Down*" so loudly to the dog that I felt that I had to duck for cover myself! A secret recurring dream of mine was to put a prong collar and leash on these "hard boot" trainers and give them a dose of their own medicine. The dream had me with the leash in my hand, the trainer kneeling on the floor. I scream "*Down*" to them, and without giving them one second to respond, I give them a hard pull with the leash. I show them a one-hundred-dollar bill and say, "You lose. You didn't respond fast enough!"

A fine example of this "hard" handling took place when Sim and I traveled to New Hampshire for a weekend of Obedience Trials that were United Kennel Club sanctioned. The Open Class was going on in one of the two rings. A woman was going to execute the Drop on Recall exercise with her Bearded Collie. The judge signaled for her to call her dog then gave her the signal to "down" the dog. She yelled so loudly and angrily that her dog dropped but looked very frightened. Again, my philosophy of "reading the dog" and trying to put yourself in his head came into play. If the dog doesn't look comfortable doing something, then change the way you are asking the dog to do it.

I began thinking about how I would teach Sim the Drop on Recall Exercise, and the first thing I knew I had to do was to break it down into small sections. I started by telling Sim to sit, then telling him to "Wait," pivot right in front of him and tell him to "Down." At close range he complied easily, but as I increased the distance between us, I could see that he was not sure what I wanted. I began using treats, small pieces of fat-free hotdog being my and Sim's treat of choice. I started again at close range, told him "Down," and when he did, I would reach down immediately while he was down and give him a treat. I very gradually increased my distance from him. I eventually was able to stand about twenty feet away, say "Down," and he would. Now I had to go back and teach him this from a stand because when executing the exercise properly, the dog is coming toward you and has to drop without sitting first, dropping directly to the down. We both did a lot of swallowing on that one.

"This is going to be tricky, Sim."

He looked at me and swallowed, appearing to try to figure out why I was tense. I took a deep breath and attempted to relax by trying Sim's signature swallow.

"OK, Bud, let's give it a try. I'm going to leave you in a stand this time."

He gave me a look and wagged his tail as though he thought my furrowed brow was funny. Usually, I had a confident demeanor when training him. His body language was confident. It was if he was telling me, "Not to worry, Mom. We can do this." Seeing this allowed me to walk about six feet away with some confidence, although not completely. I thought that when I turned to face him, he would be sitting. To my surprise, he was standing. I wanted to praise him at that point, but I couldn't. I had to go on to the next part of the exercise.

"Sim, *doowwnn*," I said, accentuating the command.

Sim looked, dropped, and then wagged his tail.

Hmm, I thought to myself. *This may not be the mountain that I thought it was going to be.* Sometimes it went smoothly and sometimes not, but I persisted patiently and gently, and he got the concept in about a week or so.

The next step was to have the dog sit, tell him to wait, walk about thirty feet away directly across from him, tell him to come, then down, then come, then finish. Sim surprised me with how quickly he put that concept together. He even appeared to enjoy it, wagging his tail while he was down, waiting for me to call him again, almost as though he thought it was our private joke. When he would come to me from the down and sit in front of me, he usually gave a little sneeze, tail wagging all the while. When I had him finish, I could hear his tail brushing the mat as he waited for me to release him from the exercise. "Good job!" I would praise him and give him a pat. He sometimes would sneeze in agreement of how good his Drop on Recall was. The whole process took about a month for Sim to execute this perfectly.

We had done our dumbbell work, and he was able to retrieve it beautifully "on the flat," meaning I threw it, sent him by saying "Take It," having him pick it up, and bring it back to me. He had learned to wait until I said "Give" to release it to my hands and then wait for me to tell him or signal him to "Finish." Now he had to learn to do what is known as a "blind retrieve" of the dumbbell. A jump is set up. The height of the jump is determined by the height of the dog at his shoulders. Sim measured about twelve-and-a-half inches, so his jump height was twelve inches. The reason it is called a "blind retrieve" is because when the dumbbell is thrown over the jump, the dog can't see it. Training gets tricky when the handler can see it and, at first, assumes that the dog can as well. Here again, I saw many dogs being mishandled because the handler would get annoyed with the dog for not knowing where the dumbbell was. When the judge tells you to "Send your dog," you tell the dog "Over." The dog jumps over the barrier *and then* and only then sees where the dumbbell is. He is supposed to pick it up and return over the jump to sit in front of you and hold the dumbbell until the judge tells you "Take it." The dog releases it to your hands and waits for you to command or signal "Finish." Again, this seemed to be an exercise that Sim enjoyed and he learned it quickly. I knew he enjoyed it because every time he saw the jump set up and the dumbbell, he heartily wagged his tail and gave me a string of his little sneezes. It seemed that he couldn't wait to do this exercise.

The last Open exercise that he had to learn was the Broad Jump. I don't know who thought this one up, but it is supposed to simulate a dog jumping over a brook or obstruction to get to you when called. There are four hurdles that graduate in length from four feet, six inches to five feet. They are each eight feet wide, and the elevation ranges from three inches for the smallest, four inches for the next, five inches for the next, and six inches for the longest board. The distance that the dog has to jump is twice the height he has to jump for the High Jump. In Sim's case, he had to jump twenty-four inches for the Broad Jump exercise. Unlike the High Jump, these are much lower to the ground, and require an extended jump by the dog. The handler tells the dog to "Wait" and walks to a position facing the right side of the jump with his or her toes about two feet from the jump. Depending on where the handler determined the proper positioning during training that worked best for the dog, the handler might be standing anywhere from the lowest edge of the first board to the highest edge of the last board. When the judge says "Send your dog," the handler will give the command or signal for the dog to jump. "While the dog is in midair, the handler will execute a ninety-degree pivot but will remain at the same spot. The dog will clear the entire distance of the hurdles without touching them and, without further command or signal, immediately return to a sitting position in front of the handler, finishing as in the Novice Recall." These instructions are taken directly from the AKC book of Obedience Regulations.

I found this exercise hard for me to grasp and then execute, let alone teach it to Sim. But I thought, just like everything else I had taught him, just take one bite at a time. This is one of the keys to successful dog training. We, as humans, understand concepts. A dog is "in the moment," so you break things into tiny pieces for them, making each moment a positive experience. The dog should never "walk" the Broad Jump boards. Some training methods suggest that you line the floor under the boards with chicken wire so that if the dog "walks" over the boards instead of jumping over the boards, there will be a very painful result. For the life of me, I will never understand why any dog trained that way would want to get within a hundred feet of a broad jump.

I knew this was another method I was not interested in. Instead, I set Sim up in front of the lowest board, and then I walked to the other side and called him. At first, he looked at me and swallowed several times. I knew this wasn't going to be easy. I decided to put his leash on. I then walked with him, stepping over the board. At first, he stopped and looked at me then jumped with me by his side. "Good boy!" I told him. We did this several times.

Then I tried the setup again. I left him in front of one board, placed myself across from him, and then called him. He jumped the board and came to a sit in front of me. When I told him, "Good boy!" he began his little sneezes that meant "I know." Little by little, the second board was added, close to the first one initially and then placed at the required eight inches away. Now I had to add the pivot, so as Sim was jumping, instead of staying in front of the last board, I would put in a small turn, stepping backward. He grasped the concept very quickly, so each time, I called him over the boards. I would go farther back on my turn. Eventually, I ended up beside the boards in the proper position for the exercise. Now I had to find the "sweet spot" beside the boards that gave Sim enough turning room but where he would not cut the corner as he came over the jump.

Finally, one day, everything came together. By breaking the exercise down step by step, not moving ahead until he understood each individual piece of the exercise, Sim was able to perform the Broad Jump Exercise. I tried it again to make sure that he really knew what he was doing. Sure enough, he did. I knew we had to practice to polish everything, and I also wanted to start looking for Obedience Trials to try him out in the Open Class. It is very unusual for a dog to qualify in Open quickly. It often takes many, many times because of the level of difficulty.

Another very important part of training, be it pet obedience or competitive, is that the dog has to be "proofed." Proofing the dog means that the dog can withstand distractions and focus on what you have commanded him to do and should do nothing else until you command the dog to do something different. An example of a proofing exercise would be that you put your dog in a sit/stay. You would then have someone else walk by the dog and have them say "*Down*" loudly as they pass the dog without using the dog's name. The dog should remain in the sit/stay. If the dog breaks the command, you know that the dog does not yet fully understand the command.

The way dogs process information once they learn a particular command is to anticipate what you are going to ask them to do.

Have you ever seen a dog go through "the whole routine?" It reminds me of a baseball pitcher or batter that has several different movements or twitches that they go through before they either swing the bat or pitch the ball. What I mean by this is that the owner tells the dog to sit. The dog sits, then lies down, then rolls over with no prompting from the owner. That is because the dog has been trained to do one trick followed by the other. The handler didn't train the dog to fully understand one command completely before going on to the next one. This is where proofing comes in again. When you are competing with your dog, many times there is more than one obedience ring being used. So let's say that you have told your dog to stay and the person in the next ring calls their dog. You don't want your dog to respond to the other handler's command and come to you. Something else that can happen is that the dog hears the judge's command and anticipates what you are going to ask the dog to do. The dog is not supposed to do anything unless you give the command. This is why we "proof" the dog against as many possible distractions as we can conjure up

Chapter 12

Love is the seed of all hope.
It is the enticement to trust, to risk, to try, to go on.

—"Fully Alive"

My friend of many years, Eva, the same Eva from whom we got Topsy, and her husband, Steve, came for a visit to ring in the New Year of 2000 with us. We hadn't seen each other in some time because they had moved around the East Coast and now were living in a suburb of Philadelphia. We had kept in touch with each other by phone regularly, however. Their Shar Pei, Brandy, had died in late 1996. Several years earlier, Eva and Steve had come for a visit. It was at the time that we had our Chow Chow, Joi. The two dogs got along very well. Brandy was a very happy-go-lucky dog. She looked forward to every day and loved meeting people. She was also very intuitive.

Eva said that she had a serious story to tell me about Brandy. She told me that soon after they had moved to the Philadelphia area, their neighbors invited them to a cookout. Everyone had met and loved Brandy and said that she was invited as well. Because she was so well trained and behaved, most people enjoyed having her around. She was doing well at the cookout, enjoying the games of fetch and catch that people were engaging her in. There was a neighbor of whom everyone thought very highly. He was the "go-to guy" whenever anyone needed help with a problem. He also was active in the different youth clubs and coached various sports for kids. As soon as Brandy saw him, her hackles went up and she growled. Eva was very embarrassed and tried to settle the dog down. Brandy continued this behavior and the closer the man came, even though he was talking nicely to her, the more agitated she became. Steve said that he would take Brandy home and apologized for her inappropriate behavior. No one could figure out what had happened. However, about three months later, the shocking news hit the neighborhood that this man had been arrested for child molestation. Brandy was able to see through all the veneer that the man put forth. We will never know exactly what she sensed about him, but she certainly let everyone know that he was not to be trusted.

Eva was still so very distraught over the loss of Brandy that she had kept her distance and had not interacted with another dog since Brandy's death. Sim acted in his usual well-behaved fashion. He kept watching her. Eva would talk to Sim but didn't pet him. Sim seemed a bit confused but respected this. That is, until the next morning. Frank and Steve had gone out together. Eva was still in bed. As far as I knew, Sim was in one of his places but not within my sight.

"Peg, can you come here?" Eva said, calling me softly.

The bedroom door was slightly ajar, just enough for Sim to squeeze through. Sim was up on the bed with Eva, quietly snuggled into her, and she was crying. Through her tears she said, "This is the first dog that I have felt comfortable enough to become emotionally attached. Sim has really helped me to get over that first hurdle. I now feel so peaceful. It is like he's a little angel."

Chapter 13

All good things come to an end, sometimes
giving way to things even better.

—"We Have This Moment"

In March, I returned to the trainer whom I had worked with before
the obedience trials the year before. We began working the Open
exercises. Sim started with enthusiasm, but as the lesson wore on,
he became "flat." So much so that when the trainer wanted me to
have him do the Broad Jump, I said no. I felt he was too tired. You
can just imagine the look I got, but it was my dog, and I knew that
something was not right with him. He slept on the drive home. The
next day, he was a little better but still seemed sluggish. I didn't work
him that day and thought that maybe he needed a bit of a layoff.
He was not eating with the same gusto he had been, and he would
have what I call "little whoops ups." I wouldn't see him "whoops up,"
but he always would "show me." If he had done it under the bed, he
would look at me, point his nose under the bed, and then look at
me again. I began to learn this signal and look where he directed me.
The frequency of this stomach upset began to worry me. However,
these episodes would come and go, and when he was feeling good,
he worked beautifully. It didn't occur to me that this could be a fore-
shadowing of a more serious problem with Sim. I proceeded to enter
him in the Open Class for the first time.

The show that I entered Sim in was being held at the Eastern
States Exposition in West Springfield, Massachusetts. When the

Breed Shows and Obedience Trials are held here, they are very well attended, with people coming in from all over the country. The atmosphere is very frenetic. If the breed people aren't grooming their dogs with blow dryers going full blast, they are running their dogs up and down the aisles to warm them up, with the treats they use dropping all over the floor. When the breed people show their dogs in the ring, they are allowed to use treats. We obedience people, on the other hand, would get disqualified if we had any treats at all on our person. We train our dogs never to pick up anything off the floor. The obedience people are trying to find a small piece of clean, treat-free ground to warm up their dogs before they go into the ring, but they want to keep their dogs calm. The lighting is harsh; it is extremely warm and crowded, and there are vendors and their wares lined up on all sides of the building. The noise from all of this is deafening.

I tried to keep Sim as relaxed as possible and lightly worked him before we went into the ring. When our turn came, the steward approached me, and I removed Sim's leash and handed it to her. I instantly knew we were going to have a problem. Sim mentally disconnected with me, put his nose to the mats, and began to sniff.

"Good morning," the judge said as she approached us and told me where to set him up for the heeling exercises. I could not guide him by the collar, but I petted and talked to him, trying to get him to connect with me again.

"Come on, Bud, we have some work to do," I said as I led him to the starting point. He gave me a brief glance that said it all. Those wonderful eyes were dull looking, and I saw disappointment in them. He as much as said, "I can't do this for you this time." My pride took over. I had practiced long and hard for this. I had paid the entry fees. People whom I knew and didn't know were watching. I knew better than Sim. We would work through this and have a reasonable presentation.

The judge asked me, "Are you ready?"

I looked at Sim and said "Watch," sweetly. He wouldn't look at me.

I said "yes" to the judge, and she said "Forward."

I said, "Sim, heel," and off I went. Sim took a few steps with me and then started sniffing obsessively at the mats. I ended up executing the heeling pattern by myself. The figure-eights were no better. He had shut down. Being fairly new to competitive obedience, I didn't know that I could have and should have told the judge that Sim wasn't feeling well and ask to be excused from the ring.

The judge showed me where to set him up for the Drop on Recall, one of his favorite exercises. I left him and went to the end of the mat. She signaled me to call him. I did, and he started slowly, almost painfully toward me, slightly tripping over his feet. She gave me the "down" signal, and I said, "Sim, down." He dropped and gave me a pained look. We finished the exercise and continued the other exercises. He did none of them. As my disappointment and embarrassment grew, I became more disgruntled with Sim. I couldn't believe what just happened. When I came out of the ring, everyone watching had an opinion. Comments like, "See, you have to be tougher with him and let him know who's boss." "Try the ear pinch. It really helps." As I was putting him in his travel crate, I gave him a treat.

A voice behind me said, "You're not going to give him a cookie after that performance, are you?" All of a sudden it dawned on me that Sim had done the best he could manage that day.

I spun around and said, "He did the best he could today. It seems very obvious that he isn't feeling well."

My tone was less than friendly. I should have thanked her because it made me realize that Sim and I were a team, and if either one of us was not up to the task, so be it. It didn't matter what anyone else thought. I knew the relationship we had, and I almost destroyed it because of my own ego. *Never again*, I thought. *I'll find out what needs to be fixed in my training of him and will fix it. I know he can do it all. Something was very wrong today.* But had I really learned the lesson Sim just taught me? At first, I was a very slow learner.

He continued to go through bouts of being "off." Either he was less than enthusiastic about his food or he might be ravenous. When he was ravenous, it usually precluded a bout of tummy upset. This showed up as vomiting and lack of energy. I wondered if a change of diet was in order. Again, I tried this and that, different supplements that were supposed to aid digestion and "unlock your dog's maximum energy." Nothing seemed to help for any period. If anything, they made it worse. In some ways, his physical problems paralleled mine. I had suffered with a hard-to-diagnose issue and was left with permanent damage and sensitivities that most doctors couldn't understand nor give me any relief from. Even after it was learned that I had been subjected to carbon monoxide for three years, there still were no answers as to how to handle my physical problems.

I took him for his annual checkup. Each time the vet would tell me, "He's a healthy boy," I was perplexed. I was still "peeling the onion." Periodically, when the tummy issue became more acute, Sim would be put on a course of medication or medications. They seemed to work, but not for very long. I even went to a different vet for a second opinion, but nothing changed. And his obedience work was a challenge. Sometimes he would work with great enthusiasm. Other times, it seemed like it was an ordeal for him to even think about it. He also began having problems with allergies. He would become very itchy and would go into spasms of "backward sneezing." This is exactly the right description. His body would stiffen, and he would "honk," seeming to breathe backward. I discovered that if I massaged the indentation in the middle of the back of his neck between his shoulders, it would ease the spasm. We then had to use different antihistamines seasonally to keep him comfortable.

The oddest behavior that I noticed during all of this was that Sim would go away from me instead of coming to me for comfort. I thought that it was probably because in his past life, he had gotten in trouble for exhibiting any normal bodily function. This was an area that I knew I had to work on. His association of not feeling well and being scolded for it was well ingrained in him. I didn't quite know how I would get him to feel at ease with me when he felt ill, but I was going to keep trying until I found the answer. I often felt sad that I hadn't gotten him as a puppy. He was such a fine animal and had been put through so much discomfort that my heart went out to him. I was determined, however, that one day we would overcome this together. Add to this the fact that Sim seemed to instinctively know when I didn't feel well, whether it was something minor as a sinus headache or major as when I broke my left ankle. He would jump up on the bed with me and either curl up by my feet, in the small of my back, or sometimes just lie beside me, putting one of his front paws in my hand. When I didn't feel well, he wanted to be physically connected to me as opposed to how he wanted to be alone when he felt poorly.

I heard about another trainer who lived in Greenwich, Connecticut. He was an AKC obedience judge, showed his dogs in obedience himself, and often was in the top four, if not the top two highest scoring competitors. Golden Retrievers were his breed of choice. He was judging a trial that Sim and I were entered in. One of the women who were competing told me that she had trained with him. His name was Art Brown. She said that he was very patient and gentle in his training style. She gave me his phone number. I called him and told him some of the problems I was having with Sim and asked him if he would be willing to meet with us. I also told him that I had a video of his poor performance at Eastern States and what I found interesting was that he had tripped over his feet on the Drop on Recall exercise. Art said he would be glad to see what he could do for us.

When Frank, Sim, and I arrived at Art's house, he ushered us into his family room. There was clothesline strung from one end of the room to the other. The line was full of all the placement ribbons his dogs had won in competitive obedience. It was almost intimidating because of the level of achievement his dogs had attained. He interacted with Sim, and it was almost love at first sight for both of them.

He couldn't get over Sim's brightness and alertness. We showed him the video. The difference in Sim's demeanor on the tape versus how he was acting with Art was quite stark in comparison. Sim was happy and animated as opposed to how stilted he was on the tape. Art then took us outside to his "training area." He had set up a regulation size obedience ring in his backyard with white regulation obedience gates. He had me work Sim. It was a bit different as both

Sim and I were not used to working much outside. However, Sim did fairly well, and Art was able to see what needed work.

He gave me some good ideas. For instance, when Art had me throw the dumbbell for Sim and Sim was looking for it, I was going to help the dog, but Art showed me by Sim's actions that he was in work mode, not confused. He said to just let Sim be and see if he could find it on his own. It was very helpful learning the difference as to when the dog would need guidance and when he was figuring out a problem on his own. I liked Art's style of training. A "hard boot" trainer would have had me use a harsh method to get Sim to find the dumbbell faster.

It showed me the difference between when a dog is in work mode, trying to understand an exercise, or when a dog does not understand an exercise at all. Art thought that Sim had potential, and we made an appointment for another lesson. We had four or five sessions with Art. He could see when Sim was "off" but could not seem to be able to offer me any idea as to why. It didn't make sense to him. I still felt that something was bothering Sim physically, but we just hadn't found the answer yet.

Sim celebrated his fifth birthday on December tenth. I still had hope that I could get him healthy and happy again to continue his obedience career. I let him rest and enjoy the holidays. As usual, he was lavished with toys from me and many of my clients. His toy chest was beginning to overflow. And every toy that he played with was in such good condition that throwing any away wasn't even a thought. Sometimes I would go through the toys to possibly sort out the ones he no longer played with and donate them to the local shelter. He'd watch me go through all of them and when I would get to the ones that he hadn't played with for a while, he would wag his tail gleefully, take the toy from the pile, and play with it for days. It was as though he had discovered an old friend again.

He developed, on his own, a very endearing habit. I first noticed it when Paula came to visit. Sim greeted her and then disappeared. As we were talking, Paula asked, "Where's Mr. Sims?"

"I don't know. I'm surprised that he isn't sitting here with us. You know how he loves to be part of everything."

No sooner did I have the words out of my mouth when Sim came running into the living room with a stuffed toy that Paula had given him.

"Look what he's got, Peg. I gave him that toy last Christmas."

"I know. That's amazing. He did the same thing with Janet the other day. I thought it was just a fluke. But when my friend Helen visited, he brought her one of the toys she had given him."

Sim ran over to Paula and dropped the toy at her feet. She threw it, and he brought it back to her. This went on for a few minutes before he then went into his "I'm a very well-behaved dog" mode, as he politely sat quietly.

Chapter 14

What is the stuff love's made of that can cause the world
to glow? Is it that you made the segments that I brought
you, well and whole? Was it when I came to recognize
the poet in your soul that I began to love you?

—"When Did I Start to Love You?"

As we ushered in 2001, Sim's health was still up and down. He could
go for fairly long periods where his tummy would be okay. But then
he would have a poor period. I kept working with the vet to try to
keep him in balance. We worked with the prescription diet, and she
had me administer medications when necessary. Sim helped me to
hone my skills to be able to "read" him, which helped to "read" other
dogs that I worked with as well. He taught me to pick up on the subtleties of the signals he was sending me. Sometimes I did very well at
picking them up. Other times, I was totally dense. One of his signals
that something was "off" with him was a type of sneeze. This was not
the normal variety. It was a deep, spasmodic episode with the sneezes
being so strong that sometimes his face would hit the floor. When I
first saw it, I laughed because it just had a very comical look about it.
As time went on, however, I realized that it was no laughing matter
and I should watch him closely.

Early in the year, I received news that Eva was dying of cancer.
She had only been ill for a short time, but the cancer spread throughout her body very rapidly. When we visited her in July, she had just
been released from the hospital. She had surgery to remove tumors

from her colon. The surgeon did the best he could, but there was an active tumor on her liver.

She put up a brave battle for about seven months. But the battle was coming to an end. She was failing rapidly, and my heart ached for her.

In February, her husband, Steve, called and told us that she was in the hospital and was going to be moved to the hospice floor. Would it be possible for us to get there to see her? She also wanted very much to see Mr. Sims. We left the next day. It was a long drive, about six hours, but Sim did well. We arrived at her house where Sim had been several months before. As soon as we got in the door, he began looking for her, sniffing everywhere, and then going upstairs, tail wagging, so sure he would find her where he had last seen her. When he couldn't find her, he looked dejected. We fed him then put him in his travel crate at Eva's house so that he would be safe while we visited Eva in the hospital. When we got there, she seemed fairly well, laughing and joking with us. Her husband told her how Sim had searched for her all over the house. I said that I would get permission from the nurses to bring him in the next morning to see her. She was very happy about this and was looking forward to seeing him.

Frank and I arrived at the hospital the next morning. I spoke to the nurses, and they said they had to call my friend's doctors to clear Sim. I presented them his therapy dog paperwork, verifying that he was up to date on all his shots and was in good health. Frank said he would wait with Sim at the desk for clearance while I went to my friend's room. I walked down the hall to her room, very excited to tell her that Sim would be in to see her very shortly.

"Hi, Eva," I said as I approached her bedside. My heart went to my shoes. She obviously had deteriorated greatly overnight. "How are you today? Oh, you can't see me because your glasses are on the table. Let me get them for you." There was no response. She was in a coma, and her breathing was very labored.

I called one of the nurses. She said that my friend did not have much time left. Frank and Sim came into the room. Before they approached the bed, I told Frank, "She's not the same as last night. It doesn't look good at all." Frank was as shocked as I was, but he spoke to her and held Sim up so that if she had any cognition at all, she would know that Sim was there. Sim's eyes widened as he looked at her and started to wag his tail. Then his eyes saddened. It was as if he knew that his friend was very ill.

We didn't stay too long because I felt that we should let her husband know that she was in her last hours if not minutes. Just before I left the room, I held her hand and kissed her on the cheek. "Good bye, my dear friend. We shared the good times and bad times together. I'll miss you." And with those words, I left her room with a cloud of great sadness wrapped around me. We stopped back at Eva's to tell Steve that she was in very bad condition and that he should go to the hospital immediately. Another friend of Eva's was at the house, and Steve said that he and Ellen would be going there shortly. Just as Frank and I were getting ready to leave, the phone rang. It was the hospital letting Steve know that Eva had died about an hour ago. If I had been told by the nurse that the end was that near, I certainly would have stayed with her.

All the way home, Sim just stayed quietly in the back seat. He seemed very "off." When we stopped for a potty break, he didn't want to eat anything, showing no usual enthusiasm for the different environment. The stress of the situation had taken its toll on him. Again, Sim the Teacher showed me sometimes, even though dogs cannot verbalize their sadness, they still are affected by it.

Sim's mourning continued for about a week. However, I continued his obedience training, hoping that it would be one of the ways to help him to get over it. There was nothing else I could do for him, and I knew that only the passage of time would bring him relief.

I took him to many different training facilities for what are known as "run-thru's" of his Open routine. Run-thru's are practice sessions where someone puts you and the dog through your routine without judging. It is sort of a mock trial. The dog doesn't know whether it's the real thing or not. Or so we thought. After much experience and "listening" to Sim, it appears that dogs do know the difference because of the level of stress that we show. Naturally, we are much more relaxed when we're practicing. Our body language says it all to the dog. That being said, it still was good practice because each training setting was different, preparing Sim for many possibilities that might take place while he was competing. His run-thru's under many different circumstances looked very promising. He was training forwardly, so I started looking for obedience trials again for him to compete in.

The American Kennel Club puts each breed of dog in one of seven groups. They are Sporting, Hounds, Working Dogs, Terriers, Toys, Non-Sporting, and Herding Dogs. Sim was part of the Toy Group, which also includes the Pug, Maltese, Chihuahua, and the Yorkshire Terrier, to name a few. They are all large dogs in small packages. I received a premium from the Toy Dog Club. A premium is a notice of upcoming shows and trials, the dates and place where they are being held, the entry form, and the list of judges for each class. The Toy Dog Club always has their event around Memorial Day weekend. I thought I would enter Sim because it might be less stressful for him. There would only be toy breeds being shown. Not that size ever bothered him. If nothing else, though, this might be a positive experience for him, whether he qualified or not.

The facility was about an hour and a half away. It was a four-day show, so we made reservations at a motel that was close to the show site. Frank and I took Sim to the site the night before to familiarize him with it. He seemed to enjoy the trip and was comfortable in the facility. The next day, we arrived at the facility and set up our chairs and Sim's crate. He seemed to be in fairly good humor but slightly distracted by all the noise and activity going on. My turn was coming, so I began to warm him up. I told him to "Watch," and he kept his attention on me as I walked him up and down the outside of the ring. People commented to me how great he looked.

When I entered the ring, he didn't fully disconnect, but I wasn't confident that he would have a qualifying performance.

We didn't quite make it this time. I put the leash on Sim, grabbed my armband, and hustled out of the ring, praising him all the way. When we got to our seat, I gave him a couple of his favorite treats. "Good job," I told him, giving him a kiss on top of his head. *Tomorrow is another day*, I thought even though I was disappointed. When I showed Sim in the Novice Class, he got his Companion Dog title in three trials. I guess that made me have unreasonable expectations when it came to him earning his Companion Dog Excellent. *It's the "Excellent" part of the title that's the killer,* I thought to myself. It seemed to me that the judging was more strident because we were no longer a novice dog and handler team.

Chapter 15

Don't let any past failures discourage you from facing
the challenges of a new day. Remember, we have all
sometimes failed. Maybe we learn more from failures
than successes. Dismiss the past and start again.

—Decision Vision

After the scores of your class are posted, you can ask the judge reasonable questions. I asked him about Sim's score on heeling so that I would know what to work on. He rudely answered me saying, "That heeling was atrocious!"

"Oh," I said. "I didn't think it was terrific, but I wouldn't have classified it as atrocious." He ignored my comment and turned to the next handler to answer her question.

I learned another very valuable lesson with that experience. Judges, though impartial, have a breed or group that they might favor. They also have their own idea of what "perfection" is. There is an obedience judge who is an engineer. He wants everything to be very exact and precise. Another judge might overlook "exactness" for spirit. This taught me to research my judges and their temperament before entering Sim. However, the judge that we were showing under the next day was known to have a very hard pencil, meaning that he was a very rigid marker. He never "gave" anyone anything when scoring.

We packed up our gear to go back to the motel and get some rest for the next day's events. Frank is an avid *Star Trek* fan and will watch the program whenever he can find it. It just so happened that there was an episode of *Star Trek* on that evening. In a humorous way, I started using the Vulcan Mind Meld on Mr. Sims. The Vulcan Mind Meld was a method that Mr. Spock used to either gather or transfer information from himself to another life form. He would place his forehead on their forehead and the transfer would take place. That night, I told Sim that his heeling would have to improve, so we were going to have a Vulcan Mind Meld session to see if it helped him. I put my forehead on the top of his head and said, "Sim, you've got to stop that lagging when we heel. You do all the other exercises like a Border Collie, but your heeling leaves much to be desired. According to the judge, today it was *summa cum lousy!*"

He wagged his tail, rolled his eyes, and swallowed. It was if he were saying, "I gotcha, Mom."

We'll see, I thought.

The next morning, we arrived at the show site and found that there were a few more entries in Sim's class than the day before. "Long days of living, training, and travel together will foster in a dog and his handler an almost clairvoyant connection, with each fluently anticipating the moods and tendencies of the other. At their best, the pair of individuals will seem a single, fantastic creature possessing six legs, two hearts and one mind" (Anonymous).

I began to warm Sim up. He was giving me good attention, was enthusiastic, and seemed to be "up on his toes." The judge was an older man, and as I said earlier, his reputation preceded him. However, he was very pleasant when Sim and I entered the ring, although I thought I saw him cast a wary eye at Sim. It is very unusual to see a Shih Tzu in competitive obedience. Some trainers will tell you that the Shih Tzu is "very biddable," meaning that they accept training. This statement is usually made with a bit of an air of superiority. However, these trainers never are seen in the competitive obedience ring with a Shih Tzu. They usually show Border Collies, Golden Retrievers, Labradors, Shelties, and many of the other breeds that have a strong work ethic. These breeds not only learn the exercises, but they also look forward to doing them. In the world of Shih Tzus, it just depends whether they feel like working that day or not.

Most of the time, they would rather have you plump up their pillow, bring them a treat, and leave the heavy lifting to another breed.

I handed Sim's leash and dumbbell to the steward, and the judge showed us where to set up for the heeling exercise. He asked me, "Are you ready?"

I looked down at Sim and said, "Watch." Sim looked up at me with those great eyes of his. "Yes" I said.

The judge said "Forward."

I told Sim to "Heel," and off we went down the right side of the ring. His heeling was spot on this time. He was with me every step of the way.

As I approached the end of the heeling exercise, the judge said "Halt." Sim was sitting right next to me.

When the judge said "Exercise finished," I praised Sim lavishly. He gave me his little sneeze again.

The two stewards entered the ring for the figure 8 exercise. Once again Sim's heeling and attention was what it should be and when we finished his eyes were brighter than before.

"Exercise finished," said the judge. I praised Sim again enthusiastically.

Phew! I thought. *I can't believe that we made it through the heeling portion without a glitch. Sim loves the rest of the exercises, so I think we're in fairly good shape. We've got four more exercises to go.*

I took a deep breath and followed the judge to the starting point of the Drop on Recall exercise. Sim was looking at me with excitement in his eyes. He executed the Drop on Recall better that I had ever seen him. He was "on" and enjoying every minute of it.

When the judge handed me Sim's dumbbell, I could see the surprise on his face. Maybe this is the first time he had ever seen a Shih Tzu work well in the Open class, if at all. As we went through the exercise, Sim did it with more enthusiasm than the one before. At the end of the exercise, I gave Sim the signal, and he came right around to my left side and sat.

"Exercise finished," the judge said, with some excitement in his voice.

"Good boy, Sim!" He looked at me with those fiery eyes. At that point, we had to move over to the High Jump for the blind retrieve. I took a deep breath. *If we get through this one, and Sim does it well, there's only the Broad Jump left*, I thought.

"Throw the dumbbell," the judge told me. I threw it over the jump. I heard Sim sneeze. The judge said, "Send your dog."

"Sim, over," I said. Sim took off and sailed over the jump, found the dumbbell, sailed back over the jump, stopping and sitting squarely in front of me. At this point, I was beginning to feel light-headed, and things were becoming a blur. I couldn't believe my eyes. Sim was in his Border Collie mode, working his heart out. I was in a fog and literally was working on autopilot. It was as though I was floating in air and watching what was going on. The next thing I knew, I was standing with Sim at the Broad Jump.

I was beginning to wonder if Sim was tiring from his great effort. I knew that he could do it, but the question was, would he do it? The judge showed us where to set up. "Are you ready?" he asked. I looked at Sim. I could begin to see the fatigue setting in, but he still looked bright.

"Yes," I said.

"Leave your dog," the judge said.

"Sim, wait," I told him, trying to let him know that I knew he was tired and that we were almost finished. I took my place on the right side of the boards, squarely between the two of them as this was Sim's "sweet spot."

"Send your dog," the judge commanded.

"Sim, *jump!*" I made my voice more emphatic, almost trying to give him the extra energy he needed to get him through the exercise. And jump he did, flying over the broad boards, striding out a few steps when he landed, looking to see that I had turned to face him, and then turning to head straight toward me, stopping and sitting at my feet.

"*Finish*," the judge said rather loudly. I signaled Sim and he strutted around me, coming to a sit next to me on my left side. "*Exercise finished!*" the judge said loudly and with great enthusiasm. His astonishment with the performance of a Shih Tzu was most evident. With that, the whole arena burst into loud applause and cheers. The judge came over to me while I was waiting for the steward to return my leash. He had a huge smile on his face and said, "Great job. He was a little slow at first, but now he seems like he's just getting warmed up." I couldn't believe it. Sim had pulled off his best performance to date.

I put his leash on, ran him out of the ring, praising him each step of the way, and gave him several treats when we got to our seats. Frank praised him lavishly as well. The woman with the Papillion said to me, "Nice job!"

"Thank you," I said to her, but I knew we still had the sits and downs to get through. If he didn't do his Stays, he would receive a non-qualifying score. My heart was in my throat, and my nerves were on edge. This time, the lightheadedness I felt was purely caused by nerves. I decided to take him outside for a potty break and to steady myself as well. Other people came up to me, complimenting me on Sim's performance.

"Mr. Sims showed them all how to do it today," the elderly man with his Shih Tzu proudly said to me. He was working on the Companion Dog title for his dog, Chuckie.

I thanked them, and I greatly appreciated all the praise, but still had that twinge in my gut because of the Sits and Downs.

We went back to our spot by the Obedience Ring. We waited for the last dog and handler to finish. I took a deep breath, took Sim out of his crate, put his leash on, and slipped my armband back on to my left arm. I walked him around slowly just to let him know we were getting ready to work again. The steward told us to line up. This usually is in numerical order. We were then ushered into the ring and shown our place. I believe there were eight of us. I took Sim's leash off and placed it and my armband behind him. The judge told us the rules of the Sit and Down exercises and that if a dog moved from its position, one of the stewards would hold the dog until the handlers returned.

Sim was sitting and starting to become restless while we listened to the judge. I was worried to begin with, and now Sim was getting "ants in his pants." I thought that I should invent some sort of glue that could safely be applied to the dog's rear end to keep him in place.

The judge asked, "Is everyone ready?"

We all answered "Yes."

He said, "Sit your dogs." Even though Sim was sitting, I reminded him to "sit." He shot me a look as if to say, "Duh…I am sitting."

The judge said, "Leave your dog." I told him to "stay," and we all filed out, being led by the steward. As we waited out of sight of our dogs, one of the handlers had a watch and began letting us know as each minute ticked by. The steward also let some of the handlers know if their dog had broken the sit. "Ten seconds to go," the handler watching the time said. The judge signaled the steward, and we returned to the ring across from our dog. Sim was sitting! I had to contain myself because we still had to wait for the judge to say "Return to your dog." If the dog broke as we returned, we again faced disqualification. I walked around Sim to return to Heel position. "Exercise finished," the judge said.

"Good boy, Sim," I told him but stayed a little reserved because we still had the five-minute Down to go through. The judge directed us to "Down your dog."

I pointed to the floor and told Sim, "Down." He looked at me with sort of devilish look on his face and very, very slowly went down. My heart was thumping. *Get a grip, girl*, I thought.

The judge told us to "Leave your dog." We all told our dogs to "Stay" and once again filed out together to wait for the five minutes to slowly tick by.

Some of the handlers were very disappointed because their dog had broken the Sit. Most took it in stride, but a few said what they were going to do to their dogs to "fix this problem." One handler actually said that she was going to take her dog to the middle of town, put a prong collar on him, and make him sit for a "very long time." I said nothing but thought how they might end up making the problem worse instead of better. Sim had taught me well that we cannot impose our will on the dog. I felt a twinge of sadness for these dogs. They love unconditionally and will usually try to do what they are asked to do. The fault, more often than not, is that the handler has not clearly taught the dog what is expected. They don't look at their training methods to see how they could improve the communication with their dog.

The judge signaled the steward, and we filed back to the ring across from our dogs. The judge said "Return," and we did. Sim was still down but had his head up, watching intently. Some of the other dogs had fallen asleep. "Exercise finished," the judge said.

"Sim, you're the best," I said to him quietly as I put his leash back on him. We had qualified and gotten our first leg toward the CDX title. The judge walked down the line, telling each handler who qualified and who did not. He told the qualifiers not to go too far because he would be calling us back into the ring as soon as he completed his paperwork, and we would receive our qualifying ribbon and find out who the top finishers were. I was on Cloud Nine.

Sim was excited as well, accepting all the attention and treats he was being given, sneezing his little happy sneeze every so often. The judge finished his paperwork and called all the qualifying teams back into the ring. He explained to the crowd how the scoring is done and that the teams have to obtain at least 50 percent of each exercise in order to qualify. You start with two hundred points and then points are deducted for each "fault" that occurs. I had no idea, at that point, what our score was. I knew he had done well and had been cheered loudly by the crowd, but there were other good competitors. The judge studied his paperwork and then announced, "In first place, in the Open Class, with a score of 189½, dog and handler 347."

Oh my God, I thought. *Sim won his Class!* A loud cheer and applause went up from the crowd. The judge handed me the blue First Place rosette as well as the green qualifying ribbon. He had a huge smile on his face and shook my hand firmly.

"Congratulations, great job," he said.

I immediately bent down and showed Sim his ribbons. "Look what you earned, Bud," I said. He looked at me, wagged his tail, and gave one of those little sneezes that were becoming his trademark.

As we were leaving the ring, one of the stewards approached me. She said, "Don't go anywhere because as of right now, you are the highest scoring team. You might win High In Trial."

I laughed. "Really?" I said. "I don't think this will last long." There were many more teams to go in the Novice classes, and any one of them might obtain a higher score than ours. Even though Sim had won his class, his score of 189½ was definitely beatable. He had lost nine and a half points on heeling, one point on his Drop on Recall, and half a point on his Retrieve on the Flat. As I said before, this judge was known to have "a very heavy pencil."

We got some lunch and sat outside in the afternoon sun. Sim's coat glistened, the golden patches looking particularly striking. He snoozed, recouping from his strenuous morning. We walked him around a bit and then returned to ringside to find out if we still had the highest score. We did, so we waited, watching each and every team. It was late in the afternoon when the last team finished. The judge gave out the scores and order of finish in the Novice A class. The steward came over to me and said, "You made it. You got High In Trial." I couldn't believe my ears. High in Trial is a once-in-a-lifetime achievement, if not a one-in-a-million chance, when you're showing a Shih Tzu. There were only three of us that had showed Shih Tzus at obedience trials. There was the elderly man with Chuckie, there was a woman from upstate New York, and me.

I kept petting and talking to Sim. He seemed appreciative of the attention but swallowed several times because he didn't understand why my excitement level was so high. The final ceremony at an Obedience Trial is the High In Trial award and another award called High Combined. High Combined is awarded to the dog and handler that exhibited in both the Utility and Open Class in the same day and received a qualifying score in each class. This is really grueling as the dog has to execute both the Utility exercises and then all the Open exercises.

The two of us and our dogs entered the ring. My head was spinning. I just couldn't believe that this was happening. I kept expecting to wake up from a great dream. The judge handed me the High In Trial rosette. It was almost a large as Mr. Sims. It was a large blue and gold rosette with long blue and gold ribbons and gold fringe. I also received a director's chair with a canvas equipment bag attached. It was imprinted with the words "High In Trial" and the hosting club's logo on the back. And still to be done was the picture with the judge. I didn't want the day to end.

As much as I thought I was being considerate of Mr. Sims, I was sadly mistaken. We had our picture taken with the judge, and he again said what a wonderful job we both had done and thought that Sim had a great future competing. We finally left after a very long day, went back to the motel, fed Sim, and then went out for a celebration dinner. I was giddy. I told Frank all through dinner how I thought Sim could qualify again tomorrow and we would have two legs toward his title. I had become complacent and forgot the difficult level I was competing in and asking Sim to repeat an unbelievable performance. It's too bad that I hadn't seen the pictures immediately after they were taken with the judge. I would have seen the stress and fatigue in Sim's eyes and face. He had put in a grueling day, with his usual schedule completely turned upside down. Instead, I thought he was invincible, forgetting one of my primary rules and what the judge in Maine had told me. Neither one of us are machines. If a machine becomes stressed, something can be fixed, repaired, or adjusted. When a living being becomes stressed, it is not only the mechanical part but the mental part that needs to be fixed, repaired, and adjusted.

Think about sustaining an injury such as a broken arm. You can pinpoint the pain and address it. But depending what medicine you have to take, how bad the pain is, how impaired you are, and how difficult your daily routine is disrupted, there is mental and/or emotional injury. Because the body is on alert to heal itself, it draws energy from the body wherever it can. The whole incident can make you feel edgy, depressed, overwrought, and possibly angry. You can't explain why you feel the way you do, but it all has to do with the healing and recovery process.

After a good night's sleep, we returned the next morning to the show site. My adrenaline was pumping. I was almost taking for granted what Sim had to do. We waited as the other Open teams worked. As the one just ahead of me started, I took Sim out of his crate to warm him up next to the ring. He gave me his attention, but the eyes were not as bright as the day before. *That's OK*, I thought. *It's a small class, and he can beat most of these dogs.* When our turn came, I removed the leash, handed it to the steward, and entered the ring. Sim was beginning to become disinterested. I tried to spark him up for each exercise. He half-heartedly executed all of them well enough to qualify before Sits and Downs. When I came out of the ring with him, I told Frank, "This is it. He'll win the class again, but I don't think he'll get High In Trial because his performance was only marginal."

Soon it was time for Sits and Downs. The judge talked to us about the rules and then started the Sit exercise. "Sit your dogs," she said. I told Sim to sit but did not connect with him as I should have. I had gotten cocky and sounded it.

"Leave your dogs," the judge said, and we lined up behind the steward and filed out of the ring. About two minutes into the exercise, some of the dogs went down, including Sim. I could feel the disappointment and annoyance spread over me.

We were called back into the ring to return to our dogs. Sim was down and looked at me. He knew I wasn't happy and it reflected in his eyes, but he also was disappointed. His disappointment was not in the situation; it was in me. We set the dogs up for the Down exercise, but my heart was not in it, and Sim could sense it. He stayed down for the five minutes, but what good was it? *He could have had first place, another blue ribbon, and another leg with only one left to go for his CDX*, I thought. *But he blew it.*

Frank tried to console me, pointing out all the people that told us how many times they showed their dog in the Open Class before they got their title. I was acting like a brat but didn't care. After all, look at all the work I had done, and all I had asked Sim to do was come through for me. It didn't have to be as good as the day before but at least qualify. We packed up the car and headed home. Sim sat in the back seat. I didn't say a word to him and barely said two words to Frank. When we got home, we unpacked everything, and I looked at the ribbons and chair that Sim had worked his heart out for. I began to come out of myself and realized how silly I had been. But the experience showed me how our emotions and expectations can take over and our common sense gets lost. I took Sim in my arms, sat down in the rocking chair, and gave him a big hug. I apologized to him for acting so stupid and selfish. I doubt he understood the words, but he understood the change in my demeanor. He wanted to get down. I set him on the floor; he looked at me, wagged his tail, and gave me his little sneeze. He then looked at his food dish and looked at me again. I knew all was well and he had forgiven me. However, he probably wondered if I finally had learned what he was teaching me.

I called Art Brown to let him know how well Sim had done. He was not at home, but his wife, Carol, took my call. I told her the great news, and she actually began to weep with joy.

"Art has told me about Mr. Sims. He thinks he's a great little working dog," she told me.

"Thanks, Carol. I take that as a great compliment coming from Art."

"I'll tell Art you called. I know he will be anxious to get back to you and hear all about the good news."

A while later he did. He was as pleased as if he had shown Sim himself. I told him of my "bratty" behavior because I was disappointed that Sim did not qualify the next day. Art took a long breath.

"I don't know Sim half as well as you do, but I do know that I wouldn't have expected him to qualify both days. The next time Sim gives you a good performance, give him at least a day off to recover his energy. He gave you a great performance, and in doing so, he depleted his physical and emotional energy. There is almost always a next time."

I took his advice to heart. This was a man who not only showed his own dogs but was an AKC judge. He must know what he's talking about. I also appreciated the diplomatic way he brought me back to reality.

Chapter 16

We cannot let the crowd do our choosing for us.
The well-worn path of the pack is not necessarily the best one.

—"Decision Vision"

After giving Sim about a week's rest from training, I began working him again. I also decided that I needed to change his groomer. Sim was less than happy going into the present shop and couldn't leave fast enough. For a day or two after the grooming, he seemed to be "off." His energy level was down, and he wasn't his usual perky self. It was almost as if the grooming had sapped his resources. I arrived early at the grooming shop to find Sim in a "drying cage." This is a crate that has a large blow dryer attached. The dog is placed in it, and the dryer is run until the dog is dry. The noise is deafening and the heat from the dryer can be downright dangerous and possibly deadly. Sim was barking because of the noise and discomfort. The groomer kept yelling at him and hitting the cage so that he would quiet down. Here is another example of how we have to be our dogs' voices. They can't tell us with words how or if they have been mistreated, but if you learn to read their actions and emotions, you can tell if they had a positive or negative experience. I knew I was never taking him back there again.

I thought that I would try the owner of the grooming shop from whom I was renting space. I had heard that there was some rough handling of dogs there, but I decided I would only have the owner groom Sim. She had been grooming for many years and did excellent work. I made an appointment and brought Sim in. He would have to stay there for the better part of the day, which did not make me very happy. However, I "went with the flow."

I arrived at the grooming shop, and once again, he was anxious to leave. The owner had groomed him, and he looked wonderful, especially his ears. She had a way of trimming them that was her trade mark. He almost looked like he had a Dutch Boy haircut, with the ears trimmed longer in the front, angled up in the back. I continued with her for three more grooming appointments. It was obvious that Sim did not want to go in and even more than anxious to leave. I knew something was upsetting him. When I picked him up from the last appointment, I noticed that his ears did not have her trademark look about them.

"Who groomed Sim today, Doris?"

"What do you mean?" she asked me, feigning shocked annoyance.

"I can tell that you didn't groom Sim by the way his ears look. You have a unique way of trimming them that no one else does."

"I'm breaking in a new groomer, and Sim is so easy to work on that I let her groom him."

"Thank you for admitting your mistake. It's very disappointing to me, but what is done is done."

I didn't want to bring him back there again for grooming. However, I was now placed in a tough position. I wasn't at all happy with the possible lack of honesty if I had not recognized that Doris had not groomed Sim. But I still had to retain a cordial relationship with her because she was renting me space for my training. Sometimes, though, doing the right thing takes priority over what is comfortable.

Here again, a word to the wise. You must be your dog's eyes and ears when they are put in the care of someone, no matter how professional these people may be or are supposed to be. I had accommodated her schedule by dropping Sim off early in the morning and not being able to pick him up until late afternoon. She apologized, but as far as I was concerned, the damage had been done. I began to wonder if this was the first time that someone else had groomed him.

Maybe Doris only did the finishing touches, such as his ears. Maybe this was why Sim was always so reluctant to go in to be groomed and in such a hurry to leave. I had missed the subtle signs Sim was giving me until it became more obvious to me. He had just taught me another very important lesson.

I was at a loss as to where I was going to take him for his next grooming, but I knew it wasn't going to be there, even though it was very convenient for me. But everything happens for a reason. I knew I had to find a groomer who was better suited to the way I expected Sim to be handled.

One day, a client of mine came in with her Toy Poodle for a lesson. The dog had just come back from being groomed. Not only was the dog calm, but he also looked perfect. "Where did you have Chester groomed, Darcy, and who groomed him?"

"Her name is Svetlana. I have gone to her with my dogs for years."

She gave me the contact information. Svetlana had her business in her home, and it was pretty much a one-on-one operation, just like my training. She had worked in a grooming shop for several years and then the shop closed. I called and made an appointment.

When we arrived, Sim seemed very relaxed. She had a large white cat that had one yellow eye and one green eye. The cat was so used to being around dogs that seeing Sim didn't faze her at all. And Sim couldn't wait to engage the cat in play. We took Sim downstairs to the grooming area. It was immaculately clean. Svetlana introduced herself to Sim, and they seemed to get along just fine. Sim looked at her and swallowed a few times. I think this was because she had a thick Russian accent and he was trying to learn her different speech patterns. She said we could pick him up in a couple of hours. This was much better than the "all-day" situations he had been exposed to. When we returned, he looked the best he had ever looked. And he was very relaxed and in no hurry to leave. We made an appointment for his next grooming and left. The shows were coming up, and he looked wonderful. I noticed over the next few days that Sim never went into his "post-grooming funk." There certainly was a positive outcome to this learning experience. Sim and Svetlana continued a wonderful relationship for many years. He was a calming influence to her when she needed it, and she was one of his favorite people. Whenever he would see her, his tail would wag, and he couldn't wait to have her work with him. He trusted her completely and enjoyed each grooming session with her.

Chapter 17

Life always offers its priceless rewards if we're willing
to pay, to work, and, most importantly, to notice.

—Rainbows Live at Easter

The shows were going to be at Eastern States again over Fourth
of July, and I decided to enter Sim. He seemed to be doing well,
although he still would have an occasional bout of tummy upset. The
day of the trial arrived. Because of the location of the show site, we
didn't have to stay in a motel. We could travel back and forth from
home. I thought that this might be an advantage and be less stressful.
Of course, I dismissed the fleeting thought that maybe Sim was not
comfortable there.

The site was as loud and distracting as it had been the last time I
tried to show him there. And it was warmer than usual. The judge of
the Open class was very pleasant and sometimes would be comical.
An example of his demeanor is that he called the out-of-sight Sits
and Downs "ups and downs." As this is such a stressful exercise for
the handlers, his humor served to help relax us. His name was Jack
Holmes. I had done my research, and he seemed to have the kind of
temperament I felt would appreciate Sim's effort, for better or worse.
The ring was next to the entrance of the site, so there was a lot of
coming and going as well as commotion.

Sim did everything well, but his heeling did not qualify this
time. He was distracted by all the activity, especially at ringside. This
time, I did not get resentful. I fully understood what had happened

and figured out that Eastern States was not a place where he was relaxed in the ring. It raised his stress level and probably affected how he felt physically.

We walked around the show site, stopping at some of the vendors to see what they had to offer. I bought a toy from one. I then bought a soft-sided travel crate and mattress at another. As we were walking along, one of the vendors who were selling mugs, keychains, and other items with the image of different breeds of dogs on them approached us. She said that she had plenty of transfers with Shih Tzus in full show coat but none with a puppy cut like Sim's. "He looks so good," she said enthusiastically. "Would you mind if I take a few pictures of him so that I can use them on my products?"

"Of course you can. He's very friendly and easy to work with," I told her.

And Sim cooperated perfectly. She would tell Frank and me how she wanted him positioned and we would pose him. She took several pictures, including Sim sitting, standing, and lying down. There was a bit of confusion at first. Frank thought she was telling *him* to sit, stand, and lie down. I quickly stepped in to rectify the situation. A few months later, one of my friends gave me a box of stationery with a picture of a Shih Tzu in a puppy cut on the front. We all agreed that it looked exactly like Sim. The markings were identical. So it appears that he became the template for the Shih Tzus with a puppy cut.

Chapter 18

The things that matter the most in this world,
they can never be held in our hand.

—"A Hill Called Mount Calvary"

I read in one of my professional magazines that there was going to be a United Kennel Club obedience trial in Pennsylvania. It was not far from where Eva had lived with Steve. I was familiar with one of the judges, and the other judge was known to be gentle and fair. I thought it would be a good opportunity to visit with Steve as well. We could combine the two for a business and pleasure trip.

I called the Trial Secretary and told her that I wanted to enter Sim in the Open trials. I also wanted to have an award set up in memory of Eva and her beloved Brandy. We agreed that there would be some kind of award for "Highest Scoring Shar Pei." It would not be ready for these trials but for the next ones in February 2002.

I called Steve and told him of our plans. He was very happy that we would be in his area, close enough to visit with him. He said that he would plan to attend the dog show to see "Sim in action." I told him that we never know what we would get with Sim. It depended on how he was feeling. Steve also said that he would contact Dottie. Dottie was a good friend of Eva's. I had never met her, but Eva had told me a lot about her. Dottie also was a dog trainer and had been for a few years.

We arrived at the hotel on Friday evening. I called Steve and told him that we were going to take a "dry run" to the show site to see how long it was going to take us to get there. I told him that I would give him a call when we got back and give him directions so that we would meet him at the show site in the morning. We had a good night's sleep, and Sim seemed in good spirits. The next morning, we headed for the show site. We had walked Sim around the area the night before. He seemed relaxed as we set up his crate at the show site.

Good, I thought. *Maybe he'll do well and qualify.*

Steve joined us with a friend, Melanie. Again, I had heard a lot about her from Eva, but this was our first meeting. Steve and Melanie told me that Dottie would be arriving soon, but they weren't quite sure what time. They were just hoping that she would be there in time to see Sim's performance.

As our turn was approaching, I began to warm Sim up, walking him outside of the ring. He was giving me good attention and looked to be ready. Dottie had not arrived yet, and Steve and Melanie were disappointed.

"We really thought she was going to make it on time," Melanie told me. "I spoke to her earlier this morning, and she said she would be here."

"Oh well," I told them. "With Sim, we're never sure whether he will work well or not. She may not miss anything."

We entered the ring, and I handed his leash and dumbbell to the steward. The judge guided me to the starting point.

"Do you have any questions?" she asked.

"No," I told her.

She smiled at us and said, "Forward."

I told Sim to "heel," and he came right along with me.

"Right turn," the judge told us.

I turned right. Sim was still with me. We were heading toward the side of the ring where the spectators were seated. "About turn," the judge said.

I executed the about turn. As I came out of it, I realized that Sim was not with me. The judge said, "Halt." I did. Sim was missing. I looked at the judge, and she had a confused look on her face. I could tell from her gaze that Sim was near the ring gate. I followed her gaze to see Sim standing perfectly still, staring at someone. The person he was looking at looked exactly like Eva!

My heart skipped a beat. Of course, I knew that it was not possible. I called Sim to me. He didn't move! He just kept staring at the woman. I went to him and tried to guide him away. He looked at me, swallowed, and looked back at the woman. I softly said to him, "I know, Bud, but it's not Eva. We have work to do."

He very slowly began to come with me but kept his gaze fixed on the "Eva" lookalike. Needless to say, he did none of the exercises. He kept looking toward the gate.

The judge looked at me and said, "Not today."

"I guess not," I said dejectedly.

When we walked over to Steve and Frank, Steve introduced me to Dottie. The resemblance to Eva was striking. She was short, not much taller than Eva had been, who was 4'11", same slightly chunky body type, glasses, dark, curly hair, and wearing Eva's trademark Mickey Mouse T-shirt and jeans. When Sim was able to actually sniff Dottie, he realized his mistake. He looked very sad. I commented to Steve and Dottie how much she looked like Eva. I bent down and gave Sim a hug. "You are a wonderful, sensitive boy," I told him. "We'll do better the next time." Again, you just never know all the variables nor can you control them. If Sim or any other dog were just a machine, it wouldn't matter. Learn well the fact that they are living, breathing, feeling, beings that have a similar range of emotions, just as we do.

Another example of "mistaken identity" happened with Abbey. Janet had recently put down their black older Labrador, Cody. Abbey had known Cody from the time she was a little puppy. We were at an outdoor obedience match. Janet was heeling Abbey off leash in the Novice class. In the adjoining ring, the Open class was in the midst of their Out-of-Sight sit exercise. There was a black Lab in the group.

Abbey spotted him and bolted from the ring, heading straight in his direction. Janet called her, but she just kept going, tail wagging furiously. Abbey thought she had found her lost friend. As she was about halfway to him, she realized that it wasn't Cody. You could literally see her deflate. She slowly stopped, her tail drooping and her head down. Her sadness was unmistakable. I said to Janet, who was highly embarrassed, "She thought it was Cody. Don't be upset with her. She is upset enough. All she knew was that he was there one day and gone the next, never to return."

From that day on, I felt that if someone had multiple dogs and one died, the other dog or dogs should be able to see their pack member at peace. I'm sure they would understand the situation, even if we did not think they could.

Chapter 19

In spite of everything,
When I look back at where I've been,
I see that what I am becoming
Is a whole lot further down the road
From where I was.

—"Hands Across the Seasons"

The therapy dog evaluator who had certified us for therapy work was going to move to another state. I had occasionally worked with him when he evaluated possible therapy teams. He suggested to me that I apply to the organization he was leaving to become an evaluator. Once he left, the area would only have one evaluator, and there was enough demand for these evaluations that one evaluator would not be enough.

I got in touch with the therapy organization. They sent me the information with what my requirements had to be. I had to write a resume, telling about my experience with dogs and the type of training that I used. I needed three letters of recommendation from professionals who worked with dogs. The evaluator who left the area was readily agreed to write a letter for me. I contacted the vet at Puritan's, whom I had worked with to help Jake the Border Collie. He said he would be happy to write a letter for me. The last professional I asked was the behaviorist at Brookside Road Animal Hospital. I had consulted with him regarding some of my client's dogs that had more serious behavioral problems. He too wrote a letter. They all felt that I had the temperament and skills to make a good evaluator.

I had a letter of recommendation from Paula, explaining how she brought Boomer to me for training, another letter from the owner of Jake the Border Collie, and a letter of recommendation from Rosemarie Laramee, the head of the Pet Partners program at a local nursing home where Sim and I visited.

I had to furnish a list of books that I had read, video tapes on training that I had studied, seminars that I had attended, as well as a list of the different breeds that I had handled. I had to include in my resume, how long I had been a trainer, my training methods, and some examples of the dogs I had trained and what issues they may have had. I filled out the paperwork and sent it in.

After several months, they contacted me to let me know I had been accepted. Sim now had another job. He would become the distraction dog for these evaluations. It appeared that 2002 was going to be a very interesting year.

In January of 2002, I received a call from a local obedience club. They wanted to sponsor an event where they could offer Canine Good Citizen and therapy dog evaluations. I told them I would be glad to evaluate for them. I had studied and read several books on canine behavior. This was one of the requirements to become a therapy dog evaluator. As good as these books were in giving me some insight in canine behavior, nothing was as informative as hands-on experience with Sim and the other dogs I trained. I felt I was up to the task of evaluating but was somewhat nervous.

If a dog and handler qualify as a therapy team, they are issued an insurance policy that is renewed each year. The organization wants us to be as close to 100 percent sure as humanly possible that both the dog and handler not only can execute the required exercises but also that their temperaments are acceptable. It was an interesting experience. There was a long list of entrants. Some teams were well prepared while others felt that "because I have such a nice dog," they should pass. Some people really wanted to bring comfort to ill people. Others merely looked at passing as another "title" for their dog. When a dog passes either or both the CGC and TD, they are allowed to place these initials after their dog's name.

Once again, human ego came into play, and the feelings of the dog came second. Some dogs executed the exercises happily, while others looked extremely stressed. I came away from the experience feeling sorrier for the dogs that didn't make it than the handlers.

I learned that when people are put into a competitive setting, they view things very differently. I was amazed how many viewed the dog as a means to an end rather than a partner. One of the teams was a woman with an Australian Shepherd. The dog appeared to be having some pain in one of her back legs. She wasn't limping but was reluctant to sit. She passed the first exercise without a problem, but this is when I noticed that she was having a problem sitting. She was able to remain at her handler's side and not try to interact with the "passing stranger," who was greeting her handler. The next exercise was where I met the handler, greeted her, and then asked if I could pet her dog. I could see from the way the dog was sitting that she was uncomfortable and the look on her face was that of pain. As I went to pet the dog, she growled loudly at me. I told that handler that immediately disqualified her from certification. The woman looked at me in shocked disbelief. "It appears to me that she may be having an issue with one of her back legs. I think she could be uncomfortable, and that's why she growled at me. I would have your vet check her to see if there is a problem."

"There is no problem. She always growls like that when someone tries to pet her."

Now I was the one with the look of shocked disbelief. How could anyone think that they could have their dog certified to go into hospitals, nursing homes, assisted living communities, or schools to interact with children when the dog growls at people? To this day, I still think that the dog was in pain. The dog's welfare should come first. The woman probably never gave a thought that if the dog's pain was addressed, the dog's demeanor would change and she just might pass the test. And more importantly, the dog's well-being was what should be the prime consideration, not the accolades of a certification. Of course, we hate our own worst traits in other people, so I was definitely the pot calling the kettle black. And Sim kept working long and hard to get this through my head.

Chapter 20

There are times when the assurance of "rightness"
may contradict human logic.

—"Decision Vision"

Sim's competitive training continued. His health was still up and down, and his enthusiasm for his work depended upon how he was feeling. My tolerance for the ups and downs was better on some days than others as well. I continued taking him to different facilities for run-thru's and entered him in several trials. The run-thru's were not bad, but he would go from bad to worse in the actual trials. Each time, I would get more and more perplexed.

I kept trying to figure out what the problem or problems were. How could he have been so good a few months ago? I fell into the trap of trying anything and everything that people suggested, other than any harsh physical corrections.

There were supplements, books, tapes, classes, even a psychic. I was getting desperate, and as the saying goes, "Desperate people do desperate things." I wanted that title so badly that I was almost obsessed by it. I was using the accomplishment as a gauge of my professional worth and ability. Although I will never be proud of this learning period, it and Sim taught me the error of my ways and made me a better, more compassionate trainer.

The pet service, supply, and care business is a multi-billion dollar business. As a professional in the industry, people will ask me my opinion of certain products such as fad supplements, foods, treats, and procedures. The Pet Psychic show on TV was getting a lot of attention. Some of my clients asked me what I thought about this. I have always been very skeptical of psychics. I felt that the saying "Even a blind squirrel will find a nut every once in a while" fits this issue perfectly. A "Pet Communicator" had set up a booth at the Toy Show.

I decided to see what this was all about and have a "reading" with Sim. There were quite a few people waiting to see her with their dogs. The booth that she had was a tent. All the other booths that were selling merchandise were in the open. However, because of the type of business she had, it was necessary to have some sort of privacy. Frank and I decided to walk Sim around a while and then come back to see if the line to see her had shortened.

We looked at what the other vendors had to offer and then took Sim outside for a short walk. When we returned, there was only one person waiting. We struck up a conversation with her. She told us her concerns about her dog. One problem was that her dog was not reliable on the long sit exercise. We began trading stories as to why we thought our dogs were having this trouble. Thinking back on it now, it is possible that the Communicator had overheard us and picked up some valuable information that she could use when "communicating" with our dogs.

When our turn came, we entered the tent-like booth. The Communicator was a rather nondescript, mousy-looking person wearing glasses. She had me take a seat next to her with Sim sitting in front of me. Frank sat in the chair to my left. She petted Sim and then asked me what my concerns were. Not wanting to give her too much information, I was sketchy in my response.

"Sometimes his stomach gets upset. This is of major concern to me. The other two things that I would like to ask him is why is his heeling so erratic, and why won't he stay in the long sit when I leave the room with the other handlers."

"OK. I'm going to connect with him now, so everyone has to be quiet."

She closed her eyes. I watched Sim as he lay at my feet. He did look up at her briefly but then kept looking at me. When I did not respond to him, he swallowed a couple of times and then gave his little sneeze. It appeared to me that he was communicating with me, not her.

She really wasn't too accurate about him, unable to tell me that he had been a rescue or about the toy that had been lodged in his tummy. And no mention of Ballerina Bear was made. Sim surely would have told the Communicator about her. She did tell me that he wasn't too bright, saying that he told her he wasn't able to figure out how to get out of her tent. Sim also told her that he didn't like the food he was eating and that he didn't like the long sit because it was boring.

I acted as though I was impressed with what she had told me. However, it merely confirmed what I already knew. I had been sketchy with the information that I gave her; therefore, she couldn't tell me much in return. If someone has some knowledge of animal behavior and human nature, the person can tell you things that sound like it came from your pet.

People have the tendency to humanize dogs and think that they react emotionally the same way a person does. For example, I have heard people say "The dog's just being spiteful" or "The dog is holding a grudge against me because I…" You can fill in the blank. Nothing is farther from the truth. Dogs do not process the same way we do. They are as honest as it gets. In fact, I have found that 85 percent of behavior problems are usually rooted in a physical problem.

Dogs cannot tell us that they don't feel well, so they may act in an inappropriate manner. This discomfort can be caused by many things. So the psychic may tell the owner that the dog is saying it does not like its food, it isn't comfortable in its current bed, needs more exercise or less exercise, or possibly doesn't like the sound of its name. It sounds reasonable to the owner, and so the owner feels that the dog has told them something through the psychic.

As far as I am concerned, if no harm comes to the dog and/or owner and the advice leads to a better life for the dog, then so be it. We are with our dog more than any psychic, veterinarian, groomer, or trainer. Most people do not educate themselves enough regarding their dog. Do you know the breed's traits, even if you have a mixed breed? How much exercise is needed to keep the breed in good physical and emotional condition? How much heat or cold can the dog tolerate because of its color or type of coat? What was the breed originally used for? What should their proper weight be? Do you read the labels on all food, treats, toys, and chews that you give to the dog? Do you make a mental note of why your dog may be feeling "off" or do you just chalk it up to "a bad day"? Do you ask your vet for and understand the instructions when your dog is on medication? This means *all* medications, including heartworm medicine and flea and tick treatments or collars. Do you ask about what side effects might occur?

If the answer you get is not clear enough for you or you are told "Don't worry about it," *look it up* online in a Physician's Desk Reference site or on the medicine's manufacturer's web site. *The Pill Book* can be easily found in book stores and some pharmacies. It gives side effects of most medications, many of which are used for pets as well, and a dog can have many of the same side effects that a human can have. It is a great reference source to have on hand and can be of help for both humans and dogs.

We cannot put our head on our dog's shoulders and assume, in human terms, what they are feeling. But if you "listen" to them by observing their different behaviors, you will begin to understand what they are "saying." The language that they "speak" is very subtle and nuanced when they begin the communication. It may be a certain facial expression, posture, even breathing patterns.

As we either ignore or don't understand what they are trying to convey, the behavior escalates. Sometimes we don't realize what is going on until the dog is figuratively "yelling" at us. Unfortunately, by the time the dog is "yelling," the problem, be it behavior or physical, may be far advanced, and turning it around will take a lot of time and effort.

A good example of this is the case of a client of mine, who had an electronic fence installed around her yard to keep her dog confined. Part of the training is to say to the dog, "Watch it," to alert them to the fact that they are getting too close to the area where they will receive a shock through the electronic collar that the dog is wearing.

I was unaware of this procedure until the dog "told" me about it. Part of my training is to teach the dog to watch you, using the word *watch*. Although this dog was an excellent student and was preparing well for competitive obedience, he refused, or so I thought, to learn the "watch." No matter what I tried, he would only give me a cursory, worried glance and then look away. As luck would have it, one day his owner mentioned to me the training that the dog had gotten for the electronic fence. Everything became perfectly clear to me. The word *watch* meant something negative to the dog, so no matter what I tried to do to make it positive, it was not going to change the dog's mind based on his previous experience with the word. I began using the word *look*, and the dog learned what that meant, so I was able to obtain the desired results. Once again, never discount what the dog may be trying to tell you. And never stop "peeling the onion."

Chapter 21

To use shock as an effective dog training method
you will need:
1. A thorough understanding of canine behavior.
2. A thorough understanding of learning theory.
3. Impeccable timing.
And if you have those three things, YOU DON'T
NEED A SHOCK COLLAR!

—Author Unknown

Another product that I was asked about, particularly in obedience
circles, was the "electronic training collar." To me, there is no place
for this in either pet or obedience training. It can cause serious psy-
chological as well as neurological damage. I don't even care for the
underground containment systems for dogs. If a temptation is great
enough, a dog will withstand the shock that it receives when it leaves
its property. However, I'm willing to bet that the dog will not withstand the shock to return to the area it left.

I purchased an electronic training collar so that I could see
it firsthand and discover exactly how it worked. When it arrived,
the packaging was very attractive, with a picture of a dog happily
working with its owner. I opened it and began to read the instructions. There were two sets of prongs, one set longer than the other.
According to the instructions, if the shorter one didn't give you the
response you wanted from the dog, change them to the longer ones.
It also instructed to use the lowest electronic stimulation setting and

then gradually work up to the one that works the best. The last straw was the paragraph that instructed the owner to be sure to frequently disinfect the prongs because they could cause infection.

I put everything back in the box and put it in the closet. My thought was that if anyone asked me about these collars, I could show them why I felt they were so cruel. After two weeks, I packed it up and returned to the company I ordered it from. I requested a refund. It appalled me so much that I couldn't have it in the house. When people get overcome with the competition aspect of the human/dog relationship and forget that they are part of a team, they will resort to anything because they feel that "Winning isn't everything, it's the only thing."

Chapter 22

The difference between a wise man and a fool is
that a wise man only makes a mistake once.

—Mr. Courley, my eighth-grade English teacher

The word of Sim's High In Trial spread in the training community,
and some people who had been competing began coming to me for
help with their dogs. I guess they felt that if I could train a Shih
Tzu that well, then I must be a competent trainer. The elderly lady,
Bev, who had shown her Pomeranian in Maine when we were there,
asked if I could fit her in for lessons. She had bred and shown Poms
for many years. This was her breed of choice. Her Pom was named
Ike and was about nine years old. Ike had done very well for Bev
but was beginning to flatten out. He had gotten his CDX title in
the American Kennel Club and needed one more leg in the United
Kennel Club for this distinction.

Bev had been training for many, many years. She was well into
her seventies and had some physical issues, including a knee replace-
ment. She walked with a bit of a limp, used a cane, and had curva-
ture of the spine. Ike was devoted to her, and even with all of Bev's
disabilities, he worked beautifully for her, winning several AKC and
UKC obedience titles.

It is hard enough to teach a dog the more advanced obedience
exercises because of their complexity and difficulty. It is even more
difficult if the handler is disabled. When Bev arrived for her lesson, I
looked at Ike. He didn't look right to me. He seemed lethargic, and

his eye whites were orange. I asked her if he was OK. She said yes, other than not training well.

I put him through some of the Open exercises, and I could see how hard he tried but how he labored to do them. I suggested that she make an appointment with her vet and let me know what happens. She called me a few days later. Ike had Lyme disease. The vet was very concerned and was keeping him for a few days for treatment. He was seriously, if not gravely ill. I told her this probably explained why he was not performing up to his usual standard. He often placed in the top three in his classes. Bev wanted Ike to be able to compete in the Utility Class, "even if he never gets the title," she told me. Bev was very sweet and grandmotherly, but when she competed, she was like a shark that smelled blood in the water. I saw her use harsh corrections on Ike and made it quite clear that I would not allow any of that in my lessons with her.

In 2000, Bev was well aware of her age and physical condition. Because of this, she decided to get a Sheltie puppy. She felt that this would be the "Silver Bullet" in the obedience ring. Shelties have a great work ethic and learn rather rapidly, but they don't take well to rough handling. Her Sheltie, Scottie, was now about two years old, and she asked me about working with him on his Novice title while Ike recovered. Scottie had the sweet-tempered Sheltie personality. He and Ike got along well, although he liked to grab Ike by the tail and playfully drag him across the room. Ike took this good-naturedly, and when he had enough, he stood his ground and Scottie would back off.

After a couple of months, it appeared that Ike had recovered. Bev wanted to start working the Utility exercises with him along with the Open work. She brought both dogs to the lessons, and we would work one and then the other. Ike was as loyal as ever, trying as hard as he was able to learn the difficult exercises. Scottie was learning the Novice exercises, but because of the necessity of Bev having to use a cane, his sessions would be up and down. She was hoping to have Ike ready to show in Utility at the August shows at Eastern States.

Bev was so used to Ike working well that she would get annoyed with Scottie when he wouldn't respond as quickly. I was very patient with her and explained many times to her why Scottie was having a problem. He had to get used to the cane. Bev didn't use her cane much at home but always did when she trained the dogs. Scottie was also having an issue with what appeared to be urinary tract infections. He would squat and whine when he wanted to urinate, take a few steps, strain to urinate, and then stop. Bev and I thought that maybe he had crystals or stones in his bladder. She said she would have the vet check him out.

We took Sim to one of the July 4 shows at Eastern States. I thought that if we took him there just to walk around without having to work, it would help him to be more relaxed and less stressed when he was in another facility for a trial. He seemed to enjoy the outing and did not appear stressed at all. I planned on entering him in the trials in Maine where he had done so well, earning the two legs of his Novice title. I hoped that this outing might help to build his confidence.

At about 10:30 p.m., Bev called.

"Peg, this is Bev. I hate to call you so late, but something is very wrong with Scottie."

I could tell from her voice that she was very concerned.

"What seems to be the matter, Bev?"

"He keeps trying to urinate, but while he's squatting, he keeps strainin' and whinin'. He won't eat nor drink anything for me either, and he keeps pacin' around like he's hurtin' somewhere."

"OK, Bev. Try to relax. Frank and I will come and pick you and Scottie up. I really think we should take him to Emergency at Brookside Road Animal Hospital."

"Thanks so much, Peg. I hate to be such a bother, but I'm really worried about Scottie."

"We'll be there as quickly as we can."

"We've got to pick Bev and Scottie up. He's having problems urinating and not eating anything for her. I can tell how terribly upset she is because she's dropping the *g* at the end of some of her words. Bev is usually very careful about that when she talks with me. And at Bev's age and physical frailty, she can't afford to get that stressed."

110

"Geeze, Peg, that's too bad. I'll take Sim out real quick so he can relieve himself. We never know how long it will take in Emergency."

Bev lived about forty-five minutes from us, and her house was on a mountain. Fortunately, the weather was good that night, and we got to her in record time. Scottie looked to be in distress, and his breath was putrid.

When we got to the animal hospital, Dr. Nastase was on duty. Bev, Frank, and I filed into the exam room. We told Bev to sit down until the vet came in. She was visibly shaken. Dr. Nastase came in and we introduced ourselves to him. I told him that Bev was the dog's owner. She stood up, looking quite frail as she leaned on her cane.

"What seems to be the matter?" he asked as he examined Scottie.

"He's having trouble urinating. He's straining and whining, but nothing is coming out of him," I answered.

"Please sit down and relax while I examine him," he said to Bev, trying to reassure her. "Is he eating and drinking at all today?"

"No, Doctor. And that's why I'm so worried about him," Bev said.

All of a sudden, Dr. Nastase looked at me and, in almost a whisper, said, "Come here and feel the dog's chest."

I did. Scottie was so thin that his chest felt like a picked-over turkey carcass. Because of his long coat, we hadn't noticed the weight loss.

Dr. Nastase began to ask Bev how much she was feeding Scottie, being very respectful to her. She said that she was feeding him the same amount as she was feeding her Pom. Scottie was a small Sheltie, so he probably should have weighed about twenty pounds. Ike weighed about eight to nine pounds. I believe that Scottie weighed about fifteen pounds that night.

Dr. Nastase took Scottie in the back to draw some blood and urine to make sure that nothing else was wrong. When he came back, he said, "Take him home and feed him anything he wants. He's very underweight. That's why he's having trouble urinating. Just be sure that you gradually increase the amount of food you give him. You can decrease the amount of food right away if a dog is too heavy. But you have to go slow and easy when you're trying to put weight on the dog. Too much too soon can cause problems such as stomach upset. It would be as if you ate too much. I'll let you know if there are any stones or crystals in his bladder as soon as I get the lab work back."

"I feel awful that I've been underfeeding Scottie. How could I have been so stupid? I've had dogs for many years and never would have thought that I could make such a mistake."

She hadn't listened to Scottie. He had begun eating his and Ike's stools to maintain himself. Bev would only become annoyed and disgusted with this habit and yell at him when she saw him do it. As is usually the case, the dog was trying to tell us something. Fortunately, Scottie recovered nicely once he was fed the proper amount of food.

Chapter 23

The future ain't what it used to be.

—Yogi Berra

Frank was on vacation the following week. We had no special plans, so I looked up different places for run-thru's for Sim to get him ready for the September shows. I found a couple. One was in New Hampshire, and the other was at a facility in the eastern part of Massachusetts. The next day, I was carrying a rather large plant from the family room to the kitchen to water it. I tripped over something and went down in a heap. Sim was right there to see if I was OK. My left ankle was throbbing badly. I had the feeling I had broken it. However, the plant didn't lose as much as a leaf.

I went to the emergency care facility not far from our house. Sure enough, the ankle was broken. Because I had had polio as a child and my left foot had sustained damage from it, the foot could not be put into a cast. It had to be wrapped, and I had to use a cane. *Shades of Bev*, I thought. It was going to take several months for it to heal, so the trip to Maine was not going to happen. "Oh well," I told Sim. "This will give us more time to work things out." And he had to get used to me with a cane.

Fortunately, because my left ankle was broken, the cane was held in my right hand. Sim did adapt to it and kept a close eye on me when we walked as well as supporting me through my recovery. He would stay by my side when I needed to sit and rest. When he had to go out, he would wait patiently as I slowly got ready to take him and was only able to walk him at a snail's pace.

Bev told me she had entered Ike in the Utility Class at Eastern States. It was going to be the third week in August. I continued to work with her to get him ready. The bout with Lyme had taken a lot out of him, and I thought that the trial would be too stressful. Bev was determined to go through with her plans. She said, "I tain't gettin' any younger, and neither is Ike." At the last lesson before the trials, I told her I would come and watch.

When I met her at the show site, she told me that Ike had been doing a lot of sleeping while they were waiting their turn. She took him out of his crate, and I could tell not only did he not feel like working, but he also wasn't feeling well. I didn't say anything because I knew she was going through with it no matter what. Needless to say, Ike didn't and couldn't do anything. When they came out of the ring, Bev was very disappointed and very rough putting Ike back into his crate. I tried to politely intervene, but she waved me off. I knew I would talk to her about it another day. She called me two days later to say that Ike was sick again. This time, the vet was extremely concerned. The Lyme disease had reemerged, and Ike hadn't fully recovered from the first bout. It was nip and tuck for about a week. He did pull through, fortunately, but I convinced her to retire him. She still had Scottie to work with.

By November, my ankle had healed. I thought I was going to be healthy for the rest of the year but ended up contracting pneumonia. Sim donned his nurse's uniform once again and stayed by my side for the two weeks I really felt ill. When I would go to bed to rest, he would be right with me, curled up behind my knees. When I would get up, he would watch me closely and seemed to curtail the amount of times he would usually want to go out for a potty break. Once again, however, my schedule to show Sim and get that elusive CDX title was put on hold.

As the saying goes, "every cloud has a silver lining." The schedule change gave me the opportunity to apply to Delta Society to become a Pet Partner evaluator and instructor. They sent me the study materials and the information as to how much time I had before I had to call them and take a verbal test. I called in and had to answer twenty-five questions. They pertained to different parts of the examination that the dog and handler would be tested on and how I would judge whether or not the team was qualified to become part of the Pet Partner's program. They specifically dealt with procedure and desirable responses to the various exercises. Some of the situations that the teams would encounter in the test were if the dog was tempted with a treat, would it understand the command to "Leave It"? Some other situations were being crowded and petted by several people, the dog being bumped from behind, staggering and gesturing people who might be yelling, just to name a few. I had to have a score of 80 percent or better. I passed with 100 percent. I wiped my brow when the examiner told me that. Some of the questions, at least to me, were subjective and more than just one answer could be possible. I was then told that I would have to go to the ASPCA, the American Society for the Prevention of Cruelty to Animals, in New York City, for a weekend practicum for both becoming an instructor and evaluator. A practicum is a hands-on seminar and test, and this was the final part of testing that I had to pass.

I excitedly told Frank the good news. He was as happy as I was. We made the arrangements to spend the weekend in New York. Even though I had to be in New York City, we stayed at the hotel on Long Island that we always used. It was close enough to the city that it would not be a long ride, but it also was close enough to our family members on the Island. It was a couple of weeks before Christmas, and the weather was very brisk. Sim wore his New York Doggie Duds jacket and made quite a hit with everyone who saw him in it. Frank and Sim were on their own while I was attending the sessions. They drove around New York City, stopping at different places of interest. Sim's favorite stop during the two days was Madison Square Park, where he left his "signature" quite liberally.

Because of the experience I had gained from the other therapy dog organization, I had no problem becoming certified after passing the test given at the practicum. However, there was one large difference between the two groups regarding the physical examination of the dog that surprised me. When testing the teams for the therapy organization that I was an evaluator for, the physical examination of the dog is very brief. The ears and front paws are examined, and an overall look was sufficient to see whether the dog was regularly groomed and well maintained. I was in for quite a surprise when the instructor that was teaching the practicum explained how "detailed" the physical exam of the dog had to be. It was as thorough as the exam a judge gives a dog when the dog is competing in the breed ring. My jaw dropped when we were told that with the male dogs, we had to examine their "private parts."

I said, "Excuse me. What did you say I am supposed to do?" The others in the class laughed, and so did the instructor. But she verified what I heard.

"This could be very interesting," I said. Once again, the class laughed. The instructor explained that when evaluating the animal to see if it had the proper temperament to be certified, we had to be sure that nothing would elicit poor behavior. I was elated because I had passed and was looking forward to what 2003 would usher in.

Chapter 24

Electrician: I think I may have made a mistake.
Homeowner: What gave it away, the flames?

—"All in a Day's Work," *Reader's Digest*

With the arrival of 2003, I thought and hoped that this might be the year that Sim would get his CDX title. He had just turned seven and was in good health, other than his continuing stomach problems. We were giving him a prescription diet, and it seemed to be helping somewhat. There were still the little episodes of upset, and I couldn't make head nor tail what triggered it. He was due for his annual physical, and as usual, I had a list of questions for the vet. She gave him a thorough exam and said everything seemed good. She had to take some blood for testing, and I had brought a urine specimen.

She took him out of the exam room so she could get a tech to hold Sim steady while she drew blood, gave him his Lyme shot, and administered the vaccine for kennel cough which is given in the form of a nose drop. Sim hated getting that vaccine because I think he felt that he wasn't going to be able to breathe. However, because of showing him and having him groomed, I didn't want to run the risk of him being exposed to kennel cough. This is an airborne illness that is similar to the flu in humans. If not treated fairly promptly, it can lead to serious respiratory problems. When she brought him back into the exam room, Sim gave one of his sneezes that I knew meant trouble. I brought this to the vet's attention, letting her know that this was the type of sneezing I had mentioned to her several times before. "It's different, Kathy. This sneeze means trouble." She said that it was probably caused by the way she had his head tilted up to administer the nose drop. We talked for a short time, and I voiced my concern about his sneezing again. She assured me that it was nothing to worry about. I left to pay my bill.

Sim's sneezing became more violent as I waited in line. He began to bring up white phlegm, coughing as he did. I told the receptionist that he was having a problem. A vet tech immediately took him back to the exam room, where the vet gave him an injection of Benadryl. He was having an allergic reaction to the Lyme vaccine. She marked his chart accordingly. I was now certain that when Sim violently sneezed, it was a harbinger of a physical problem. *Lesson learned*, I thought. *Listen to your dog, you know him best!*

Although Sim's work was good, it still was unpredictable. Something was bothering him but nothing I could really pinpoint. I did take him to a United Kennel Club trial in New Hampshire. He had been there for many run-thru's, so I thought he might be comfortable and less stressed there. Sure enough, he earned an Open leg. The United Kennel Club, as with the American Kennel Club, requires that the dog earn three legs to be awarded the title. *One down and two to go*, I thought. Even though Sim had qualified, I could tell that he did not have any enthusiasm doing it. I would find out soon what the problem was. Another session of "peeling the onion" was coming.

One morning, after eating his breakfast, he went under the dining area table and began to shake. I knelt down next to him. It had a familiar look about it, much like when the toy came up. I tried to soothe him, but the shaking persisted. I called my vet. They couldn't see him until two o'clock in the afternoon, so I said I would take him to Brookside Road Emergency. I hung up and was just about ready to leave when the phone rang. It was my vet's office. They said they would see him immediately.

It was my usual vet's day off, so I saw the vet who started the practice many years ago. He was very experienced and very concerned about Mr. Sims. He did blood work, wondering if Sim had Addison's disease. Addison's disease is when the adrenal gland stops producing enough cortisol and aldosterone, a hormone that regulates levels of sodium in the blood. When sodium levels go down, potassium levels go up and blood pressure goes down. This causes the heart to beat faster to compensate. However, the high levels of potassium prevent the heart's natural pacemaker from speeding the heart rate. What the vet was looking for in the blood work was possible evidence of low sodium in combination with high potassium.

He gave me some medication for his stomach and said he would call me with the results. He also gave me some worming medication just in case there was a parasite issue. If not, the worming medication can act as a soothing and coating agent on his stomach.

The next day, my regular vet called to say that the blood work was fine. She told me to continue the meds and let her know in a few days how Sim was doing. It was up and down. When I let the vet know, she thought that Sim might benefit from a different prescription diet formula. We tried it, and it helped, but something was still "off." He just wasn't himself, and I could see the discomfort in his eyes. I finally said to her, "Let's scope him and/or do an ultrasound." I felt that Sim should have an ultrasound of his gastrointestinal tract. This procedure would show what, if anything, was wrong in his stomach and intestines.

I wasn't sure what the answer was, but we had to get to the bottom of the problem. The vet looked at me and said, "You know it will be expensive." I told her it didn't matter. What mattered was Mr. Sims's health. She said she had to contact Liz Schaler, the internist who would perform the scoping and then would let me know when the scoping would be done.

I told Sim, "Don't worry, Bud. We'll get you feeling better again soon."

Within a few days, they called with the time for the appointment. I dropped Sim off in the morning and waited anxiously all day to hear the results. When the vet called me, she told me that Sim had a bad ulceration in the duodenum area, just about where that toy had lodged for all that time. He was on five different medications, including Prednisone. I cringed when I heard about the steroid because of the side effects. The vet said that she was not happy about it either, but it was only for a short term, and if we didn't do it, the ulcer could perforate and bleed. If that happened, Sim would be in real trouble. He also had inflammatory bowel disease. It is a manageable digestive disorder but is unpredictable and tricky to stabilize. Any sort of stress, be it physical or emotional, can set off a bout of IBD. The meds seemed to help him, and he began to act like his old self within the next few weeks. We then resumed training.

Chapter 25

It's best to look at others from the inside out.

—The Franciscan Friars

We also resumed visits to the local nursing home where Sim was one of the favorites. The nurses would have a list of patients that requested a visit with him. On one visit, a nurse asked us if we would go into a certain room. She said that the woman there "did not have much time left" and would like to see him. I entered the room with the nurse and saw someone in the bed—quiet, motionless, and facing away from the door. I looked at the nurse. I'm sure my look transmitted my concern. She gave me a reassuring look as she softly spoke to the patient.

"Someone special is here to visit you, Miriam."

Miriam boosted herself up on her elbow. "Who is it?" she asked.

"His name is Mr. Sims, and he's a very handsome gentleman," the nurse answered.

The nurse motioned to me to put Sim on the bed. I lifted him up and placed him on the bed with Miriam. He seemed to sense what was happening and very gently cuddled into her as she stroked him.

"Oh, he is very handsome," she said. I could see the look of joy come over her face. After twenty minutes or so, the nurse asked Miriam if she was getting tired.

"Yes, I am, but I thoroughly enjoyed my visit with Mr. Sims."

She smiled and thanked us. Sim gave her a little lick on her hand, which was unusual for him. I gave him a hug as I removed him from the patient's bed and told him what a great job he had done. I later heard that she had passed away later that night. ·

There was another resident of the nursing home who usually sat outside of her room in the hall. She was in a catatonic state, meaning that she sat with her eyes closed, not noticing anything that was going on around her. Until, that is, someone with a dog approached her. Her eyes would open wide and she would become very animated.

Sim and I approached her. I gently touched her on the arm to ask if she wanted to visit with Sim. Her eyes opened, and at first, they had a dull, empty look about them. Then she saw Sim. Her eyes lit up.

"I had several dogs growing up. In fact, I've had dogs most of my life," she told me. "One was a Cocker Spaniel named Charlie. Then there was the Dalmatian named Chance. Charlie was a real character. He would let me put him in my doll carriage and push it all around the village I lived in. People would stop and tell me what a cute 'baby' I had. And Chance loved ice cream. When I would take him for a walk in the village, he would steal the ice cream off cones that children would be holding as they walked by us. I wish I had a nickel for every ice cream cone I had to replace."

She talked about having been a schoolteacher and said that she taught reading. As she petted Sim, she would recount these stories and didn't want us to leave. When we had to leave, she would say goodbye, hoping to see us again, and then she would return to her inanimate state. It was as though a switch was pulled with her going from inanimate to very animated, relating to the dog, to inanimate again. I swallowed hard to get rid of the lump in my throat. However, it made me realize the amazing impact that all the therapy dogs have on these residents and the great value their visits have.

Chapter 26

Don't waste time learning the "tricks of the trade."
Learn the trade.

—H. Jackson Brown Jr.

What seemed to become a pattern was that it would take Sim a few days to recover from the effort he put into these visits. As I thought about this, I finally was able to put together the fact that he also required time to recover from training, run-throughs, and trials, and even the therapy visits he loved. I began to be much more particular about his schedule, making sure not to overwork him. I started "peeling the onion" again.

Sim enjoyed his work as the "distraction dog" in the CGC and TD evaluations, and he took it very seriously. The more of this work he did, the fussier he became about the manners of the dogs being tested. Hence, he earned the title of Manners Police. If dogs that were waiting to be tested started horsing around with each other, Sim would strut over to them and give them a look. I don't know exactly what that look said, but the dogs would stop their antics and lie down. Sim would then strut away with an air about him as if to say, "I settled those clowns down. They need to behave themselves." This was a particular crowd favorite, especially because the size of the unruly dogs made no difference to him, and his size did not stop the other dogs from picking up his message. He also would do this at obedience trials if he felt it was necessary to keep order. The word

Shih Tzu means "lion" in Chinese. There wasn't a doubt in my mind that Sim exuded this part of his heritage loud and clear.

One of the most memorable times was when we were sitting watching the other competitors. There was a lady who had two Dobermans sitting near us. The two Dobies started wrestling with each other. Sim watched for a short time and then approached them. Again he only gave them a look, and again, these two large dogs complied. It made me begin to notice that the more training a dog has, the more particular they become about the behavior of a less mannerly dog. Their tolerance for poor behavior is very low.

What it also brought sharply into focus for me was that dogs have the ability to read and understand body language almost flaw-lessly, especially ours. We can try to fool them with our words, but they can see right through it. This becomes extremely import-ant when training. If we don't know what we're doing, the dog can tell. I have seen people acting as if they know exactly what they are doing, especially in the obedience ring, and then shrug and think the dog is "stupid or stubborn" because the dog didn't give the desired response. Many times, the problems stem from the training. If the dog is becoming confused with an exercise and the handler allows his or her frustration to take over rather than to break things down, the dog associates the handler's frustrated body language and dissatisfac-tion with that exercise, and the exercise becomes something unpleas-ant. This can cause the dog to be stressed, sometimes to the point of shutting down or developing an obsessive-compulsive behavior to deal with the stress.

Now the handler has two problems to deal with. Not only does the handler have to work with the dog to accept and enjoy the exer-cise but also reverse the negative emotional impact that has occurred. This can sometimes become an insurmountable problem, so it is bet-ter not to push the dog to this point to begin with. I will expand on this in a later chapter.

Each dog, as well as each breed, has its own pace of learning. Some exercises come easier to certain breeds than others. For exam-ple, take the Scent Discrimination exercise in the Utility Class. There are ten articles used for this exercise, five of which are wooden and five of which are metal. One of the articles is "scented" by the handler by rubbing the article between his or her hands. The article is then placed with the remaining unscented ones in a pile. A Blood Hound might learn this exercise very quickly, where it might take an English Bulldog a long, long time to even understand the concept of retrieving the article, let alone scenting out the proper one. We often make the mistake of trying to rush the dog rather than breaking the exercise down and respecting the dog's learning process.

To make matters worse, after we have taken a lot of time to teach an exercise and the dog "gets it," we then overload the dog by expecting the dog to perform many repetitions of the exercise perfectly. After about the third repetition, the dog begins to think that it is doing something wrong. The dog thinks, *Why else am I being asked to continue to keep repeating this unless I'm not doing something right?* Because the dog wants to please us, the dog starts to make changes in how the exercise is being performed. This gets the handler aggravated, and rather than to do something different with the dog for a few minutes and then return to the original exercise, the handler gets more forceful and the whole exercise falls apart.

Another mistake that is commonly made is pushing the dog to the point of stress. The dog has been working on an exercise that has been difficult to learn. Then once the dog has begun getting it right, instead of letting the dog enjoy his accomplishment, we introduce another difficult exercise. When is enough *enough*? It takes a dog thirteen weeks to fully understand and grasp an exercise. This does not mean that you cannot teach the dog more than one thing at a time, but rather, you should teach something difficult mixed with something easy and pleasurable. It may be just a small part of another difficult exercise but something the dog has fun with.

The point that I am making is that when working with your dog, you should be pleased with what you get when the dog gets something right. When a "miracle" is delivered, know when to say when. Both of you should be able to savor the moment and feel proud of the accomplishment you and the dog have made. Tomorrow is another day. If today's training session was mutually enjoyable and you are satisfied with the results, it will make tomorrow's training session something the dog will look forward to and not dread. Learn your dog's limits and know when to stop. You always want to end a training session on a high note, leaving the dog wanting more.

Chapter 27

No matter how dire the situation, keep your cool.

—H. Jackson Brown Jr.

I continued practicing with Sim. When he was having a good day, he would do well. I had become more astute at being able to "read" how he was feeling. The maintenance regimen of medication and the prescription diet were keeping him somewhat in balance. I received the premium for the September shows in Maine and felt that the judges were a good fit for Sim. I asked the vet if she thought that it would be all right to show him. She said that he appeared to be well enough. "Just be sure to keep the stress level down," she recommended.

I planned our trip carefully. Janet and her husband were going to be there as well with Abbey. Sim would have one of his pals there, so that should add some fun to the trip for him. We all met on Friday evening and had dinner in the hotel where we were staying. Then we all called it an early evening because we had to be at the show site early in the morning.

Neither Sim nor Abbey qualified that day, but they both seemed relaxed. Both Janet and I felt that they would do better the next day. They had the opportunity to get used to the facility, so we considered the first trial a "run-thru."

There was a restaurant that Frank had read about, and we all agreed that it sounded like a great place to try. Frank asked one of the clerks at the desk of the hotel for directions to it. We fed and walked Sim, put him in his crate, and left for dinner. The restaurant was about an hour or so away. When we got there, we had to wait thirty minutes to be seated. The four of us chatted away, Janet and I going over how the dogs did at the show, Frank and Brian looking at the yachts that were docked by the restaurant. We had a leisurely dinner and then headed back to the hotel. We talked a short while longer and then headed to our respective rooms.

When we got into our room, Sim looked at me from his crate. I greeted him and was just about to let him out when Frank said to me, "Someone's been in our room and has gone through our things." Nothing looked out of place to me. Frank showed me how his soft-sided suitcase was exactly where he left it but that it was turned inside out. Other than that, there was no evidence that anything was disrupted. I checked the dresser drawers and found where our video camera and related equipment had been stolen. I then let Sim out of his crate. He was a little unsteady on his feet and began to vomit. The burglar or burglars must have given him something to keep him from barking. We called the desk to report the burglary.

The same desk clerk that Frank had gotten directions from answered the phone. He asked Frank if we wanted him to call the police and offered no sense of urgency about the event. Of course we wanted to report it to the police. More important than that, however, was if Sim was seriously harmed. He vomited several times and then gradually seemed to recover. Needless to say, I had him excused from the trial the next day. There was no way that I was going to put him in the obedience ring after the stress he just had gone through. I was just pleased that Sim was getting over the experience. I was beginning to feel that my boy had a little black rain cloud over his head. Try though I might to manage his stress level, it was almost an impossible task.

What we took away from this experience were two things. First, you never can be prepared for every situation. No matter how vigilant we may try to be, things will happen. For instance, we may be very careful with our credit cards, never letting them out of our possession. However, sometimes identity thieves put card readers on the equipment where we have to swipe our cards. Next thing you know, your identity has been compromised. Second, you never, ever ask a hotel clerk for directions. Anyone listening to the conversation would get a good estimate of the amount of time our room would be vacant. They had more than enough time to get in and get out of our room. We went to the show site the next day just to watch and give Sim the opportunity to be there and not have to work. I kept my fingers crossed that the break-in had not caused him irreparable emotional damage.

Chapter 28

Never deprive someone of hope;
it might be all they have.

—H. Jackson Brown Jr.

Every situation, even a bad one, can be a learning experience. You can never be in control of every situation, but that doesn't mean that you can't try to adjust as things change. This became quite clear as my work with Bev, my elderly client, continued. Her physical difficulties increased. She now had to use a walker instead of the cane. It was almost impossible for her to be able to train Scottie with a regular style walker. We researched the problem, and she found a triangular-shaped walker that had three wheels. One wheel was directly in the front and then one wheel on each side. It also had hand brakes on the handlebars. This made it possible for her to operate the walker with one hand and hold the dog's leash with the other. It took a while for both Bev and Scottie to get used to the equipment change, but with some practice, it all began to come together. Getting everything polished and ring-ready was going to take a lot of work, but it appeared that it was going to happen. My greatest challenge was to keep Bev from becoming impatient with Scottie. She was asking a lot from him. He was a willing worker and learner, so he gave it his "all" each time we practiced. I hoped that they would be ready early in 2004 to begin to enter trials and earn his Companion Dog title with both the AKC and UKC. I had to help Bev adjust her training to her physical issues.

During this year, the American Veterinary Association had changed the guidelines for vaccination protocol. Research was showing that excessive vaccinations appeared to be causing a host of disorders including cancer, allergic reactions, and autoimmune diseases. They were now recommending that instead of vaccinating a dog every year for distemper and parvovirus, titers could be taken to see if the dog's immunity to those diseases were at acceptable levels. When the dog was brought in for its annual physical, the vet would take blood and have the blood tested for the titer levels. The higher the titer level, the more protection against that disease the dog has. If the level falls below a certain level, then a vaccine is given.

A titer is a measurement of how much antibody to a certain virus (or other antigen) is circulating in the blood at that moment. Titers are usually expressed in a ratio, which is how many times the blood could be diluted until no more antibodies could be found. If the blood could be diluted two times only with no more titers, it would be a titer of 1:2. If it could be diluted one thousand times until no more antibodies could be found, it would be a titer of 1:1000. The only exception to titering was the rabies vaccine, which is given every one, two, or three years, whatever period is mandated by state law. In exceptional cases, a vet will have titer testing done for rabies if a dog has shown serious allergic reactions to vaccinations or has an illness that could be compromised by the vaccine. I felt comfortable with this and spoke to my vet about it. She agreed, and Sim never had another distemper or parvovirus vaccine again. Year after year, his titer level was always very adequate.

Just as I had to help Bev adjust her training to her physical problems, I had to think what the best protocol for Sim's vaccinations was. It took some getting used to, but after researching the pros and cons, I felt confident that titering was in the best interest of Sim's health. Little did I know that this learning experience would play a large role in Sim's and my life later on.

Chapter 29

There is no right way to do something wrong.

—Unknown

In 2004, I became a member and began regularly attending a local dog obedience club. Sometimes I would participate in a Level 3 class. This class was for dogs that had a lot of obedience training and/or competitive experience. It gave Sim the opportunity to work in a different place around dogs that he wasn't use to. I felt this was especially helpful with the out-of-sight Sits and Downs. There were several different instructors.

The head instructor had owned and trained German Shepherds. His assistant also had German Shepherds. One of the woman instructors had Corgis and the other woman instructor had Schipperkes. Schipperkes are small black dogs that are known for their toughness. They have almost foxlike faces with high-set ears and weigh about eighteen pounds.

The style of the class depended on which one of the instructors was teaching. Some had harsher methods of corrections than others. I always followed the general directions but never used any method that I felt was not in Sim's best interest.

Fortunately, I had a background in training and had very set ideas as to what I would and wouldn't do. Other people who brought their dogs to class depended solely on the instructions that were given. They thought that the professionals would only give them useful training information. This was not always the case. Each dog is an individual. What one dog can tolerate, another cannot. If something doesn't look right to you, *don't do it, and never turn your dog over to anyone else in the class unless and until you are certain that they are not going to inflict any harm, either physical or mental, on your dog.*

There are times when something may look harmless and it might very well be. However, always keep your relationship with the dog uppermost in your mind. Many a human/dog relationship has been irreparably harmed when the owner just accepts instruction without thinking it through first. This also applies to dog training books, tapes, DVDs, and TV shows. Most TV shows are prerecorded and tapes are edited. What may appear to be an instant solution because the dog responds positively immediately isn't necessarily the case. It may take many times and sometimes a more responsive dog to get the desired effect. The "demonstration" dog may have been put through the exercise many times without success. Harsh training methods may have been used, such as an electronic collar. However, you only see the dog respond positively after only one or two tries. This can give you an unfair expectation as to how quickly your dog can give you the required response. It also may not be a long-term solution, possibly creating more problems.

For instance, if treats are used for a desired response over and over again, what happens when there are no treats available? Does the instruction include follow-through or what to do if that method doesn't work? Always remember my motto, "There's more than one way to teach a dog to sit." If the training advice is limited, then your training success will be as well.

I brought Sim in to the club one evening for an Open run-thru. The instructor was Judy, the woman who owned the Corgis. The instructor with the German Shepherds, Paul, was sitting and observing. He looked at the set-up in the ring with the High Jump and Broad Jump. This indicated to him that we were going to do Open work. The expression that then came over his face made him look as if he had just taken a big swallow of sour milk, fully expecting Sim to fail. Of course, Sim showed him that not only could he do the exercises, but he could also do them with great style and flair. From that day on, Sim became a favorite of this instructor. He would greet

Sim with much enthusiasm and say, "I really like this little dog!" Once again, Sim lived up to his heritage. He may look like a lamb but could roar like a lion!

Chapter 30

If there is a better way to do it better...find it.

—Thomas A. Edison

Judy began asking me my advice about one of her Pembroke Welsh Corgis named Sandy. Corgis are long, low, tailless dogs. They have foxlike heads with oval brown eyes and medium-size erect, high set ears. Their coat is medium-length, which lies flat and is somewhat coarse to the touch. They are often associated with Queen Elizabeth of England, as this is her breed of choice. Over the years, the Queen has owned over thirty of these dogs. Recently, she introduced a Corgi/ Dachshund cross known as the *Dorgi*.

Sandy was fawn and white in color. He was an older dog, and Judy had trained him through the Utility level of obedience. However, he needed one more qualifying score to get his Novice or Companion Dog title. His problem was the Sit/Stay exercise. He would become so stressed that he would lie down and start rolling on his back. I told her I had a couple of ideas, and I would be more than happy to try to help her. She made an appointment with me to see if we could solve the problem.

When she and Sandy arrived for their appointment, I put them through the Novice exercises. Sandy did well until we got to the Recall. Judy set him up where I told her to and told him to sit. I said, "Leave your dog."

She told him, "Stay," and began to walk forward. As she reached about six feet away from him, he began to roll. I could see that it was

135

almost an obsessive/compulsive behavior. I asked her if anything had happened to cause him to react this way. She couldn't think of anything. According to her, it just started to happen one day. I was surprised at her response because she was a trainer. It would have been helpful to be able to pinpoint when and why the problem started, but I could only work with what I had been told.

"Judy, I would suggest that you use the word *wait* when you leave Sandy for the recall rather than *stay*. The change may take his mind off his nervousness. Plus, it will make him notice that after you tell him to wait, you will call him to you. When he hears 'Stay,' he will get to know that you will always return to him."

What was so significant to me was that the dog was comfortable until she passed the six-foot point. That is the length of a standard training leash. I told her to practice leaving him and only go about two feet away then go back to him. It worked well. I gradually had her increase the distance she walked before she returned. We tried this at six-inch increments. All went well until she reached the six-foot mark. Then he would lie down and roll side to side.

She became annoyed, walked over to him, and replaced him in a sit, verbally letting him know she was very displeased with his behavior. I could see the stress increase in him. He had a worried expression on his face, as though he didn't understand what was happening or why he was being corrected. I pointed it out to her and told her that I thought we had a starting point to identify the problem. It seemed to me that the problem had been made worse because when he broke the sit, she would harshly set him back into the sit. To make matters worse, she had been working with one of the other trainers at the club, who also would harshly replace Sandy when he broke. Sandy now associated the idea of a Sit/Stay to be unpleasant. Because this issue had been going on for so long, it had become strongly ingrained in him. It was not going to be easy, but we were willing to try to correct it.

I started by having her take a few steps away from him after telling him to "Wait" instead of "Stay." The "Wait" command is given with the left hand. The "Stay" is given with the right hand. I wanted to see if that would change the exercise enough for him that he would be able to relax. I then had her go right back to him and give him a special treat. Little by little, we were able to extend the distance she would go before returning to him. Eventually, she was able to go out of sight, and he seemed to be comfortable. All of this took quite a while, and he did revert back to the old behavior every so often. However, we both felt that if the conditions were right, he could earn that elusive title.

Sandy was about eleven years old, about a year and a half older than Sim. They became great friends. Sim had a calming effect on Sandy. We began to call them Grumpy Old Men. They both had very set ideas as to how other dogs and people should act. Sandy was called The Fun Police because he would whine and bark loudly when people would clap or get rowdy at a trial. As was noted before, Sim was The Manners Police. The two were quite a pair.

Judy entered Sandy in a Corgi Specialty. A Specialty show is where only a specific breed is entered to compete. Judy asked me if I would attend the show with her. She said I could bring Mr. Sims as well. We both thought that this was a good environment for Sandy because it would be less crowded and less frenetic than a normal show. Of course, everyone asked me about Sim, and I told them he was studying to become a Corgi. He did a good job keeping Sandy calm. When we took them out for potty breaks, they would walk along together, sniffing here and there and then comparing notes with each other. Sandy didn't qualify that day, but he did show improvement. He stayed sitting for about forty-five seconds before he began rolling. Judy and I both felt that we were headed in the right direction. The takeaway from this was that the gentle training, plus Sandy's confidence being built, with Sim's help, was working.

Chapter 31

It takes as much stress to be a success
as it does to be a failure.

—Emilio James Trujillo

AKC had introduced a new class called Rally Obedience, more commonly known as Rally-O. It was going to become a titled class in 2005, meaning you and your dog could compete and earn titles similar to the other obedience classes. The difference between Rally-O and the competitive obedience we had been practicing was that you were allowed to talk to your dog throughout the competition. There is a course set up with each station numbered, and the exercises are done in numerical order. Each station has a sign that instructs you what to do. For example, one station may say "Sit your dog." You then move on to the next station which may say "Right turn." The next one might say "Fast."

In Rally-O Novice, the course is done on leash. I had been asked to do therapy dog evaluations at a facility that was offering run-thru's of regular obedience classes as well as Rally-O. I had time before the therapy dog evaluations started, so I entered Sim for an Open run-thru. It was outside, and even though the weather was nice, I wasn't sure how well he would perform. The trainer who put us through our paces had been training for many years. She was just amazed with how well Sim worked and surprised how good he was because of his breed. Here was another trainer that thought a Shih Tzu had no work ethic whatsoever. His workout here gave me confidence that he might do better the next time I showed him in a trial.

In the afternoon, they offered Rally-O run-thru's. Frank was watching the teams as they worked and asked me if I was interested in taking Sim through. I said no. I didn't want him to become confused working with me in regular obedience, where I could only give him commands when I was directed to by the judge, and in Rally where I could talk to him all the while. Frank said he would like to try it. I had trained Sim to be able to do all the exercises, so Frank felt it would be easy. They did so well that the trainer that put them through said they should compete.

Judy had joined us and put Sandy in Rally-O as well. He did well also, and there were no long Sit/Stays, so rolling would not be an issue. We thought that this would help to give him some confidence, and he seemed to enjoy the work. Frank and Judy decided that they would like to compete in Rally-O and would begin practicing for the trials next year.

Sim seemed to be feeling better most of the time. We had made another diet change. The vet suggested a fish and potato prescription diet. When a dog suffers from inflammatory bowel disease, sometimes the diet has to be changed on a fairly regular basis. If a dog begins to adversely react to the diet he is being feed, the protein source in the food is considered to be the biggest cause. The dog is then prescribed a protein source that he has never been exposed to and, therefore, has not built up an allergy to it. There are several "unique" protein sources. Duck, rabbit, kangaroo, venison, quail, and fish may be tried. I wondered if I had to learn to hunt and go on a safari to get some of these exotic meats. Years ago, when there weren't the choices that there are now, lamb was used because most dog foods were red meat or chicken based. However, as lamb became a popular ingredient, it was used more and more. More dogs had been exposed to it and its effectiveness as a "unique" protein source was no longer viable.

As usual, when we started the new diet, Sim seemed to tolerate it and showed some improvement. However, after about a month on the fish diet, I began to notice that right after he finished a meal, he would start scratching at his sides and underarm area. It appeared to me that he was quickly becoming allergic to it. I watched this progress for about a week and then let the vet know. She said that we should try duck and potato. As soon as we made the change, the itching after meals subsided. *Keep peeling that onion*, I thought. *Eventually, we will find the root cause of all of this.*

The trials in Maine were approaching. I entered Sim for Saturday and Sunday. Saturday, he did not qualify. Again, it appeared that he was getting used to the surroundings, even though he had been there many times before. He was becoming a celebrity and had many fans who made a big fuss over him and cheered him on. The next day, he earned his second Open leg. And this time he beat some of the big boys, including an Australian Shepherd, a Golden Retriever, and a Labrador Retriever, to name a few of the more work-oriented breeds, placing second. It had only taken three years, but considering how his physical problems held him back, I was extremely proud of him.

Bev was there, showing Scottie in the Novice Class. She was using the wheeled triangular walker. They did very well until the Stays. Scottie broke the Sit/Stay to follow Bev. She was very disappointed that day. However, they continued to work, and Scottie earned his Novice title in November that year. It was quite an accomplishment and showed that with the right kind of practice and handling, both the dog and handler were able to overcome some tough obstacles.

Chapter 32

Funny, isn't it? Sometimes you have
to be silent to communicate.

—Monica, *Touched by an Angel*

One morning in November, I was going about my usual chores when I began feeling a searing pain in the lower left quadrant of my body. It became so strong that it literally made my knees weaken. I looked at Sim, who was staying unusually close to me, and said, "Something's wrong, Bud. I have to lie down." As usual, Sim dutifully followed me into the bedroom. I carefully lowered myself onto the bed because the pain was so intense. It was difficult to find any relief or comfortable position. Sim waited for me to get as comfortable as I could under the circumstances and then very carefully and gently jumped up on the bed and curled up behind my knees. At first, he sat up as though he was keeping watch over me and then lay down. The pain was constant. No matter how I tried to change position, it only got worse.

The phone rang. It was Frank with his usual lunchtime call. I could barely speak to him. He asked me what was wrong. I told him, and he suggested that I call our doctor. I said I couldn't talk any longer, let alone call the doctor. Frank said that he would let the doctor know what was going on with me.

A short time later, the phone rang again. I didn't want to answer because I felt so terrible but did anyway. It was Dr. Connelly. He wasn't sure what was going on but called in a prescription that was supposed to relax my colon. He thought that possibly was the origin of the pain. I called Frank to let him know what the doctor said and to ask him to pick up the prescription for me on his way home. Sim had stayed by my side all day.

Later in the afternoon, Sim gave me his "Excuse me, but I have to go out" look.

"Well, Bud, I'll do the best I can, but we're going to have to take it slow and easy." I put his leash on and took him out. The pain was so strong that I felt dizzy. Sim walked slowly with me, stopping to relieve himself as quickly as possible. He then turned and headed for home.

As soon as we got in the door, I headed for bed again with Sim close behind. Frank came home early and had the prescription with him. He gave me one of the tablets. According to the directions, I was to let it dissolve under my tongue. I did and waited to see if there would be any relief. The pain stopped getting worse but didn't get any better. In the meanwhile, Frank fed Sim and then took him out again. Sim returned to my side after he had eaten and had the opportunity to relieve himself. I was miserable. It was now about 9:00 p.m., and I had been trying to get some relief all day.

One of my clients, Marianne Lynch, was a physician's assistant. Frank called her and told her that I was feeling very poorly. She said she would be right over. She asked me some questions and thought that either I had a urinary tract infection or a kidney stone. She gave me an antibiotic and told me that if it was a kidney stone, the antibiotic would do nothing. If it was a urinary tract infection, it should help. In either event, she told me to call my doctor the next day and let him know.

"I hate to see you in so much pain, Peg. You're always so strong and don't let things get to you. I can tell that you are really ill."

"Thanks, Marianne. I appreciate your help and concern. Sim is taking very good care of me. He hasn't let me out of his sight all day." I was in such pain that every word I spoke seemed to make the pain worse.

"I've been watching him keeping a close eye on me to be sure I didn't do anything to upset you. He's like your Guardian Angel now. But I well remember all the times that you were his."

I mustered a weak laugh.

"We're quite a pair. We've been through a lot of ups and downs together and have always supported each other."

"You sure have. I really think that it was destiny that brought the two of you together. Feel better and be sure to call the doctor tomorrow."

She gave Sim a pat on the head and left. I felt blessed that I had someone to turn to. It made me think of all the wonderful—and not so wonderful—people that I had met through my business. And Sim was an essential part of all of it.

The antibiotic gave me some relief within an hour. I reached over and petted Sim and said, "Whew, that was a tough one, Sim, but I think I'm OK now." He jumped off the bed and returned shortly with one of his toys, a large orange octopus that he liked to have me throw for him. I told him, "I don't think I can throw it, Sim. Mom still needs to rest." He looked at me, swallowed, placed the octopus against my legs, and then put his head down on it, using it like a pillow. I was finally able to go to sleep in comfort. Once again, our mutual caregiving was in full view.

The next morning, I felt fine. I called the doctor and let him know what had happened. He said to continue the antibiotic. Since the antibiotic seemed to help, he felt that there was no kidney stone and was just glad that I was feeling better. In thinking about this conversation in hindsight, the words of H. L. Mencken come to mind: "For every complex problem there is a solution that is concise, clear, simple, and wrong."

Chapter 33

Whether you think you can
or think you can't—you are right.

—Henry Ford

The groomer that I had been renting from was making some changes to her business, so I had to find another space for my training. I called my vet. She said that she would get back to me after she made a phone call. In about ten minutes, she called me back. She said that I should contact the CEO of Brookside Road Animal Hospital.

They had some space that I might be interested in. I contacted him and we set up an appointment for the next day. Brookside Road Animal Hospital was renting a very large space at Hay Market Square, a shopping center near the animal hospital. They had set up a canine therapy facility. Any dog that had knee, hip, elbow, or other joint surgery or needed exercise because of obesity would be given an evaluation by Dr. Houghton, the head surgeon at Brookside Road Animal Hospital, and he would set up a program that would best benefit the "patient." The space was complete with an above-ground swimming pool, an underwater treadmill, a massage therapy room, and an exercise room. The business was closed Sunday and Monday so the exercise room space would be available to me for those two days of each week.

We agreed on a fair amount for monthly rent, and I was ready to go. The only hitch was that this space would be available only for a year. The canine therapy unit was going to be moved to half of the building that housed my vet. Brookside Road Animal Hospital owned that practice, and it was a satellite facility in the neighboring town of East Islip. By moving the facility to their building, it also allowed them to tailor everything to their best advantage. For instance, the pool would no longer be above ground, but rather, they could chop the floor and install an in-ground pool. This would make it much more convenient for the dogs to be able to get in and out of the pool.

The CEO told me that when their lease ended or the construction of the new facility was completed, I would be welcome to use the conference room at Brookside Road Animal Hospital. It would only be available on Sundays. I was fine with this arrangement, but because of the way my business was growing, I thought that I should at least look to see if I could find something where I would not be as restricted. I began looking at places that I could lease so that I wouldn't be constrained as to when I would be able to train. I had gone from two and a half days at the grooming shop to two days at the therapy facility. In a year or so, I would be down to only Sundays.

And so the search began. It is difficult to find appropriate space for dog training for several reasons. Landlords are often put off by this type of business because of possible cleanliness and noise issues. No matter how much you may to try to put their minds at ease about these issues, it is a losing battle. I guess if it were my property, I would be resistant as well. Another issue is size. Training is a space hog, particularly when you're training for competition. A commercial building is leased by the square foot per month. Because I needed a reasonably large space, the cost per month was going to be prohibitive. Unlike a retail store that can divide each section of square footage and figure how much money will be generated per square foot, I could only try to estimate how many dogs per day or month I would have to train just to meet the rent. I also needed to be in a location that would be safe for women coming for an evening lesson. And in most cases, it was usual procedure to have to sign a three-year lease. It was a daunting task, to say the least.

At one point, I thought I had found a place that would work well for me. The location was pretty good, and the size and layout of the space would work well for me for pet and obedience training. The landlord had his hair salon next door. Frank and I both felt that this would work well. The rent would be a little bit of a stretch each month, but my business was continuing to grow. So much so I had a list of people who were waiting for an opening in my schedule so they could get an appointment and begin training. We talked to the landlord to tell him that we liked the space.

He was glad to hear of our decision and then proceeded to tell me how I should run my business.

"You should consider adding doggie daycare to your services," he said. "It's the going thing now, and you could make a fortune. The space is large enough to handle the dogs for this part of your business. It's easy money. You really should do this."

"Give me a couple of days to think about taking this space. I'll call you back."

"You'll have to call me back in two days because there is some-one else interested in taking over this space."

I was not interested in doggy daycare, and the space that was available to me was not large enough for this type of service to be done properly, nor was there any yard outside for the dogs to "potty." They would have to be walked on a busy main thoroughfare. It would have been a disaster waiting to happen. Plus, there were already several doggy daycare businesses in the local area. I didn't appreciate him telling me how my business should be run. I certainly wouldn't tell him how to give someone a haircut or permanent. So I had to walk away from the potential space.

It bothered me, but I knew I had to keep any emotion out of it. The arrangement would not have made good business sense. Little did I know that I had made one of the best decisions possible. At times, life will throw us a curveball that we least expect. There was one headed right for me that I had no idea was coming. I knew I had a place to practice my trade, and if in a year, I could only work on Sundays, so be it. I have learned throughout my life that God always has a plan. It may not be the one we were working on, but things get put into proper perspective, and we find out about it when we least expect it.

Chapter 34

Success is never final, and failure is never
fatal; it's courage that counts.

—Unknown

My client Paula's dog, Boomer, had badly injured his knee and
needed surgery early in December. He had ruptured his anterior cru-
ciate ligament, commonly known as ACL. Although we were not
sure exactly how it happened, it most likely occurred on two separate
occasions. The first one could have happened when Boomer caught
his foot in a small hole in the grass, landed awkwardly when catching
a ball, or slipped on a wet or icy surface. Any one of these scenarios
may have created a tear in the ligament, weakening it. The second
time he may have engaged in any of these activities probably completed the tear or rupture. The surgery is somewhat intricate.

Post-surgery rehabilitation is very important so that the healing process takes place properly and the affected leg becomes strong
again. Paula brought Boomer to the canine therapy facility where I
was doing my training. Boomer was somewhat comfortable there
because he had been there for lessons with me many times. I met
Paula there to watch and see how Boomer reacted to the therapy. In
all the time I knew him, he was a pushy, independent, self-assured
fellow.

This day, however, I saw another side of him, and it tugged
at my heart. He was very tentative, taking a long time and much
encouragement to go into the pool. Even though he was tethered

to a long line and had on a flotation vest, he was very unsure and uncomfortable to take that first step. The therapist and Paula kept encouraging him with treats as they stood in the pool, and I stood beside him at the edge of the pool, talking to him softly, trying to build his confidence.

He finally took the plunge. He was able to swim the prescribed number of laps but was not relaxed. He was then moved to the underwater treadmill. This helps the dog move his legs easily and build the muscle tone without straining them. Boomer seemed a little more confident with this exercise than with swimming in the pool.

When this exercise was finished, he was given a shower to wash off the chlorine from the pool, then dried. We then moved to the massage room, where the therapist massaged him and showed Paula how to do the same thing at home. The therapist also showed Paula some exercises that Boomer should do. One of them was like a doggie push-up. He had to stand and then lie down then stand again. This was to help strengthen his leg muscles as well. Boomer went through several sessions at the facility and the work that Paula did with him at home. He healed nicely and regained his outgoing personality as well as being able to walk normally again.

I bought Boomer a pair of doggie boots for Christmas. Paula told me that it took Boomer a few minutes to get used to them but was walking well with them.

I thought that it would be nice for Sim to have a set of boots as well to keep his feet warm when we went for our walks. He sometimes would have to stop when his feet got too cold or when the snow would pack up between his toes, and I would have to take the "ice balls" out for him. I bought him a set of red boots. When they arrived, I couldn't wait to try them on Sim. I showed them to him, and of course, he gave me "the swallow." I didn't know what a production this was going to be.

I gently put the first one on his right front paw. He looked at me and held his paw up. I told him he was a good boy and put his paw on the floor and gave him a treat. He looked at me again and swallowed. I put the second one on his left front paw. He held it up; I put it down. "Two down and two to go," I told him. I put the boot on his right rear paw. He held it up; I put it down. I put the last one on his left rear paw and fastened it as I had the others. He held it up; I put it down. I stood in front of him, and he looked at me, wide-eyed, and swallowed. I took a treat and started to walk slowly so that he would follow me. He just stood there, staring at me.

"Come on, Bud," I said. "You look very handsome with your new boots on. It will keep your 'footsies' warm and the ice won't hurt your toes." He didn't move; he just looked at me and swallowed. I went to the kitchen to get a few more treats to entice him to walk with me. Before I could get back to the family room where I had left him, he was standing next to me in the kitchen. And he was barefoot.

"What happened to your boots?" I asked him. He just looked at me, and I almost could see him chuckle, although he just gave me a little sneeze. I walked into the family room with Sim close behind. He started trotting around the room, showing me where each of his boots had fallen. It appeared that he had shaken them off. I laughed so hard the tears were rolling down my face. Sim just stood, looking at me with his tail wagging enthusiastically.

"Guess these are going back from where they came. Right, Bud?" He looked at me, tail still wagging, sneezed, and swallowed. That was an absolute "*Yes!*" So I repackaged the boots and sent them back.

I still wanted something to keep Sim's feet warm and dry. I happened to see an ad in one of the specialty dog magazines. Someone had invented dog boots that would stay on. The boots were made of suede. They were then attached to "socks," and each "sock" had a suspender attached. The fabric parts of the suspenders were attached to each other in the shape of an *X*. The *X* went across the dog's back and then each boot and sock hung down to each paw. I called the company. They told me that I would have to make a tracing of one of Sim's front paws as well as his height and chest measurement. Once they got this information from me, it would probably take about two weeks before I got them. If I wasn't happy with them, they could be returned.

When they arrived, I examined them. They looked very cute. The boots were light-brown suede. The socks were light blue, and the suspenders had a light-blue background with red and yellow stripes.

I showed them to Sim. "I think they're pretty jazzy, Bud. What do you think?" He gave me the swallow. "We'll try these and see how you like them. If you can wear them, they'll keep you nice and warm and dry." He just looked at me and swallowed.

"Okay, Sim, let's give them a go." I carefully and gently put each paw into the sock and worked the sock up his leg until his paw was in the boot. I gave him a treat when each paw and leg was covered. When I had completed the task, I took a treat and started to walk, telling Sim to come along with me. At first, he just stood there looking at me as if to say, "Not again." But very gradually, I got him to walk. The first few steps were awkward. I'm sure they must have felt odd to him. We kept walking around the house, first down the carpeted hall, then into the kitchen, then into the family room. He seemed to be getting the hang of it and appeared to be comfortable with them.

Success, I thought. I took them off after our little training session and hung them on the brass hat rack in the family room that held Sim's wardrobe. His wardrobe consisted of a cable-knit pastel print turtleneck sweater, a black jogging suit with a white stripe down each side, a yellow rain slicker, which he wasn't really comfortable with, a maroon jacket with an autumn leaf motif, and of course, his New York Doggie Duds coat. The neighbors would watch for Sim when Frank walked him early in the morning to check out Sim's outfit. I think they may have planned their wardrobe by what Sim wore. They often told me how they couldn't wait to see what he was wearing each day.

This brings me to a very important point. If you put an article of clothing on the dog for his or her comfort, warmth, and/or safety, that's fine. However, I don't agree with people who put costumes on their dogs. People usually do this around the holidays, particularly Halloween. Some dogs, though few, are comfortable with this and actually enjoy it and the attention it brings. Most, however, are not comfortable. If you really look at your dog's face after they are "dressed up," you will usually see discomfort and sometimes even embarrassment. Most of the model dogs in the dog catalogs never really look pleased being dressed up like a doll. Some of the Hollywood stars dress their dogs up and treat them as though they are "little kids in fur coats." Then they wonder why their dogs have behavior problems. Think of yourself in a foreign land where you don't speak the language. The people are very nice to you, but they insist on dressing you in a large bumblebee costume. Truthfully, would you really enjoy this or would you feel that being dressed like that was undignified? Dogs have dignity just as we do. We should never do anything at any time that takes their dignity away. This holds true whether we are playing with them or if they are at the point in their life where they may be coming to the end of time with us.

Several days later, we had a light snowfall. *Time to try the boots*, I thought. I put the boots on Sim and then put on his leaf jacket. He looked great and I told him so. At first, he was unsure about the boots, but once we got out into the snow, he really enjoyed the protection they gave him. He started to gallop through the snow, pushing his face into it and scooping some into his mouth. When he brought his head up and looked at me, he had snow all over his face. He was having a great time. As we walked along the street so that he could relieve himself, he trotted along and seemed to appreciate the fact that his feet were warm, dry, and comfortable and he wasn't slipping and sliding. *Great*, I thought. I had made a good choice. *Sim will be able to enjoy his walks every day even if we have a bad winter. We'll be able to go from our street to the next one where the kids are. They love to play in the snow, and Sim loves to interact with them, tunneling in the snow, catching snowballs that they threw to him, and just being rowdy in general. We'll also be able to walk through the woods so Sim can track the scents of the little critters that burrow under the snow. And best of all to him, he'll be able to climb to the top of the snow drifts and mark them, letting the other dogs in the neighborhood know that he is "king of the hill."*

Chapter 35

It's not whether you get knocked down;
it's whether you get up.

—Vince Lombardi

In 2005, I continued practicing with Sim, hoping that this would be the year that he would get his Open or Companion Dog Excellent title. Frank continued practicing Rally O with Sim. There was a training facility that had classes on Monday night. We attended them as often as possible. Sim seemed comfortable working there and enjoyed the Rally O work with Frank. As usual, Sim's energy and ability to work enthusiastically varied with his physical status. Again, his demeanor was unpredictable, but when he felt well, he worked well. Frank was getting more comfortable with Rally O, and he and Sim worked well together.

In February, I began organizing Sim's obedience trial schedule. I knew that I couldn't show him at Eastern States in the Open class because he became too stressed there. However, I thought that Frank might be able to try Sim in Rally O there because of Sim being on leash throughout all the exercises. Eastern States shows would be a four-day event during Fourth of July week.

I knew that Frank had to work him in a trial before that one in a more relaxed atmosphere. The Toy Club was offering Rally O this year during their Memorial Day shows. I thought that this was a good starting point for Sim and Frank. Sim was familiar with the facility and had gotten his High In Trial there.

The man who was going to be judging on the first day was Ed Phipps. I had seen him many times and always looked forward to the day that I might be judged by him. He always seemed very fair, impartial, and had a good sense of humor, which helped to relax the handlers. Sim had shown under Ed at Eastern States and it was a disaster. Sim did next to nothing because he was so stressed in that environment. Ed was very patient and just said that Sim would do better another day. I had a feeling that, in this case anyway, Frank was going to be more nervous and stressed than Sim as this was his first time in an obedience trial competition. I was cautiously optimistic. Hopefully, Sim would be feeling well and would enjoy the work.

In late March, I began my spring cleaning. One morning, as I began taking apart the dining area, I began to feel a dull ache in the left lower quadrant of my body. I shrugged it off, thinking that I had possibly pulled a muscle while cleaning the other rooms. Unfortunately, in a very short time, the dull ache began to transform into a familiar piercing, burning pain. *Not again*, I thought. Sim was under the dining area table, once again being the project manager. I was ready to start washing the walls and woodwork. "Well, Sim, everything is ready to go, but I have to lie down and see if I can relieve this pain." I walked down the hall to the bedroom and carefully lowered myself down on the bed. I heard Sim's collar tags jingling close behind me. He jumped up on the bed and curled up behind my knees.

I stayed there for about twenty minutes. I thought I was feeling some relief. "Okay. Sim," I said. "I'm going to try to get some work done." I got up and headed toward the dining area. Sim was not far behind me and took his place under the table again as I began to scrub the wallpaper. After fifteen minutes or so, the pain began to intensify again. "Time for a break again, Bud," I said. Sim lifted his head and looked at me.

I took a couple of aspirin and headed down the hall. This time I made it to the bed before I heard Sim coming down the hall. He got to the doorway of the bedroom and shook his head, collar tags jingling, alerting me to his presence. He carefully came up on the bed and stationed himself at my feet. The pain was becoming more intense again. After twenty minutes, I began to feel slightly better. Sim sat up and gave me his "Excuse me, but I have to go out" look.

"I know, Bud. Give me a minute to get myself together." Sim looked at me and gave me the swallow. I got up slowly. Sim jumped off the bed and walked next to me. I got his leash and took him out to potty. He crossed our street to the nearest telephone pole and relived himself fully. It sounded much like a water fountain turned on full force.

"What a good boy," I said to him. "You really had to go!"

We went back into the house, and I gave Sim a treat for being so patient and tried to continue my work. The phone rang. It was Paula. As soon as she heard my voice, she asked what was wrong. I said, "Oh, I have this stupid pain again, and I'm in the middle of cleaning the dining area. I can work for about fifteen to twenty minutes, and then I have to lie down and rest."

There was a short silence, and then she said, "Did you ever think about stopping the work you're doing?"

She told me to get some rest and she would check in on me the next day. I continued the pattern of cleaning, resting, cleaning, and resting in twenty-minute intervals several more times. Sim constantly kept a close eye on me and always curled up on the bed with me. The last few times, he actually curled into my back as though he was acting like a heating pad. However, when I would get up to start work again the last few times, his demeanor began to change. His ears were flat against his head, and he walked slowly. It was almost as if he was thinking, *How many times am I going to have to get up on the bed, get down from the bed, and watch her go up and down the ladder? I'm getting worn out trying to take care of her.*

The look on his face made me laugh. I gave him a hug and said, "Thanks, Sim. You've done a great job taking care of me." He gave me a kiss on my cheek, which was unusual because he was never a real "kissy face" kind of dog. When Frank got home, I told him I thought I'd better go to the walk-in clinic. "I probably have another urinary tract infection. It feels just like the last time."

The doctor examined me, agreed that it probably was an infection, and prescribed an antibiotic. Within a couple of days, I felt better. However, that curveball was getting ever closer.

The Toy Show was fast approaching, and I had entered Sim in both the Open Class and the Rally O Novice class. He seemed to be feeling fairly good on a more consistent basis. However, because Sim would be working with me in the Open class and Frank in the Rally O class, I didn't want to overdo anything and have him become too stressed. The regular obedience classes were going to be held in the morning and the Rally classes would follow in the afternoon. The only judge that I was familiar with was Ed Phipps. Unfortunately, he had never seen Sim at his best. *Maybe three will be the charm*, I thought. And it would make me very happy if Sim got his Open title with Ed.

I entered Sim in the Saturday and Monday classes. We made arrangements to stay at the motel Friday night but decided to go home after the Saturday classes. This would allow Sim to spend a night at home before returning to the motel Sunday night for the Monday classes. I was hoping that this would help to keep him relaxed.

Saturday morning, we arrived at the show site. We ran into many of the same people that we would see there year after year. It was almost as if it was a big family reunion. We would exchange stories as to how our dogs were doing both in their training and health issues. There was always something new to learn. It might be about the latest health fad or exercise regimen for the dog. Foods that would "help your dog concentrate, work like a champion, have great energy." Supplements that would give your dog the "edge to win." Most of these I discounted because Sim was so sensitive that he wasn't the type of dog that I could try many of these ideas with. Some of them sounded too good to be true.

Again, I heeded the advice of the judge in Maine who told me to always remember that we are the brains of the team. Never put your dog in jeopardy, no matter what the situation. Some of these fads sounded plausible. They had "testimonials" that said how well the product worked or how quickly positive results were seen. I had to keep in mind that these people were all competitors, and when you are competing with a dog, you never are sure how your team-mate is going to react in the ring. Everyone is looking for an edge, something to make things more predictable. Sim taught me that no matter how well we plan, organize, practice, and even pray, there never are any guarantees as to what you're going to get on any given day. This one was going to be memorable for more than one reason.

As usual, we set up near the obedience ring. I watched as Ed judged each team. Our turn was coming soon, so I started to warm Sim up. He was giving me attention, and though he didn't seem very enthusiastic, I thought he might do well. When we entered the ring, Ed told us where to set up for the heeling exercise. Sim performed all the exercises but seemed sluggish. Ed said to me, "So far, so good. Let's see how the sits and downs go."

Good, I thought. *Maybe today will be the day.* When the last team finished, the steward starting calling us to line up for the Sit and Down exercises. We filed into the ring and went to our assigned places. I removed my armband and Sim's leash and put it behind him. Ed gave the usual instructions and then told us, "Sit your dogs."

I told Sim, "Stay." As he was already sitting, I thought that I could reinforce the "Stay."

Ed told us, "Leave your dog."

I again told Sim to "Stay." He looked at me and swallowed. We filed out of the ring to our "hiding place," led by the steward. We were all chatting with each other to ease the tension, and no one was watching to see if any of the dogs went down. Ed signaled the steward to bring us back into the ring. I took my place across from Sim, *and he was sitting.* My heart skipped a beat. *Today he will get his Open title,* I thought hopefully.

Ed walked over to me, trying hard to keep from laughing. At first, I couldn't figure out what was going on. He said, stifling a giggle, "Your dog went down at about two minutes into the exercise and stayed there until ten seconds before I called everyone back. He then sat up. It was almost as though he had a little watch on and knew that you would be coming back shortly, so he had better be sitting up just the way you left him. I'm sorry."

Oh well, I thought. *I guess the sun, the moon, the stars, and all the planets weren't lined up correctly for me today.* You either begin to have a sense of humor about these things or you have a nervous breakdown. I prefer the former to the latter. Sim did hold his down stay, so his overall performance wasn't bad, although he obviously did not qualify.

Stan, the elderly man there who also showed his Shih Tzu, Chuckie, greeted me when I came out of the ring. As I said before, Shih Tzus are not known for their work ethic. His dog was about two years younger than Sim. He laughed and said to me, "With these guys, you never know what you're going to get. My dog knows his routine perfectly, but if he's not in the mood, he won't do anything. He does everything great at home and where I train."

"Welcome to the club," I told him.

After we had lunch, Frank began to warm Sim up for Rally. Another difference with Rally as opposed to regular competitive obedience is that the handlers are allowed to go into the ring and walk the course to see what heeling pattern will be like based on what order the signs are set up in. Frank handed me Sim's leash and went in with the other handlers to get a feel for the set up.

I knew that he was nervous, so I said to Sim, "Mr. Sims, you're going to be the pro here. This is Mr. Frank's first time in the ring, so make us proud." He looked up at me, wagged his tail, and swallowed. When Frank came out of the ring to wait his turn, he said the course looked "doable" for Sim. I told him about my conversation with Sim, and I thought they both would be fine. As it worked out, they did great and qualified. Frank was so excited that he couldn't stop telling me how well Sim did with him.

He said to me, "I really had it easy. You trained him. I just had to guide him."

I looked at Sim and discreetly winked. He looked back at me and gave me one of his "I know" sneezes. Frank wanted to have his picture taken with Sim and Ed. I told him he very much deserved the honor. He and Sim had done a great job. We returned on Monday. Sim again did not qualify in regular obedience but got his second qualifying score in Rally O. He and Frank needed one more qualifying score to earn the Rally Novice title.

Chapter 36

All great achievements require time.

—Tommy Joseph Schwartz

The Corgi Specialty was coming up again in June, and Judy was working Sandy to get him ready. We both felt that he had a good chance to get his Companion Dog title this time. They were also offering Rally O at the specialty, and she and I felt that Sandy would have no trouble getting a qualifying score in that class. He was enjoying Rally O in practice, and it seemed to be giving him more confidence. Once again, she asked me to join her and to bring Sim along. Sandy and Sim went into their "Grumpy Old Men" routine to everyone's delight, Sim keeping the unruly dogs in line and Sandy continuing his role as the "Fun Police," barking his disapproval of any clapping or cheering. Judy and I set up our chairs near the obedience ring. The two dogs settled themselves next to each other.

As Sandy's turn in the ring was approaching, Judy began to warm him up, walking him back and forth by our chairs. He looked good and was giving her his full attention. She entered the ring, and the judge showed her where the starting point for the "Heel on Leash" exercise was. Sandy did very well and seemed relaxed. He executed the Figure 8 exercise almost effortlessly. The stand for exam was faultless. They set up for the "Heel off Leash" exercise, and again, Sandy did a great job. The last exercise was the recall. Judy told Sandy to "sit."

The judge said, "Leave your dog."

Judy told Sandy to "wait" and began to walk to the other side of the ring where she would then turn and call him when the judge signaled her. As she got about half way from Sandy, he began to roll on his back. I held my breath. I wasn't sure whether or not the judge would excuse him from the ring. Instead, Judy turned to face him when she reached the designated spot.

The judge said "Call your dog."

Judy said cheerfully, "Sandy, come!" In an instant, he went from rolling obsessively on his back to flying right toward her and sat squarely at her feet.

The judge told Judy that she was amazed that Sandy stopped rolling and came to her the instant she called him. She had some points deducted for the exercise, but otherwise, he did well.

When it was time, Judy and Sandy entered the ring for the Sit and Down exercises. Sandy was placed three dogs away from where Sim and I were sitting ringside. The judge told the handlers to sit their dogs. Judy looked at Sandy and reminded him to sit.

"Leave your dogs."

All the handlers in unison told their dogs, "*Stay!*"

I was concerned that the voices might make him edgy. Judy and the other handlers left their dogs and took their places across the ring, turning to face them. The judge began timing the Sit exercise for the one-minute required time. A couple of the dogs dropped immediately. About thirty seconds into the exercise, Sandy started rocking and dropped his nose, aiming at the floor. *Uh-oh*, I thought. He then looked to his left toward Sim and me. I froze. I didn't want to make any move or gesture that might make him start rolling. Sim sat watching Sandy and swallowed.

"Return to your dogs," the judge said. I let out a huge sigh of relief. Sandy had held the Sit! Now he had to maintain a Down for three minutes. If he, by chance, started rolling and stayed down, he would get points off, not disqualified. However, if he rolled and disturbed the dog on either side of him, he would then be disqualified.

The judge said, "Down your dogs."

Judy gave Sandy the command and he went down, adjusting his body into a comfortable position.

"Leave your dogs," the judge said.

Sandy kept his gaze riveted on Judy. At about the two-minute mark, he looked away from her. I kept my fingers crossed that he was just relaxed enough that he didn't have to stare at her. *Forty-five seconds to go*, I thought to myself. *I think he just might make it.* Sandy stayed still.

"Return to your dogs," the judge said. Judy returned to Sandy, and both she and I began breathing normally again. The judge said, "Exercise finished," and the crowd applauded. Sandy, of course, started his little Fun Police howl.

Judy had him quiet down as the judge went to each entrant and told them whether or not they qualified. Sandy did it! He finally, after many years, got the Companion Dog title. Judy and I hugged when they came out of the ring. Sim and Sandy gave us a look as if to say, "So what's the big deal?"

We got some lunch, fed the dogs, and then went outside to walk around and relieve our stress. The dogs trotted along together, as though, in their own way, they knew the accomplishment that had occurred and were enjoying the victory. Later in the day, the Rally O competitions were held. Sandy did beautifully and earned his first qualifying score in that class.

My advice to Judy paid off. She became more patient with Sandy and was rewarded with a more confident, relaxed dog.

Chapter 37

You may have to fight a battle
more than once to win it.

—Lady Margaret Thatcher

Judy had been a trainer for many years, and she had also judged many obedience matches. She told me that there was a match coming up in a couple of weeks on a Saturday and asked me if I would like to judge the Novice classes. She would be judging the Open and Utility classes. I was elated. This was a great opportunity, and I was looking forward to it. My first experience with Sim in a match was very positive and had given me the encouragement to continue training and showing him. I hoped that I could help to encourage other people the same way the first judge encouraged me. I thought that it would also be beneficial to be at the other end of the pencil. It should help enhance my skills as a competitor.

The match was going to be held outside in a field. This was the same setup as my first experience with Sim. Judy said that there would be a canopy covering the area. The day may be hot, but at least there would be cover from the sun or rain.

The Friday afternoon before the match, I began to feel that searing pain again. *Oh no, not now, not again*, I thought. I took it easy that day with Sim always close by, keeping watch over me. "Well, Bud, I'm not going to fool around with this. When Mr. Frank comes home, we're going to the clinic."

I thought that if I got antibiotics again and had a good night's sleep, I would be fine the next morning. I was miserable all day. When Frank came home, he immediately could tell something was wrong by the way I looked. I told him I had "that pain" again and wanted to go to the clinic.

The doctor there examined me. I told him this was something I had twice before and antibiotics seem to help it. He told me the same things I had heard before. If it was a kidney stone, the antibiotics wouldn't help. If it was a urinary tract infection, I should feel better in a few days. When we got home, Sim was waiting for me at the door. He had a worried look on his face.

"I'm going to be OK, Bud. I have to take some medicine and get a good night's sleep."

He gave me his "I'm with you" swallow. I was just hoping that I was going to be able to participate in the judging at the match the next day.

I got up at 6:00 a.m. to start getting ready for the day. I ate something and immediately took another antibiotic. I was excited and was very much looking forward to the assignment. However, the longer I was up, the more I realized that the pain was still very much present and becoming more prominent. I took a shower, hoping that the warmth would help ease the incessant, burning pain that I felt.

By 7:30 a.m. I knew that I couldn't fulfill my promise. That was the worst part of it for me. I would be inconveniencing the club that expected me to be there, and Judy was now going to have to work on her own. It put her in a bad light because she had told the club that all the classes were covered for judging. I called the contact at the club and got no answer. I left a message and apologized, explaining what had happened. Then I called Judy to let her know that I wouldn't be able to work.

"Did you call the club?" she asked. I could hear the annoyance in her voice, and I can't say I blamed her.

"Yes, but I had to leave a message. I'm really sorry about this, Judy, but I literally can't stand up, let alone judge today."

She gave a heavy sigh and said, "OK. I'll talk to you soon."

I took it easy for the next few days. The pain had eased to some degree, but I still was quite uncomfortable. Sim stayed with me, always keeping a close eye on how I was doing. Once again, he adjusted his own schedule of walks, seeming to know that it was an effort for me to take him out. When he did go out, he relieved himself very quickly. *What a great little guy*, I thought. He, once again, was acting as my Guardian Angel.

On Tuesday, I decided that I had to go back to the clinic. Something was not right, and I wasn't feeling much better. I made an appointment with Gayle Peters, the physician's assistant there. She had taken care of me when I had pneumonia, and I felt very comfortable working with her. When I told her what had been going on, she asked me if anyone had taken a urine sample. I said that they hadn't and were assuming that the pain was being caused by either a kidney stone or a urinary tract infection.

She said that she wanted some blood work and urinalysis done. The clinic had an in-house lab. Within fifteen minutes, she had the results in her hand.

She said to me, "Something doesn't add up here. Nothing points to either a stone or infection. I'm going to make an appointment for you for a CAT scan." She left the exam room.

Uh-oh, I thought. *Now I'm going to do the "Shih Tzu swallow."*

She came back in a very short time. "Your appointment is for tomorrow afternoon. They will let me know the results, and I will call you as soon as I hear something." I thanked her and drove home in a bit of a daze. I didn't expect this turn of events.

When I got home, Sim was waiting for me in the same spot he was in when I left. I looked at him, the anxiety of the situation flowing over me. I sat down next to him and gave him a hug. "Sim, I don't know where this is going, but we'll get through it. You're always there for me, and knowing that helps me more you than know." He swallowed and then gave me one of his "I *do* know" sneezes. "You and I have to go easy about this with Mr. Frank. I don't want him to get too upset."

When Frank got home, I told him the news, trying to make light of it. "The CAT scan is just a precaution because nothing showed up in the lab work. I have to be at the imaging center at 2:00 p.m."

Frank looked at me and said, "OK. I'll work half a day and be home to take you there. We'll leave at 1:15."

"Thanks, Frank." The look that passed between us said it all. We were hoping it was nothing serious.

The next afternoon I arrived for the CAT scan. The technician asked me a few questions and then began the procedure. As usual, they don't tell you anything.

When she was finished, she said to me, "You're just about finished. I just want the doctor to double-check the films."

Gayle called me midmorning on Friday. She was very direct and straightforward. "Got the results of the CAT scan, Peg. You have a large tumor in your uterus. Who is your gynecologist? I'm going to *fax* this report to him." That invisible curveball was now just a few feet away.

I gave her the information. My gynecologist was located in Connecticut. She said to keep in touch when I found out anything and wished me good luck.

I took a deep breath. I was feeling different emotions all at once. They ranged from relief in that the source of the pain had been found to fear of not knowing what I was going to face. At about 4:00 p.m., the phone rang. I had butterflies in my stomach, and I broke out into a sweat, almost not wanting to answer the phone. I picked it up.

"Hello?" I said tentatively, wanting it to be the doctor and yet not wanting it to be the doctor.

"Mrs. Lovelock, this is Dr. Savage. Forgive me for being a bit unorganized, but it's 4:00 p.m. on a Friday, and I just got your CAT scan results from the fax machine. I'm reading it as we're talking."

"That's all right," I told him. I could hear the rustling of paper and the doctor musing to himself.

"OK. Now I've got the full picture. It appears that you have a tumor the size of a large cantaloupe in your uterus. You're going to need surgery as soon as we can make the arrangements." That darn curveball whizzed by my head, almost knocking me out.

It was obvious that I had no choice in the matter. The only question I could think of at that moment was, "How do we proceed?"

"Well, first I want you to go to the hospital for an ultrasound. Call my office on Monday, and they will tell you what day and time your appointment will be. After that, I want you to have some blood work done. I'm checking for certain cancer markers in the blood, so it will take a little time before I get all those results back. In the meantime, once I get the results from the ultrasound, I'm going to want to see you for an examination and consultation. We have to move fairly quickly here because I don't want that tumor to either twist or burst."

I was not a patient of Dr. Savage. The gynecologist that I usually saw was on vacation for two weeks. I could wait for him to do the surgery if I wanted, but Dr. Savage wanted to get things lined up ASAP. "I'll call your office on Monday to get things started and we'll go from there," I said.

"Great. Have a good weekend, and I will see you soon," Dr. Savage said.

Have a good weekend, my rear end! I thought. "Hey, Sim, wait 'til I tell you about this Dr. Savage who hit me over the head with a sledgehammer and then tells me to have a good weekend."

Sim looked at me as if he knew I was exhibiting false bravado. He put his paws up on my knees, wanting me to pick him up. I did and he snuggled his head under my chin. I could feel the hot, angry tears rolling down my cheeks, landing on the top of his head. He looked up and licked my face. I couldn't help but smile. My buddy was giving me support in the only way he knew how.

"Thanks, Bud. Now we just have to tell Mr. Frank what the schedule is going to be. He's going to be very worried about me, so we have to be calm and act like it's no big deal. We'll just have to go step by step as Dr. Savage explained it to me."

Sim looked at me, gave me another kiss, and swallowed. I know it was his way of saying, "We'll get through this together, Mom."

At dinner that night, I explained to Frank what Dr. Savage had said. I told him that Monday I would call and find out when the appointment for the ultrasound would be. Frank said that as soon as I found out, he would take that day off from work. I also told him that Dr. Savage wanted specific blood work done, making light of the cancer marker testing. I just said that I thought that was just normal protocol before surgery.

"You and I will sit down with Dr. Savage when I get the appointment for my exam with him. He'll go over everything with us. Think of any questions you may have. He sounded very nice on the phone, and I feel very comfortable with him. Unless he seems different when we meet him, I will probably have him perform the surgery." Frank looked very concerned but tried to be upbeat and reassuring.

I called Dr. Savage's office on Monday and was told that my appointment for the ultrasound was for Wednesday afternoon. While Frank and I were on the way to the appointment, we talked about the different possibilities. I told him that basically I felt healthy, other than when the pain surfaced. I thought that the way I felt was a positive indication.

We didn't have to wait long before I was called by the technician. She ushered me into the room where the ultrasound was going to be done. She said that she would do some preliminary testing, and then the radiologist would come in and do more extensive testing. I asked the radiologist if I could look at the screen to see what was causing me all this trouble. He said just for me to turn my head in the direction of the screen. I saw what appeared to be a black soccer ball! "Oh, my," I said to him. "That's really something." I had a physical reaction to what I saw, similar to watching a horror movie. I broke out into a cold sweat, then flushed, and then felt nauseous.

He said, "It sure is. But the good thing is that it is perfectly round. Cancer has fingers and no defined shape. I'll get these results to Dr. Savage, and he will call you. Most likely it will be tomorrow."

I got myself ready, and the tech walked me out of the room to the reception area where Frank was waiting for me. She could tell from my demeanor that I was upset. I was no longer joking and laughing with her.

She said, "We will never know until the actual surgery is done and you definitely need surgery, but it looks about as good as it could. It has a defined shape, and that's always a positive sign. Good luck with everything."

I thanked her. As Frank and I walked back to the car, I told him what both the radiologist and technician said. "I know the whole idea is pretty scary, but they seemed optimistic. Let's see what Dr. Savage has to say when he gets the results."

When we got home, Sim was waiting for me. As I walked from the garage into our family room, he approached me with his tail wagging, and he was extending his right front paw. This was his special greeting that he gave me when I got home no matter the duration of my absence. He then went to his overflowing toy box and picked out the orange octopus. He brought it to me so we could play fetch. "I guess you're pretty optimistic too, Bud." He gave a playful growl with his mouth full of the octopus and then shook the toy vigorously. He seemed to be giving me his encouragement in the only way he knew how at that time. *I'm blessed*, I thought. *Sim is truly my best friend. He has an uncanny way of knowing how I'm feeling and just the right way to interact with me to make me feel better.* With that, Sim gave me one of his "I know" sneezes.

Chapter 38

In the middle of difficulty lies opportunity.

—Albert Einstein

I had no idea that the next event in my life was going to help me to understand even more what the life of a dog seems like to them. I was going to be put in a situation that I had no control over and was at the mercy of the people around me. They would dictate what and when I would eat, sleep, walk, eliminate, and have visitors. I had to depend on them for everything and had little or no say in the matter. During this time, I would have to interact with people who thought they were doing what was best for me, and I would have to accept it, no matter how much I disliked it. The one advantage that I had compared to dogs is that I spoke the same language as they did and could communicate my discomforts or dislikes. That didn't necessarily mean that my likes and dislikes would make any difference. It was an educational, sometimes scary, sometimes humorous few days.

On Monday, I received a call from Dr. Savage's office. I was scheduled for a 2:00 p.m. appointment on Wednesday. When we got to his office, I had to fill out the usual paperwork that any new patient fills out. I was edgy. I just wanted to get the examination over with and then have the consultation with Dr. Savage. Before I knew it, his assistant called my name and led me to the examination room. She gave me a gown to put on and said the doctor would be in very shortly.

I didn't have to wait long at all. Dr. Savage was a pleasant-faced man with a medium build and white, thick hair. He went over what his thoughts were given the results of the ultrasound. "It's just as I thought. No surprises here," he said.

He then finished his examination and said to meet him in his office. I told him that Frank was with me. He said that he would have his assistant show Frank where the consultation would be.

Frank and I sat across a large desk from Dr. Savage. This time, I noticed his twinkling blue eyes and his sense of humor. This helped to put me at ease. Frank and I agreed that we wanted him to do the surgery.

"OK. Thank you for having confidence in me. I'm going to schedule it as soon as possible. I'm concerned that the tumor might burst and cause a greater problem. However, I want to wait for all the blood work to come back so that I know exactly what I'm dealing with. I'm going to schedule an oncology surgical team in the operating room with me. We'll get the tumor analyzed immediately. If anything doesn't look right, the team will be in place to take over the treatment. Any questions?"

As comfortable as I felt with Dr. Savage, hearing those words was like a punch in the stomach. It made everything that much more real. Frank asked a few questions such as the length of the surgery and how many days would I be in the hospital. Dr. Savage said that since I was in good physical condition, if the surgery was just routine, it should only take a couple of hours. I would most likely be in the hospital for three to four days. He also told Frank that the recovery from this kind of surgery took quite a while. He said, "She may feel like going out to dinner in about three months, and it could very possibly take a full year before she is all better. I'll be in touch as soon as I get the blood work back and have a time and date for the surgery." Frank and I shook hands with him.

As we headed home, we went over things. I told Frank how much I liked and trusted Dr. Savage. "It was fate that he is handling my case. I'm sure everything will be just fine." All of a sudden, a realization struck me.

"Frank," I said excitedly, "can you imagine how difficult it would be for us now if I had found a place for my training business and had signed a three-year lease? I won't be able to work for quite a while. We could have been financially ruined!"

Frank was silent for about fifteen seconds. He then let out a huge sigh of relief. "I never gave that a thought, but you're right, Peg. We could be in a very tough position right now."

"Well, Frank, I guess everything happens for a reason, even if we don't understand why it happens at the time. This makes me feel even more confident that the surgery is going to go well and I am going to be fine."

When we returned home, I began calling some family members and friends. Everyone was very supportive. I told all of them that I thought everything was going to be fine. I felt well, and to me, that was an indication that this was just an annoyance, nothing very serious. When I called Judy, I said to her, "I told you I wasn't able to stand to do the match. I felt really badly about that, but now we know why."

She laughed and said, "When you say you can't do something, it's for a very, very good reason!"

Chapter 39

In order to succeed we must first believe that we can.

—Michael Korda

Frank and Sim were going to compete in Rally O at Eastern States during Fourth of July weekend. Once again, Ed Phipps was going to judge their Rally class on the first day of the shows. In competitive obedience, at that time, you had to qualify under three different judges. In Rally O, the team only had to qualify under two different judges. So even though Frank and Sim had earned their first qualifying score under Ed, they were able to show under him again. Another difference between Rally O and competitive obedience was that if you earned your title, you were able to immediately sign up to compete on the next level in a trial held the very next day. In competitive obedience, you had to wait until the paperwork was sent in to the AKC before you could go one to the next level. We arrived late morning. It appeared that Frank and Sim would be going into the ring around noon.

The Rally Novice class was packed and running well behind schedule. The stewards told us that Frank and Sim had quite a wait ahead of them. Frank told the steward that he had to go back to work. They talked to the judge and agreed to make them the last entry. They told us to return at about 3:30 p.m.

We headed home, and then Frank went on to work. He said he would be back at 2:30 p.m. and that should be enough time to get to Eastern States by 3:00 p.m. I tried to give Sim a bit of a rest so that he would be relaxed for the afternoon. We played fetch for a short time, and then he was ready for a nap. Frank was right on time at 2:30 p.m. We drove over to Eastern States, parked the car, and walked in. As luck would have it, they were calling for Frank and Sim. We weren't going to have the chance to relax for even a minute. "Good luck, guys," I said, giving Frank a good luck kiss on the cheek and Sim a kiss on the top of his head.

The two of them went into the ring. I made myself scarce. I didn't want Sim looking for me instead of paying attention to Frank. They did well and qualified again. Frank was elated. Sim seemed to take it all in stride. We were amazed that Sim was able to perform well with all the back and forth that had happened. He received his qualifying ribbon as well as a special red, white, and blue ribbon because he had earned his title. The letters RN for "Rally Novice" would now be added to his name. His full name now became UCD Mr. Sims, CD, RN, TDI, CGC. He now had thirty-two ribbons for his accomplishments in AKC and UKC.

Not bad for a dog that just needed a second chance, I thought. I was so proud of him I wanted to give him a special treat, but because of his tummy issues, I had to just give him many hugs and kisses. He was pleased with them and gave me "the swallow" several times, along with a couple of sneezes and kisses.

Frank and I walked over to the Trial Secretary's office to register Sim for the Rally Advanced class. Since he had gotten the Rally Novice class today, he could be entered in the higher class. After a day of rest, we would come back and try him out in the more difficult class. This class mirrored many of the exercises that Sim had to perform in the Open competitive class, and all exercises had to be performed off leash. This was going to be a challenge for Frank. Throughout the Rally Novice class, he was able to keep Sim on leash. It was going to be another story altogether off leash.

Sunday, we arrived back at the show site and set up Sim's crate by the ring where Rally Advanced was going to take place. There were some people whom we knew from the obedience club that I occasionally attended. They had placed their chairs close to the ring so they could watch each entrant. They were particularly excited to watch Sim and Frank.

We walked Sim around and found a small area to practice in. Sim seemed relaxed and upbeat. He was a little distracted but kept his attention on Frank. We were pleased with the short practice and headed back to our seats. Sim was going to be put back in his crate for a while to relax. As we were approaching our seats, a woman with two German Shepherds that were not under control came up behind us. The two dogs lunged after Sim, growling and snapping at him. Sim was startled because he didn't see them coming. The woman with them did nothing other than to look annoyed at us. I grabbed Sim's leash from Frank to get him away from the situation and to examine him to be sure he hadn't been injured by the other dogs. He seemed to be physically OK, but I could tell from his expression that he had been shaken up. I grabbed some of his hotdog treats and walked him briskly, talking to him and treating him constantly. I was trying to help him clear his mind. Again, no matter how well you prepare, you just never know what unexpected incident may occur. I brought him back to his crate and told Frank that I wasn't sure what Sim was going to be able to do.

"Just go easy with him and don't worry about how well he does. He's had a bad experience, and I think he may not be focused on what he should be." Sure enough, when their number was called and Frank took Sim into the ring, I could see from Sim's body language that he was upset. Frank took the leash off and handed it to the steward. Sim was trying to keep an eye on me rather than paying attention to Frank. I knew this wasn't going to go well.

This incident helps me to make a very important point. When a dog is involved in a traumatic experience, the "fight or flight" reaction is activated. Hormones in the body such as cortisol and adrenalin flood the system in preparation to either fight or run from the situation. The dog can stay in this heightened level of physical stress anywhere from two to seven days. If there is more than one incident in a day, each incident compounds the other. For example, if a dog encounters three stressful situations in one day, it may take six to twenty-one days for the dog's chemical levels to return to normal. I knew the best thing that we could do for Sim was to get him home where he could relax and recoup from his experience. I was just hoping that he would not associate this incident with going into the ring with Frank.

Chapter 40

I've had a perfectly wonderful evening.
But this wasn't it.

—Groucho Marx

Dr. Savage called me on Tuesday to say that he had received the results of the blood work he had been waiting for. "Nothing enough to make me twitchy," he told me. "You're scheduled for surgery Friday, July 15, at around 7:15 a.m. The hospital will be in touch with you to confirm everything. See you then."

"Thanks, Dr. Savage," was all I could muster. I called Sim to me and gave him the news. "Now listen, Bud, I'm going to be away for a little while. I'm sure Mr. Frank will bring you to the hospital to see me. Everything is going to be fine, and you and I will be back in action before you know it. So maybe you should enjoy the rest."

I felt an odd feeling of uncertainty mixed with a little fear. The more I prepared and talked about the surgery, the more real the situation became. And the more real the situation became, the more I felt a bit unsettled. It all had happened so quickly. Getting the news about the tumor when I thought it was a urinary tract infection was like going in for a manicure and having your hands cut off. "Stop your negative thinking," I told myself. "You're going to be fine. You're in great hands with Dr. Savage. What will be will be. And you have Mr. Frank and Sim waiting for you to get home and have everything back to normal."

We left the house very early Friday morning. I had to be in the hospital by 5:00 a.m. Before I left, I gave Sim a hug. He looked at me with sleepy eyes, not quite sure why I was up and about in the middle of the night. "OK, Bud. This is it. I'm off to get everything taken care of." Sim's eyes became more alert, and he snuggled into me. I gave him a kiss on top of his head and deeply inhaled his special scent. He looked at me and swallowed, then gave me one of his kisses. "Thanks, Bud. You're a good boy. In fact, you are my best boy."

As we drove to the hospital at 4:00 a.m., there was no traffic at first. Everything was eerily quiet. Frank and I went over things such as that he would wait until the surgery was over and be there for me. He would then leave for work and come back in the evening. I also went over Sim's meal schedule. Of course Frank knew it by heart, but he let me go over it.

As we were reaching the hospital, the sun was just beginning to rise. It no longer was pitch black but not quite daylight yet. We went to the reception area and signed in. The receptionist told me to have a seat and someone would be with me shortly. The nurse came over to us to start the preparations. She said that Frank could stay with me until they took me to the waiting area just outside of the operating room. She began taking my temperature, blood pressure, and pulse. Dr. Savage had told me to fast and have a clear liquid diet the day before and I had complied. The nurse asked me about this and wanted to know what time I last had a drink. I told her that I had taken a shot of gin at 10:00 p.m. the night before. Her jaw dropped.

I said, "Well, it's a clear liquid, right?"

She began to laugh, which helped break the tension that I was feeling. She completed the prep work, and it was time to head for the operating room holding area. Frank walked along next to the gurney, holding my hand. We gave each other a little kiss.

"Drive carefully," I told him.

"You, too," he said. The nurse laughed at our exchange and said how devoted to each other we were.

"We've known each other since high school," I told her.

The automatic door opened, and the nurse wheeled me into a dimly lit room. It had several cubicles with curtains dividing them.

She said that Dr. Savage would be with me shortly. I was wearing a hospital gown and hairnet. *I must be making a real fashion statement with this outfit*, I thought to myself. Other doctors were with their patients, going over what their procedures would be.

"I didn't recognize you," a voice said to me. I looked up and saw a man in green scrubs and a hairnet.

"It's Dr. Savage," he said to me.

"Didn't recognize you either. These outfits are really something, aren't they?" I replied.

"OK. I'm just about ready for you. Are you OK?"

"Considering everything, I'm as good as I'm going to be for now."

"See you in the OR," he told me. A nurse came along and moved me to a spot just outside of the OR. There was a clock over the OR door. I looked at it. The time was 7:05 a.m.

Guess we're going to be right on time, I thought. The nurse said she was going to start the IV with "a little something to help me relax." I looked at the clock again. It was 7:10. That was the last thing I remembered. The next recollection I had was Frank walking next to the gurney as I was being taken to the recovery room.

I don't remember the short conversation between us. I went back to sleep. At some point, I was moved to a room. I woke up for a short period, and the nurse told me how to operate the pump with the pain medicine in it when I felt the need for it. She also said that my IV would be changed periodically. It was keeping me hydrated and nourished for the time being. My recollection of the rest of that day is very fuzzy, to say the least. I do remember Frank coming back in the evening to visit me. He brought me a vase with pansies in it. Pansies are one of my favorite flowers. As a child, I always liked to pick them and look at all the different "faces" each one had.

Again, I was dozing. Things began to come more into focus later that evening. My roommate was going home the next day. We struck up a conversation. She said that I would most likely have a private room because she doubted that anyone else would be brought in over the weekend. Early Saturday morning, Dr. Savage came in to see how I was doing. He said everything went well and looked good, although nothing was for certain until the lab work came back.

"It was the ugliest damn thing I've ever seen," he told me, eyes twinkling. I laughed.

"It's a wonder you weren't in pain all the time. The tumor had pushed your organs all over the place. As soon as we get the IV out, which will be later in the day, you will be able to have something to eat. You were in such great physical shape that I don't think you lost any more than a tablespoon of blood. How are you feeling?"

"I really don't feel too bad, just a little beaten up." He laughed, gave me a pat on the arm and told me he would see me Monday. He thought I would be there until Tuesday.

"Not if I can help it," I told him. I wanted to get home as soon as I could.

He smiled and said, "We'll see about that."

In the afternoon, I could hear the commotion of the nurses and aides giggling and talking baby talk. Frank and Sim walked into the room. A wave of homesickness swept over me. It had only been a day, but I missed them terribly and I felt very lonesome. My eyes filled with tears. I didn't want Frank to see my distress, so I rubbed my eyes, making it appear as though I had just woken up from a nap.

"Oh," I said. "Now I know what all the fuss was about." Frank gave me a kiss on the cheek and put Sim up on the bed next to me. Sim looked worried. He checked me out thoroughly, very carefully, and then moved to the foot of the bed.

With that, a nurse and aide came in, supposedly to take my temperature and pulse. However, they made a big fuss over Sim, petting and talking to him, telling me how they would steal him when I wasn't looking. Sim was cordial to them but was much more reserved than usual when he met new people. He stayed at the foot of the bed, keeping a wary eye on them when they got close to me.

"Good boy, Sim. They're good people, just doing their job to help me feel better." He looked at me and gave me his Shih Tzu swallow but still kept a close eye on them. They left and Frank, Sim, and I visited for a while. I was beginning to get sleepy. We said our "drive carefullys."

"See you later," Frank said. I settled back down and began to doze again when the nurse and aide came back into the room.

"We're here to remove the IV and pain pump. You'll be able to have dinner tonight."

"Great. I'll look forward to it."

"We'll get you up to walk around a little bit after dinner." I didn't feel that good yet, but I thought if I had a good meal, I'd be ready to try it.

My thoughts went to the saying "What doesn't kill us makes us stronger." I guess I had just gotten a crash course in strength. Sim came to mind and how much he had been through with physical problems.

I rested, reading a little bit then dozing. Dinner finally arrived. *Great*, I thought. I was really hungry. The aide set the tray up for me and removed the stainless cover.

"Enjoy," he said and left.

I took one look at the tray. There was clear soup, weak coffee, milk, and vanilla custard/pudding. *I'll start with the pudding*, I thought.

I took one mouthful, which was one mouthful too much. It was awful. *I'll save the rest for Frank. Maybe it's the anesthesia that's making things taste bad.* I drank the soup and coffee. At least I felt a little full. This certainly wasn't the meal I was hoping for. I had "fasted" the day before the surgery and only had IV fluids the day of the surgery and half of today. I was hoping for some "real" food.

When the aide came in to take my tray, I asked her why I wasn't given anything substantial to eat. She said it was part of the orders that Dr. Savage had left. I had to be on a restricted diet for a couple of days. A bit later, a nurse came in to check on me. She said that it would be helpful if I got up and walked around a bit. She helped me out of bed and then held on to my arm. My legs felt a little weak, but as I kept moving, I could feel them getting a bit stronger. We walked halfway down the short side of the hall, past the nurses' station. She turned around, and we headed back to my room. I said that I would like to sit in the chair for a bit rather than to go back to bed. I asked her if I could walk a little further later when Frank came.

She said, "That would be great. The more walking you do, the faster you'll get out of here." I made a strong mental note of that remark.

One of the aides came in and asked me if I wanted anything. I could have coffee, tea, juice, soda, or Jell-O. "How about some Jell-O and some ginger ale?" I suggested.

A short time later, another aide came in with a tray for me. It had Jell-O, ginger ale, and another container of the custard that I had saved for Frank. *I'll try it again*, I thought. *Maybe it will taste better now*. I took a spoonful. It tasted no better than the last batch I had tried earlier. *Well, now Frank has two containers of this if he likes it.*

I did some reading for a while; then I started to doze.

I woke up to Frank gently patting my hand. "How are you feeling, Peg?"

"Not bad but hungry. I saved some custard for you. Maybe it's my taste buds, but I think it's awful." I handed Frank the container and he took a mouthful.

"It's good. I'll take care of it for you."

"There's no accounting for taste," I said, chuckling. "How about taking me for a spin around the hallways? Walking is supposed to be helpful."

"Sure," Frank said. "We'll just go slow and easy." He helped me out of the chair. We walked out of the room and turned right. There were a few rooms that we had to go past, and then we were in a lobby area that had an oversized couch and some easy chairs.

There were several pictures on the walls. The pictures were relaxing scenes. Some were beach scenes, forests, and pleasant fields. We passed this area and continued to the end of the hall. If we had continued walking, we would have entered another wing of the hospital, so I suggested that we turn around and head back to my room. I was getting a bit tired at this point. When we got there, I told Frank that I thought I should sit up in bed instead of the chair. He helped me get back into bed and then sat next to me.

"Dr. Savage thinks I will be here until Tuesday. I'm hoping to get out by Monday. I miss you and Sim. How is he doing?"

"He misses you but he's eating well. He just seems a little lost without you there," Frank said. "I keep telling him that you will be home soon. He just looks at me and swallows then mopes. I try to get him to play with his toys. He'll play for a short time and then just mopes again." I smiled.

"He's Mom's boy for sure," I told Frank.

We gave each other a kiss and "drive carefullys," and Frank left. I began watching the baseball game.

All of a sudden, one of the nurses called me on the intercom. "Did you ring for a nurse? Do you need anything?"

"No, I didn't," I answered.

"Was it Mr. Sims by any chance?" she asked me, giggling.

"No, Mr. Sims has left the building," I answered.

We both laughed and she said, "What a great little dog he is." I agreed, although I told her I was very, very partial.

"You certainly should be. He's a real special little guy. Have a good night."

I thanked her and started watching the game again. I was feeling pretty good but had a twinge of homesickness again. I wanted to be back with Frank and Mr. Sims.

Chapter 41

When you come to the end of your rope,
tie a knot and hang on.

—Franklin D. Roosevelt

I awoke at about 1:30 a.m. I could hear the staff bringing someone into the room. They pulled the curtain between the two beds. I heard the voice of an older woman. She sounded as though she was in some pain. A male voice asked her how she was feeling and called her "Mom," so I surmised it was her son. Then I heard an older man's voice telling her she was going to be OK. The older man said that he would be back to see her later in the day and to get some rest. She asked him if he was sure he was all right. He told her he was fine. Her son said that he would have Dad stay at his house for the night so he wouldn't be alone. I heard them leave, and then I heard some of the medical staff come in.

They asked her some questions. She began complaining, saying, "Oy, the pain!" She said this several times. One of the nurses said that she would be back with some pain medication and something to help her sleep. She quieted down and went to sleep. I knew she was sleeping because I could hear her snoring.

I closed my eyes, trying to go back to sleep. *I want to go home right now*, I thought. I began saying some prayers and then I apologized for feeling selfish. *This is a hospital, dummy, not a five-star hotel. Did you think you were going to have a private room until you went home?* I thought to myself. Thinking back about it now, I'm sure that the medications I was on also added to my emotional frailty. It made me wonder, when Sim was feeling "off" when on medication, was this how he felt emotionally too? *Tomorrow's another day. Maybe I'll have something good to eat for breakfast.* And then I went to sleep for the night.

I woke up at about 6:00 a.m. The hustle and bustle was starting. The nurses and the aides were going room to room to check the vital signs of the patients. They came into the room. The curtain was still drawn between the two beds. The nurse came over to me first, took my temperature, pulse, and blood pressure. She marked my chart and then went to the other bed to check on my new "roommate." She asked the woman how well she slept.

"Oy, I barely slept a wink," she said. I smiled to myself because I had woken up a few times, and each time I did, I could hear her snoring.

This is going to be fun, I thought to myself. The nurse told her that someone would be in to take her breakfast order in a little while. I began drooling. I wanted some real food, and since I love breakfast, this was going to be good. I thought of Sim watching for any scrap of egg, English muffin, or any other part of a hearty breakfast that might be shared with him.

She didn't say anything to me, though. Hmm. Probably just an oversight. They'll take the two orders together, I thought, hopefully.

"Can I get eggs, dear?"

"How would you like them?" the aide asked.

"Scrambled, not too dry, please. And I'll have a lightly toasted bagel with cream cheese on the side."

"Would you like any juice and coffee or tea with that?"

"I'll have orange juice and a cup of coffee with half and half on the side."

"Anything else?"

"No, that will be fine."

I was starting to chomp at the bit. *I'll have the same thing*, I thought. *That will make it easy*. I waited in anticipation. *She should be coming over shortly*, I thought. *Wonder what's taking her so long?* I waited and waited and waited. It soon dawned on me that she wasn't going to take my order. *Oh well. Maybe eggs would be too difficult to digest, but certainly I must be getting something tastier this morning.*

I called over to my roommate through the curtain. "Hi, I'm Peg. May I push the curtain back?"

"Sure, dear. I'm Dorothy."

I pushed back the curtain between the beds. Dorothy was a woman in her seventies with a full round face and attractive features. She obviously had recently had her hair done. It was champagne blond in color and styled in an "up do." She had a frosted peachy-pink manicure. I, on the other hand, probably looked like death warmed over.

"How are you feeling?" I asked her. She said that she hadn't slept a wink most of the night because of pain. Her son had been driving her and her husband, Gabe, back home after visiting the grandchildren. They were traveling on Interstate 84 in Connecticut. It seems that they had gotten broadsided by either a van or truck. She said that her back and neck were sore. Her son and husband were not hurt, although she worried about her husband because he had just come out of the hospital two weeks before. He had undergone a minor heart procedure. With that, her phone rang. It was Gabe, calling to see how she was feeling.

Soon, I heard the food cart coming. *Yay,* I thought. *I'm looking forward to a good breakfast.* The aide gave Dorothy her breakfast because her bed was nearest to the door. The aroma of the eggs and toasted bagel wafted through the air to my nostrils. She then brought me my tray. As I lifted the stainless-steel cover, I looked with anticipation. "Here we go again," I said to myself. I almost wanted to cry, and the frustration inside of me was growing. I couldn't smoke to ease my anxiety, and there was no comfort in the food I was being served. There was a carton of skim milk, cooked cream of wheat, orange juice, coffee, and the ever popular custard container. I immediately put the custard on the side table for Frank. At this point, I never wanted to see custard again. The cereal wasn't bad but very bland and tasteless. *Old toenails would probably have more taste,* I thought to myself. I was tempted to ask Dorothy if she would share some of her breakfast with me.

"They keep trying to convince me that this custard, or pudding, or whatever it is supposed to be is good. I wouldn't feed it to my dog, but Frank sure seems to like it." She gave a little chuckle but was very busy enjoying her breakfast. I felt like a dog looking in the butcher shop window at a prime steak but couldn't get to it.

"Well, Dorothy, I'd better get up and walk off my breakfast. The doctor wants me up and moving." I got out of bed, went into the bathroom to wash my face, brush my teeth, and comb my hair. *What a mess*, I thought. *Maybe a little lipstick will help.* I came out, put on my robe and told Dorothy to issue an Amber Alert if I wasn't back before lunch.

As I walked by the nurses' station, returning from my walk, one of the nurses asked if Mr. Sims was coming in for a visit today.

"I don't think so. My husband has enough to do at home trying to keep up with the chores that I usually do. And I think Mr. Sims might become more stressed coming to visit me and then leaving without me." She agreed but said she thought he was just "the best."

"You and me both," I told her.

I entered my room and got back into bed. I began to read one of the books I had brought with me. The nurse came in to check our vital signs again. Then to my surprise, Dr. Savage came in to see how I was doing.

"Did you bring me a Whopper from Burger King?" I asked him. He laughed heartily.

"You can laugh, but I'm looking for some real food. I don't think I'm eating the right food to support my system trying to heal."

"Not quite yet. Your system was so stressed that I want to go easy on it." He examined the incision and said that I was really healing nicely.

"So do you think I can go home tomorrow?"

"I'll be back to see you late morning or early afternoon tomorrow. We'll see how you're coming along."

"And will you bring me a Whopper for lunch?" I asked him, giggling.

"Now you're pushing it," he said laughing. He patted me on the hand and left. The thought of facing more of that custard distressed me, even though I had no intention of eating any of it. *Now I understand how a dog feels that doesn't like his food because it disagrees with him in some way, I thought to myself.* "*The owner continues to feed the same chow to the dog, and when the dog won't eat it any more, the owner accuses the dog of being finicky or spoiled. If I don't get some real food soon, spoiled is going to take on a whole new meaning.*"

An aide came in to take Dorothy's lunch order.

"I can't listen to this," I said to myself. "I'm sure I'm going to get that darn custard again and Dorothy is going to get something really delicious."

All I heard Dorothy say was, "That sounds good, dear. I'll have the special." When the aide left, Dorothy started fiddling with the remote again.

Our lunch arrived. Dorothy had a turkey sandwich with Swiss cheese and a side of pasta salad. "This looks great," she said.

I lifted the cover on my lunch. I had clear broth, apple sauce, coffee, and custard. Once again, I pushed the custard to the side of the tray. I picked up my cell phone and called Frank. "Hi, it's me. Can you do me a favor?"

"Sure," Frank said. "What do you need?"

"When you come to visit me, can you stop in the hospital gift shop and see if they have a Dixie cup? This custard is driving me crazy."

"Really?" Frank said. "I love it."

"Good for you. I'll probably have three or four cups of it by the time you get here. See you in a while. Love you,"

Frank said, "Love you too." I hung up.

"How long have you been married, dear?" Dorothy asked.

I told her that Frank and I had known each other since high school. We had dated other people but kept coming back to each other. We had been married for thirty-five years.

"You must have been married very young, dear," she said. "You don't look old enough to be married that long."

"It's the custard, Dorothy. It must have some youth hormones in it."

With that, Dorothy's husband came in to see her.

I got up and said that I would go for a walk so they could have some privacy. I headed for the area with the comfortable furniture. There were some tables with magazines, so I sat down for a little while and thumbed through one that looked interesting to me. My sense of humor was coming back. I kept thinking of Dorothy's personality and quirks, and I had to control my laughter before I went back to the room. I also could feel a pulling sensation from my stitches.

Laughter is the best medicine, but I've got to be a little careful here, I thought. *I'm already in stitches and can't wait to get rid of them.* After a while, I got up and started walking my "route." To break the boredom, I began visualizing being in the obedience ring with Sim. I practiced squaring my corners when I turned left or right and executing the proper footwork on the about turns. It made the walk more interesting, and I was able to keep going for a longer period. After four laps, I decided to go back to my room to rest.

I said hi to Dorothy and Gabe and sat down in my chair. I began reading a book when Frank came in. I was so glad to see him. The diet was getting to me, and I was beginning to feel even sorrier for myself.

"How's things?" he asked me.

"Good," I said.

"Really?" he asked. "You look a little down."

"I'm dying for some real food. I asked Dr. Savage if he was going to bring me a Whopper tomorrow. I did ask if I can go home tomorrow. He said it will depend on how well I seem to him. I don't want to stay until Tuesday. I think I can recoup just as well at home. How is Sim doing today?"

"Same. He really misses you. I'm trying to keep him as steady as I can. He'll be fine as soon as you get home. How about we go for a 'spin' around the halls?"

Frank and I made the right turn out of the room and headed for the lobby area. "Wait until I tell you about Dorothy and Gabe. They are such nice people, but I feel like I'm in a sitcom."

"It's good to see you laughing," he said to me.

"I'm hangin' in there, but I really want to go home. By the way, did you get me the Dixie Cup?" I was eying a small brown paper bag that Frank had been carrying.

"Holy smokes! I almost forgot. Here it is."

"Hey," I said. "I'm the one that's full of medication, not you."

"I'm in a fog with all of this. It just doesn't seem right when you're not at home with me."

"Soon," I said as I was enjoying every last spoonful of the Dixie Cup.

"Let's walk a little more, and then I'll have to head for home. I have a big day at work tomorrow, and I want to get everything set up. I want to be ready to leave work when I know what time you will be ready to leave."

"OK," I said. "You don't have to come back tonight. I understand that you're trying to get everything in order."

"You're that sure that Dr. Savage will release you tomorrow?"

"Oh yeah. I'll bet you a two-dollar scratch lottery ticket."

"You're on," Frank said. We walked back to the room. Gabe had left, and Dorothy was talking to someone on the phone. I decided to sit in the chair for a while. I had brought a book of crossword puzzles, and my mind felt clear enough to try one.

"I'll start with the easiest level and see how well I do," I told Frank.

"Don't cheat and look at the solutions in the back of the book," he said then gave me a kiss and said he would be back sometime after dinner.

"Drive carefully," I told him.

"You too," he said.

Frank arrived for his evening visit. "How are you doing tonight?" he asked.

"OK, but dinner was the same old, same old. It's getting very tiresome. I saved you the custard again."

"Good," he said.

"What did you have for dinner?" I asked.

"The ziti bake that you made for me. It was very good."

"I'm glad you enjoyed it and had a good dinner, but I don't want to hear about it. I'm ready to eat old sneakers if I can find any."

"Poor Pegs. It'll be OK. You'll be home tomorrow. I'll even stop at Burger King or McDonald's on the way home if you want."

"Thanks, Frank. I'm just grumpy."

"I understand," he said offhandedly.

I could tell that Frank was preoccupied with something. He wasn't himself. He seemed testy.

"Are you OK?" I asked him.

"Oh, it's just getting everything ready for work tomorrow. We're really busy right now and everything is coming to a head all at once."

"Why don't we go for our 'evening stroll' up and down the hall a few times and then you can go home. Get some rest. This has been hard on you too."

We took a short walk, and then Frank left.

The morning started out with the usual routine. The aides came in and checked our vitals. They asked us how we were feeling. Dorothy said, "Not too bad, but I didn't sleep a wink all night."

The aide taking my pulse asked me how I was doing. "Other than being ravenously hungry, I'm feeling pretty good. I think I may go home today. I'll see what Dr. Savage thinks when he comes by later. Could you sneak something good to me?"

She laughed. "Let me see. Maybe we can add some crackers to your diet today."

"Well, whoop dee doo. I never thought I would live to see the day that crackers would seem like a gourmet meal."

"I'll check our little kitchenette when I finish with the other patients and see what I can find for you."

"Bless you," I said, both of us laughing. *No wonder a dog will scour the floor for crumbs just to have something better than his usual kibble, although some kibble would be mighty tasty to me right now,* I thought.

I got out of bed and went into the bathroom to wash my face and comb my hair. I wanted to start packing up my toiletries in anticipation of going home. When I came out, Dorothy said, "You're up and about early."

"I'm hoping to go home today. It all depends on what Dr. Savage thinks, so I'm getting my things together, just in case. How much longer will you be here?" I asked her.

"I'm not sure, but I may be able to go home tomorrow. I can't wait to be back in my own bed again. I haven't slept a wink all the while I've been here." With that, an aide came in to take Dorothy's breakfast order.

I must have lost so much weight that I'm invisible. They can't see me to ask me what I want for breakfast. You would think that they can hear my stomach rumbling, though, and that would give them a clue that I'm here, I thought to myself, bringing a smile to my lips.

In a short time, breakfast came. Dorothy had her eggs, toasted bagel, cream cheese, coffee, and a Danish. I had my cooked cereal, juice, skim milk, and of course, that custard. Just as I finished, the aide came in with a handful of unsalted crackers. "Boy, do they look good," I told her. "Thanks. I'll save them for when I get back from my walk. They'll be a real treat." The aides had begun to understand my sarcastic sense of humor.

I was just getting ready to leave when Dr. Savage came in. "How are you doing this morning?" he asked me.

"Good but very, very hungry. Did you bring me an Egg McMuffin or the Whopper you promised?"

He laughed. "Sorry, I forgot. Let's have a look at your incision." I got back into the bed, and he examined me.

"Looks darn good to me. I'm going to tell the staff that you can go home today."

"Fantastic," I said.

"It's going to take a while for the staff to get all the paperwork and instructions together, so you'll be here for a while, but you will probably be out of here just before dinner."

"Great, but I'll really miss the custard." Dr. Savage gave me a quizzical look.

"It's awful. The hospital must serve it so that no one gets too comfortable and wants to stay longer than necessary."

"You're too much," he said, patting my hand. "I'll see you in my office on Friday so I can make sure everything is healing the way it should be."

I left the room and made the left turn, walking past the nurses' station. Things seemed busier than usual. I guess several new patients had been brought in overnight. I turned at the end of the hall and headed toward the other wing. As I passed the visiting area, I saw a man dressed in blue scrubs working on his laptop computer. He smiled and said "Good morning," as I walked by. I smiled and returned the greeting. I walked to the end of the hall and walked a bit farther into the other wing. It was even busier there, so I turned and left the area.

Guess I'm going to have to stick to my usual route, I thought. I walked along, again visualizing being in the obedience ring with Sim. I could feel my strength gradually coming back.

I was on my fourth lap when the man in the blue scrubs looked up and said, "Well, you're doing very well this morning. When did you have your surgery?"

"Friday. The doctor wanted me to stay until tomorrow, but I'm determined to go home today. I just saw him and he's given me the OK to leave," I replied.

I continued my walk and did another two laps. The man in the scrubs was still in the visiting area. I told him that I was into the home stretch and was going back to my room. He said, "Do you realize that you have walked almost a quarter of a mile?"

"You're kidding," I said smiling.

"Well, there are 5,280 feet in a mile. One of your round trips is probably close to 260 feet. You've walked six laps. I would say you're in very good shape." I understood what he was saying, although my mind was still not working up to speed, so the math formula escaped me.

When I thought about this encounter later on, I realized that without meaning to, I sometimes overworked Sim when practicing heeling. If I was really trying to perfect and polish his heeling, I would repeat the heeling pattern over and over again. It now was put into perspective for me that I may have been making his disdain for heeling worse rather than better. I may have made him heel miles, going against my own philosophy of never working on an exercise so much that the dog dislikes it and wants no part of it.

Chapter 42

Happiness makes up in height
what it lacks in length.

—Robert Frost

When I returned to the room, Dorothy was reading a magazine. She looked up. "How did your walk go?" she asked.

"Good. I'm getting stronger by the day," I answered.

I got dressed in the same outfit I had arrived in, black linen pants, an off-white knit T-shirt, and a black and white plaid jacket. I didn't put the jacket on yet, but I felt better with some real clothes on. I packed up my overnight bag with my robe, slippers, and nightgown. I checked to be sure that I had everything that I brought with me. I even put on a little bit of makeup. "Oh, you look nice," Dorothy said.

"Well, at least I look fairly human again," I said.

The aide came in to take Dorothy's lunch order. When Dorothy finished telling her what she wanted, I asked the aide if there was any chance that I was going to get some real food for lunch.

"I'll check," she said.

"Not good," I said to Dorothy. "Those words are a nice way of telling me no. It's going to be the same thing all over again, but maybe they'll add some crackers," I said, rolling my eyes.

I called Frank at work to let him know that I could leave. "Great, Peg. Do you know what time?"

"No, but Dr. Savage said everything should be ready so that I can be discharged before dinner. Don't rush. If you get here around five o'clock, I think we'll be fine."

I hung up, feeling good that I was finally able to go home but a little worried that I wouldn't be quite as independent as I was used to being.

In a short while, Frank came in.

"Maybe you should go out to the nurse's station and see how things are coming along," I suggested to Frank.

"Good idea. Maybe I can get things moving." Frank was only gone for a short time. When he came back, he said, "The nurse will be in shortly with some papers for you to sign, to go over some post-op instructions, and a wheelchair."

The nurse came in. "Everything is in order for you to leave. You just have to sign these papers. One of the papers is Dr. Savage's home care instructions. You have no restrictions on eating. You can take a shower, but don't do anything strenuous until you see him on Friday."

"Great. It all sounds wonderful to me. Where do I sign?" The nurse laughed and showed me where to sign. She gave me copies and the instruction sheet.

I got into the wheelchair. The nurse said, "Give Mr. Sims an extra pat for me when you get home."

"I sure will," I told her. I couldn't wait to get to the car. When we got to the parking garage, Frank carefully helped me into the car. We thanked the aide who was helping us. As we pulled out of the garage, I reached into the glove compartment for my cigarettes and lighter. "Can't wait for that first puff," I told Frank.

He said, "You were able to go without smoking for four days. Why don't you try to quit now?"

"No way. I've been waiting for this moment. However, I'm proud of myself that I didn't need the nicotine patch they offered me. Maybe the pain meds made a difference." I lit the cigarette and took a long, slow puff. I started to cough. Frank cast a look over at me.

"You all right?" he asked.

"Oh, I'm just fine. I just have to get used to smoking again," I said, trying not to gag.

"How about some M&Ms?"

"Let me finish my cigarette first; then I'll get into the M&Ms." I took another couple of puffs. I was beginning to feel a little light-headed. I put the cigarette out and opened the package of M&M's. I counted them out and divided them equally between Frank and me. "I never knew how good these were. It just goes to show how much you appreciate something when it's not readily accessible." I finished my M&Ms and began to feel sleepy. I put my head back on the headrest.

"You OK?" Frank asked.

"Just a little sleepy."

"Take a snooze. We'll be home before you know it."

"But who's going to drive if I'm sleeping?" I asked Frank.

"You haven't lost that sense of humor while you were away. Put your head back. I'll wake you as soon as we get home." The next thing that I remember was that we were making the turn on to our street.

Just like Sim, I thought. *He has that sixth sense when he's close to home.*

Frank opened the door from the garage into the family room. There was Sim, twirling around, making little sneezes, coming toward me with his right paw extended. "There's my boy! Let me sit in the chair, and I'll give you a big hug and kiss." He quieted down as I slowly lowered myself into the chair. Then he put his paws up on my knees. Frank lifted him on to my lap. Sim was making little soft crying sounds because he was so happy to see me.

"Well, Bud, that's quite a greeting. I guess you really missed me. I missed you, too." I gave him a big hug and a kiss on top of his head. He cuddled into me and gave me kisses on my cheeks and chin. Then he jumped down and grabbed the orange octopus toy. He shook it for a minute and then came over to me, placing the toy on top of my feet and then putting himself on top of the toy. His tail was wagging, and he was making little sneezes. "I'd love to play with you, Sim, but I have to change my clothes and get comfortable then we'll all have dinner. What do you think?" He gave me a big Shih Tzu swallow and then a sneeze.

I unpacked my overnight bag and glanced at the instructions that were given to me. I put on something more comfortable and was really looking forward to my first real meal. Helen had dropped off a casserole, and it smelled wonderful. Frank had put it in the oven to warm it up. I thought I was ready to eat a horse. Sim stayed close by as I unpacked. It appeared that he didn't fully relax until I put the overnight bag away. I could almost see him heave a huge sigh of relief.

"I'm here to stay, Bud. I'm not going anywhere. How about some dinner?" Sim gave me his little sneeze and raced down the hall to the kitchen. Frank had fixed his meal.

"Do you want to do the honors?" Frank asked.

"Sure do. I've missed giving Sim his meal." I put down his dish. He looked at me and swallowed. Because of the way I had trained him, he knew that he couldn't start eating until I told him it was okay.

"OK, Bud. *Bon Appetit.*" He began eating, thoroughly enjoying every bite.

Frank said, "That's the happiest I've seen him since you went to the hospital. He's really your boy."

"I know. He's so special. I don't know what I would do without him."

Frank gave me a quizzical look. "How about me?"

"I guess you're okay. But I don't have to listen to Sim babbling on and on about nonsensical things, nor do I have to worry about making sure the toilet seat is put back down after he pees."

I lit my after-dinner cigarette. Sim watched the smoke curl upward from the cigarette to the ceiling. He gave a couple of little sneezes. The thought crossed my mind that I might consider quitting. It was very fleeting. *After all,* I thought, *I don't drink alcohol. I exercise every day. Dr. Savage didn't make a big deal of it and it is one of the few things that I get enjoyment from.* Sim looked at me and swallowed. I was almost positive that he would have preferred to live in a smoke-free environment. Could he have secretly joined the Environmental Police while I was in the hospital?

Chapter 43

Cheer up, the worst is yet to come.

—Philander Johnson

I rested quite a bit the next few days. I guess I was run down because of the energy the tumor had sapped from my system and now because of the healing process. Although I felt a bit edgy not doing anything, as this was never my style, I somewhat enjoyed just reading and watching some TV. There also were many, many phone calls from family and my students to see how I was doing and if there was anything they could do. Flowers and fruit baskets were arriving by the truckload. Frank came home at lunchtime to walk Sim. He would also bring in the mail. Every empty flat surface, other than the floor, was covered with cards wishing me a speedy recovery. There were also some helium-filled balloons with get well wishes imprinted on them. I found it overwhelming. "Well, Frank, I guess I know what it will be like when I die. This is like a dress rehearsal, seeing the outpouring of caring from everyone." Frank nodded in agreement but did not at all appreciate my sarcastic sense of humor on this subject.

I had an appointment on Friday to see Dr. Savage for a post-op examination. I was hoping that Frank would be able to take me. I would not be able to drive for six weeks. Unfortunately, he was busy at work. He said that he could take me on Monday. I told him that Dr. Savage was emphatic that he wanted to see me one week to the day of the surgery.

"That's OK. I'll ask Helen to take me." I was more than very disappointed. I have always been very independent, and this surgery had rendered me dependent on Frank for things that I had always handled before. I guess, because of the healing process and medication, I was emotionally brittle. I could feel the anger bubble up in me. Helen was more than happy to take me for the appointment. When I told Frank, I told him with an air of "So there. I can take care of myself."

Dr. Savage continued to be very pleased with my progress. He also said that my lab work came back with no indication of cancer. I was so relieved that my knees felt weak. I asked him when I could start getting back to "normal."

"It's going to take a while. I want to see you in six weeks to see how your incision looks. You can resume some normal, light housekeeping and exercise in about two weeks. Don't overdo anything. You will start something with lots of energy and begin to feel tired. Don't try to push past the fatigue. Stop and rest."

"How long will the emotional piece last?" I asked him.

"Give me an example." he said.

"I have these ups and downs. I look at the huge outpouring from friends and family, as well as my students, and I know how much people care about me. Then Frank can't make this appointment with me, and I feel very lonesome. It's not as though Frank isn't doing anything. He's taking care of the dog, he's getting my meals ready, and he even stays close when I take my shower at night so that if I need him, he's right there for me. But all of a sudden, I begin to feel like Mr. Sims is my only friend in the world."

"Mr. Sims?" he asked with eyebrows slightly raised.

I laughed. "Mr. Sims is my dog. He is my best bud. We've been through a lot together and have a very special bond."

"Oh. You had me worried there for a minute," he said, his blue eyes twinkling. "What you're feeling is normal. It will come and go just like the discomfort you're feeling. It will gradually be less and less. As I told you and your husband before the surgery, it will probably be a year before you are back to your old self again."

"I don't want to be my old self again. I want to be my young self."

He gave me a big hug. "Keep that sense of humor, Peg. You're going to be fine. I'll see you in about six weeks. If you have any problems, call me."

When I came out of his office, I stopped at the desk to make the next appointment. Helen stood next to me and said that she would bring me back if Frank couldn't.

"Thanks, Helen. I really appreciate it. Hopefully, Frank will be able to make it next time, but I feel better knowing I have backup."

"Do you want to stop anywhere on the way home?" she asked me.

"No thanks. I'm beginning to get tired, so I think this will be my outing for the day."

Helen left and told me to get some rest because I looked tired. "I will. I know Sim will keep his eye on me."

As soon as she left, the phone rang. We had made arrangements with a contractor to have new siding installed on our house. The date for this was made before we knew about the need for my surgery. "We will start installation on Monday morning," he told me.

"What time?" I asked.

"My crew will be there by 8:00 a.m."

"How long do you think the whole project will take?" I asked.

"Probably about two weeks, give or take. Some of it will depend on the weather. If it rains, we will lose time. If not, we may finish sooner."

"OK. See you then." I hung up the phone, feeling like my world was falling apart. I sat down and Sim immediately sat at my feet looking up at me. "Sim, I just don't get it. I'm supposed to get some rest, and now there's going to be all these clowns crawling all over the place."

Sim jumped into my lap and put his head under my chin. I hugged him, and the tears started. He just stayed with me while I let out my anxiety. As the tears subsided, Sim licked them from my cheeks. I looked at him and smiled. "Thanks, Bud. You always know the right thing to do to make me feel better." Let's go take a little nap. I think I'll feel better. The weekend is here, and Mr. Frank will be home with us."

I was awakened by Frank gently talking to me. Sim sat up to greet him but made a barrier between us with his body.

"Good boy, Sim," Frank told him. "I'm just waking her up so we all can have dinner." Sim wagged his tail and gave a little sneeze.

"Guess what, Frank? The crew will be here early Monday morning to start the siding. I'll have to be up and ready early. They're supposed to be here by 8:00 a.m. on the dot." Just telling Frank about this made me begin to feel edgy.

"That's OK. We'll get through it," he said, trying to be reassuring.

WE'LL get through it? I thought. *I'M the one that's going to have to put up with the noise and inconvenience."* I could feel my anger rising again. I reached over and stroked Sim. He settled down next to me again, as though he knew that I needed him to help me relax.

"I'll set up for dinner. It will be ready in a few minutes." Frank gave me a kiss on the forehead and left the room.

"Well, Sim, I guess I'd better get moving. Maybe I'll feel better after dinner." I got up, and Sim jumped off the bed. He headed down the hall to the kitchen.

Frank fed Sim and was setting up dinner. My appetite was good, but I still was not able to eat a lot at one sitting. As we ate, we went over the things that had to be done to prepare for Monday. The furniture on the patio and deck had to be moved out of the way. All my hanging plants and planter boxes had to be moved so that they wouldn't get damaged. The flowers that were planted in front of the porch were probably going to be ruined, but there was nothing we could do about it. As we went through each item, I felt edgier and edgier.

I also was starting to get concerned about the household chores that I usually did: the dusting, changing the bed linens, the laundry, cleaning the bathrooms and kitchen, vacuuming, and washing the floors.

"I think I can do some dusting, Frank. But I can't do the other things yet. The laundry isn't hard to do, but I can't go up and down the basement stairs several times to get it done."

"Don't worry. I'll help you."

"How are you going to finish everything that has to be done outside and do the inside chores as well?" I asked.

"We'll get it all done," Frank said.

I was getting so stressed about all of it that I couldn't think straight. My mind was whirling around as though it was in a windstorm. I lit a cigarette to help calm my nerves. Sim looked up at me, gave me a little sneeze, and then swallowed.

"I know, I know. You don't like the smoke. I'm so uptight that if I don't smoke them, I'll chew them."

Sim knew from the tone of my voice that I was upset. He walked away and came back with his plush watermelon slice. He had a way of squeezing his squeak toys that was unique. He almost made them sound as though he was tapping out Morse Code. There were several short, rapid-fire squeaks followed by a long, drawn-out one. He would continue this pattern for a while then drop the toy out of his mouth and roll on his back on the toy. His body pressure on the toy made it squeak. He then would, while still on his back, stretch his neck and reach around to grab the toy. Once he grabbed the toy, he would stand up and shake from head to tail. Sometimes the pattern would start all over again or he would just stand there looking at me as much as to say, "What do you think about that?"

It always made me feel cheerful and positive. "I don't know what I would do if I didn't have you, Sim."

Saturday came, and Frank was doing his chores in the yard. He was as fussy with the outside of the house as I am with the inside. He mowed the lawn, edged the gardens and made sure they were free of weeds, then did his string trimming, making sure that the lawn had very defined edges. When he finished, he came in and said that he would take care of some of the things that had to be moved after Mass. He showered and changed.

"I'll be home in about an hour," Frank said. He looked at Sim and said, "Keep an eye on her, Mr. Sims. Don't let her get into any trouble." Sim gave him a knowing swallow.

"Maybe I'll dust a little while you're gone."

"Just don't overdo it, Peg." We gave each other the usual "drive carefullys," and Frank left.

The living room dusting went smoothly, so I went from room to room, just taking my time. As I moved to the bedrooms, I heard Sim jump off the couch. He joined me in the bedroom. "I'm OK, Bud. Thanks for checking on me. But don't tell Mr. Frank that I did this much." He just gave me a knowing look and went back to his perch on the couch. "I guess Frank must be on his way home, huh, Bud?" Within five minutes, I heard the garage door open. "How did you know to do that, Sim? Were you giving me a heads up so that I could put the dust cloth away?" Two little sneezes and tail wag made me think he gave me "Yes."

After dinner, I said to Frank, "I hate to bug you, but the bed has to be changed, the laundry has to be done, so on and so forth."

"I'll get up early and finish up outside, then you can guide me through each chore and what has to be done." This sounded good to me, but again, the edginess began creeping over me. I was so used doing things my own way that just the thought of someone else doing it was like hearing fingernails on a chalkboard.

"Um, there's something you don't know about." Frank looked at me seriously.

"What?" he said with a worried tone.

"Well, when I vacuum the living room, you know that I take Sim's blanket from the floor, put it on the antique couch together with whatever toys he has on or around it? When I turn my back and start vacuuming, Sim grabs the blanket with the toys and flips it off the couch. He then picks one of the toys and rolls on it. I think it's very funny, but you may find it disruptive."

Frank looked at me and started to laugh. "First of all, I can't believe that you never mentioned this to me before. Second, I can't wait to see this. It must be hysterically funny." I breathed a sigh of relief.

Sim and I had our own little rituals that we thought were great fun but other people might think that they were silly. This is just another dimension of owning a dog and having a good relationship with each other. Humans and dogs each have their individual quirks.

We have to learn to live with them, respecting each other's behaviors as long as they are appropriate. When they are not, intervention is required.

And this cuts both ways.

There are things that we do that the dog may not be comfortable with. For example, Sim didn't like me to try to brush his teeth. I got the impression that he felt it was disrespectful for him to have his mouth or teeth so near to my hand. After many, many tries, I finally realized that whether I used beef-flavored toothpaste on a toothbrush, a soft tooth sponge, or even just some peroxide on a cotton pad, it was unacceptable to him. I never had a problem combing and brushing him as well as cleaning his face. But he never accepted having his teeth brushed. On my side of the coin, I did not like to play tug-of-war. I felt that it is a game that is natural to the dog, one they usually win. This puts the owner in a submissive position as far as the dog is concerned. Of course, Sim loved to play this game and would try to get me to play it with him at every opportunity. Only on rare occasions did I play it with him and made sure I always won. This meant that when I felt the game was over, I would tell him to "give." This kept the pack order in proper perspective. The more interaction you have with your dog and the more you educate yourself to your dog's individual personality traits, the more solid the bond and understanding between the two of you becomes.

Reinforcing the pack order with the dog, whether it is a single-dog or multiple-dog household, is extremely important. Within the dog pack, social order is worked out among the players. However, because we are people and think as people do, we sometimes confuse the dog or dogs. We tend to favor the "underdog," feeling that it is being bullied or picked on. The problem with this thinking is that if we chastise the "dominant dog," it only makes matters worse. The "dominant dog" feels that it is justified in feeling superior and will retaliate against the "lower dog." If this "lower dog" needs us to fight its battles, in the superior dog's mind, the "lower dog" is truly the wuss he thought it was. This is nature at its finest, the survival of the fittest. Even though these dogs have been domesticated, they still have inherent traits. The best way to manage this kind of relationship is to remain neutral. If there are any squabbles, tell both dogs to "knock it off" and have them go to their crates or different rooms. Of course, if there are serious fights and/or bloodshed, the issue should be reviewed with your vet, who may recommend the advice of a certified veterinary behaviorist.

On Sunday, true to his word, Frank finished his outside chores by lunchtime. After lunch, he asked me how I wanted him to proceed with the household chores. Being an only child and having no one when I was growing up to split chores with, I always organized my chores so that I was multitasking. While the laundry was in the washing machine, I would either vacuum, clean the kitchen or bathrooms, or wash the kitchen floor. Frank, on the other hand, was more compartmentalized. He wanted to work on a project, seeing it to its conclusion, before starting another one. I knew that this was going to be a point of frustration for both of us.

When you try to change someone's natural set of traits to fit yours and they don't understand your way of thinking and you don't understand theirs, a serious misunderstanding is sure to ensue. And it did.

Sim, who was observing this exchange, quietly but deliberately put himself between us. I guess he saw our body language and could tell from the tone of our voices that this was not a friendly chat.

"I don't tell you how to do your chores in the yard. Don't tell me how to arrange my chores in the house." I could feel my frustration building.

Most of it was because I felt helpless that I couldn't do what had to be done. Sim looked at me and swallowed, keeping his back to Frank. He then yawned with a little soft cry at the end of it. In dog speak, this is one of the ways a dog calms himself in a stressful situation, but it also is a way to break tension in the pack.

"It's OK, Sim. We're not heading to Divorce Court quite yet. Let's move you so we can get this floor done." I cast a glance at Frank. He was still not happy with the situation, but in order to keep the peace, he agreed with my plan. *I can't wait for my two-week rest period to be up. This is going to drive me crazy*, I thought. Frank got through the chores and did a good job.

When he was finished, I gave him a hug. "Thanks for helping me. I'm just not used to this."

Frank woke me up early Monday morning. In a cheerful voice, he said, "Time to get up. The work crew will be here today to start the siding." I pulled the covers over my head.

"I look forward to having the work done, but I'm not looking forward to all the chaos."

The crew arrived a few minutes before 8:00 a.m. There were the two bosses that owned the company and about ten college-aged kids. Everyone introduced themselves to me. "We'll try not to bother you, but we may have to come in to use the bathroom," one of the bosses said.

"Not a problem. And I have water, soda, and Gatorade in the fridge, so don't be afraid to ask if you want something to drink."

"Thanks. We'll probably take you up on the offer."

"By the way," I said, "this is Mr. Sims. He's very friendly and well trained. Just be careful when you come in and out. I don't want him to follow you outside."

They assured me that they would be vigilant and not let Sim get out of the house. The crew dispersed around the house. They began removing the old shingles, replacing them with the sheathing that the siding was going to be attached to. The noise level began to build and build. There was the ripping sound of the old shingles being removed and the sheathing being nailed into place.

Sim looked at me and then gave me the Shih Tzu swallow. He jumped up on the antique couch so he could get a better look at what was going on. At first, he stood on the couch looking out the window at all the activity. He looked at me, looked out the window, and looked at me again as if to say, "Holy cow! Do you see what they're doing?"

I assured him that it was fine. He sat down on the couch with his head resting on the back so he could keep his eye on all the activity. I sat in the chair next to him reading. In a few minutes, the front doorbell rang. Sim jumped off the couch and headed to the door. I got up and opened it. One of the young fellows asked if he could use the bathroom.

"Sure, come on in." I showed him where the bathroom was and turned on the light for him. Sim followed us. I told Sim that everything was fine. He sat outside of the bathroom door until the fellow came out. Sim then escorted him to the door. The fellow patted Sim and went back to work.

A few minutes later, another worker came to the door. I showed him where the bathroom was. Sim sat guard once again outside of the bathroom. One by one, all the workers came in. Sim continued his vigil with each one. When the last one left, he took his place again on the couch.

The noise was incredible. I wore a headset to listen to the radio. The noise was so bad that I couldn't really hear what was being said on the program. Frank came home for lunch, brought in the mail, and took Sim out for his walk.

The workers were sitting on the lawn eating lunch. Sim went to each one, giving a cursory greeting but letting them know that he was not about to become their best friend. Frank told me how much these grown men enjoyed Sim and how they could tell that even though he was a small dog, he was not a pushover.

"How are you doing with all the noise?"

"Well," I said, "I don't have much of a choice, do I? I think this is going to be the worst part. I'll ask when they finish up today if this noise is going to go on for a while." Frank had some lunch and then left to go back to work. The crew also had finished their lunch and began working again. The crew had moved to the back of the house. Sim was snoozing on the couch in the living room as I sat reading and listening to the radio. One of the workers came in the back door. In a flash, Sim was off the couch, heading toward the kitchen, growling fiercely. He raced to the threshold between the family room and kitchen, keeping the worker at bay.

"Whoa, big guy," the worker told Sim loudly. I couldn't move as fast as I usually do, so it took me a bit longer to react.

"It's OK, Sim. He's fine." Sim turned and looked at me, tail wagging.

"I thought you said he was friendly," the worker said to me, seeming to be a bit embarrassed because a Shih Tzu had held him at bay.

"He is. I had major surgery about a week ago, and Mr. Sims is just doing his job protecting me."

The worker gave a nervous laugh and headed to the bathroom. Sim was close behind, waiting in the hall and then escorting the worker out. "Good boy, Sim. You're too much. I think you would fight to the death to protect me if you had to." I patted him on the head and gave him one of his treats. He looked at me, eyes sparkling, and swallowed.

Tuesday was a little less noisy and chaotic. The worst was over, and the installation was coming along well. The workers still came in and out to use the bathroom and were very pleasant. The worker that Sim had cornered the day before must have repeated the story to his colleagues because every time they came in, they showed Sim a healthy respect. I think Sim raised his stature with them. The episode reminded me of the Fonz on the TV program *Happy Days*. You never saw Fonzie fight with anyone, but he had the reputation of being tough and nobody wanted to test him.

A neighbor called on the pretense that she wondered how I was feeling and when she and her husband could come to visit me. However, she told me how much the noise of the residing was bothering her. I apologized.

"It shouldn't be much longer until they are finished. As soon as they are, I'll let you know and we can make a date for a visit."

"Sounds good to me," she said. "Take care and we'll see you soon."

I hung up the phone. "So, Sim, what the devil do people want me to do? Was I supposed to tell the crew to *quietly* remove the old shingles and *quietly* nail in the sheathing? I give up. Oh well, maybe I'm just more sensitive. Things usually don't get to me and I laugh, but right now everything is making me agitated." Sim snuggled into my leg, looked at me, and swallowed. It dawned on me that he was the only living being that I could be totally honest with. I could tell him anything. I could complain when friends and Frank annoyed me. I would tell him when I thought something was unfair. I could have political conversations and vent my frustrations. And sometimes, I could just be quiet. In each case, he seemed to understand and was patient until I finished feeling put upon. He also shared the laughs when something or someone tickled my sense of humor. He knew the difference and when to be serious and when to look at me with bright eyes and a wagging tail.

Chapter 44

Spend your life lifting people up,
not putting people down.

—H. Jackson Brown Jr.

Judy called me to see how I was feeling. She told me that she was going to enter Sandy in a Rally obedience trial. It was going to be held on August 18 in Fitchburg. She wondered if I was going to enter Sim.

"I'm not up to showing him in his Open class, but Frank certainly can show him in Rally again. Do you want us to meet you there or do you want to follow us?"

"Why don't Sandy and I meet you at your house and I'll follow you guys?"

"Great. I'll tell Frank and see if he'll start going to practice on Monday nights again. I can't wait to start working him again. Maybe by the time the Maine show comes around in late September, I'll be able to enter him."

"Glad to hear that," Judy said. "When will you be able to hold your classes again?"

"I'm not sure, Judy. I'll see Dr. Savage in about three weeks. I'll ask him when he thinks it will be possible."

"The club wants to have you come and do therapy dog testing. After you see Dr. Savage, maybe we can set a date."

"Sounds good, Judy. I'm looking forward to going back to work as soon as I can."

Frank took Sim to practice Rally on each of two Monday nights before the trial. He seemed to think that Sim was doing well, although he said that Sim seemed to be restless because I wasn't there. The day of the trial came around. Judy pulled into our driveway. She took Sandy out of her car so that he could stretch his legs. Sim greeted him and the two dogs started their "Grumpy Old Men" routine, sniffing, marking, and remarking each other's scent.

"OK, guys. That's enough. We have to get going. You'll see each other when we get to Fitchburg," I told them.

The drive went well. I was feeling just a little "off." Nothing serious, but I could feel that my strength was not back to normal yet. The facility was up on a hill. It wasn't very steep, but it was strenuous enough for me, and I began feeling a dull ache in my back. Frank and Judy walked slowly for me, and both dogs seemed to sense that I couldn't move any faster. When we entered the facility, we set up our crates and folding chairs. I had just sat down when a woman approached me. "You probably don't remember me, but you certified my Shepherd as a therapy dog about two years ago."

"You look vaguely familiar to me. Is your dog here? I probably would recognize him faster than I would recognize you. How are you both doing with your therapy work?"

Her eyes filled with tears. "We lost him recently. But we made many visits to the local nursing home before we learned that he was ill."

"Oh my. I'm so sorry to hear that. What happened to him?"

"He developed diabetes. We gave him insulin shots, but eventually his system couldn't handle it." She leaned over and gave me a hug. "Thank you so much. When he passed the test and became a certified therapy dog, it was one of the happiest days of my life. And he enjoyed every minute when we made our visits to the nursing homes." She gave me another hug and walked away.

I fought back the tears because I was so touched by her story. I also was amazed that she remembered me. "I guess you never know when you truly touch someone deeply. But sometimes you do find out, and it makes you realize that every time you interact with someone, you leave your impression with them." I wasn't addressing anyone in particular, but Judy and Frank acknowledged what I said.

"Let's walk the boys around the facility so they can relax," Judy suggested. There were some vendors set up, and we decided to see what they had to offer.

"Oh, look," Judy said, "I use this supplement for my dogs. I think I'll buy some. What about trying it for Sim? If it doesn't do anything for him or disagrees with him, I'll buy it from you." I picked up a package to see what it was made of. It was sea kelp with brewer's yeast. It was supposed to boost the dog's immune system, among other things. I talked to the vendor about it. She said that most people swear by it, and they see a big difference in their dog's energy and overall health.

"What have I got to lose? I'll buy a small package and try it."

"Start with about half the recommended amount to begin with. Go with that amount for about a week and then gradually increase the amount until you're up to the dosage that he requires for his weight," the vendor told me.

"Oh, I'm very careful with him. He's very sensitive. I just hope that this supplement helps him."

We headed back to our seats so that the dogs could relax before their turn in the ring. They both were in Rally Advanced now. This meant that they would be working off leash. Judy and Sandy went into the ring. It appeared that Sandy did well. We began to clap when he finished the last exercise, but Judy looked at us and shook her head. When she came out of the ring, we asked her what happened.

"I missed a station. It was my fault, not his."

"Gee, Judy, he looked good," Frank told her. "What luck. But it just shows how we can make a mistake when we're nervous as easily as the dog can."

She was disappointed but was gentle with Sandy. I was glad to see that she didn't let her disappointment get the better of her and then take it out on the dog. Sim and Frank went in next. They did well, and Sim qualified. He now had two legs in Rally Advanced and needed one more for the title. Frank and I were very excited but kept

our enthusiasm low key. Part of being a good competitor is both winning and losing graciously. We kept the conversation light with Judy.
"There's always tomorrow," I told her.

"I know," she said with resignation in her voice.

Chapter 45

Good judgment comes from experience, and
experience comes from bad judgment.

—Anonymous

I was anxious to try the new sea kelp and brewer's yeast supplement.
I was hoping that it would help Sim and give him the boost of health
on a consistent basis that he needed. As directed, I started him off
slowly with just a quarter of a teaspoon sprinkled on his meal. He
sniffed his food bowl and then backed up from it. *Maybe if I add a
little bit of cheese to his dish. He probably is getting the different odor
from the supplement and doesn't know what it is. The cheese will entice
him.* I added a little bit of Swiss cheese to his meal. He sniffed the
dish again and began eating happily. *Good. Let's see what happens,* I
thought. A couple of hours after Sim finished his meal, I noticed him
licking his paws, and his eyes were watering slightly. *His allergies must
be acting up. I did notice the golden rod and ragweed in full bloom on
our walk,* I thought to myself. I gave him one of his allergy pills. In a
short time, he seemed to have gotten some relief.

Over the following days, I continued trying the supplement.
Each time I added it to Sim's food, I had to add something to entice
him to eat it. After eating, he would show symptoms of an allergic
reaction. Sometimes he would be licking his paws; other times he
had watery eyes or sneezing. I was beginning to realize, to my dismay,
that it was the supplement.

I called Judy and told her what was happening. She thought that he might be allergic to the brewer's yeast. She said that she had some plain sea kelp supplement; she would give me some of it, and she could use the one I had purchased. This sounded good to me. In reading about this supplement, it appeared that the sea kelp had the most beneficial qualities to boost Sim's immune system.

After we made the exchange, I added the sea kelp to his meal, starting again with just a quarter of a teaspoon. His recommended full dose was two teaspoons a day. He didn't hesitate eating his meal, and I didn't have to add any enticement to it. Maybe we were going to make some progress. On the second day, he ate his meal, and a short time later, I heard him scratching. His eyes were watering and slightly pink. I checked his ears. They were slightly pink as well. I called Judy and told her that Sim couldn't handle the sea kelp, and I would give it back to her.

I was disappointed, but I wasn't going to force something on him that obviously disagreed with him. "I should have known when I had to add the cheese to get you to eat it," I told Sim, apologizing for being so dense and not recognizing what he was trying to "tell" me. He had shown allergic reactions to fish. Was I that dense that the words *sea kelp* didn't ring any bells with me? "It's just like when I was in the hospital and they kept serving me that awful custard, Sim. But no one added any M&Ms to it for me. If they had, I just might have eaten it. I'm sorry that I didn't get your signals sooner. I hope that my mistake didn't make you too uncomfortable." He just looked at me, blinked his eyes, and gave me the swallow.

There is a saying that dogs know the difference between someone kicking them and tripping over them. One is a deliberate act whereas the other is an accident. I'm sure Sim knew that I had made an honest mistake and only had his best interest at heart. I made a mental note about this incident, thinking that I would have to be more careful with anything that I gave him.

It was time for my follow-up visit with Dr. Savage. Frank was able to drive me to the appointment. I asked if he wanted to come in with me and if he had any questions for the doctor. He said that he couldn't think of anything and would stay in the waiting room.

When Dr. Savage came into the room, he was happy to see me. "You're looking great," he told me. "How are you feeling?" I told him that I thought I was making progress but still had ups and downs physically and emotionally.

"When do you think I can go back to work?" I asked him.

"I'm happy with your progress, but I don't think you should start training again until mid-October. I don't want you to risk sustaining any injury to your incision. It's healing beautifully, and I think by then, you will be fine. You'll probably feel stronger as well."

"Do you think I can show my dog in Obedience the third week of September in Maine?" I asked.

"As long as you get enough rest and don't put yourself in any risky situations, I don't see why not."

"Thanks, Dr. Savage. I now have something to look forward to. When do you want to see me again?"

"As of today, I'm releasing you. You know you can call me if you have any problems, but I think you're coming along just fine."

Dr. Savage gave me a big hug then handed me my chart to take to the reception desk. As soon as I got into the reception room, I told Frank the good news. "I'll fill out the forms for the trials in Maine. The change of scenery will do all three of us a world of good," I told him. "It will be like a mini vacation. The other good news is that I can start my training classes again. The group that has been working on Canine Good Citizen and Therapy Dog certification will be glad to get going again. I'll just have to see whether I feel well enough to go back to work in mid-October or so. I think Judy was talking about scheduling testing sometime in December, just before Christmas."

When I got home, I filled out the forms for the two obedience trials. The judges for the two trials were women. I had shown Sim with one of them before. The other one had been the trial secretary for the United Kennel Club show that had taken place while I was in the hospital. I felt comfortable with both of them. "I don't know how you're going to do, Bud, but it will be interesting to see how I feel in the ring again."

On Saturday, the judge was the one that I had previously shown with. She not only was an obedience judge but was also a veterinarian. She was a tall, gangly woman, almost imposing but very pleasant. When our number was called, Sim and I entered the ring. I felt a bit detached from the situation and a little bit weak. My hand trembled slightly when I handed the steward Sim's leash and dumbbell. The judge showed me where to set up for the heeling exercise. *I might be pushing it*, I thought as she asked if I was ready. When I answered "Yes," I could tell that my voice was not as strong as it usually is.

"Forward," she told me.

"Sim, heel," I said. Again my voice was not as strong as it should be. I started walking forward, following her directions to go "fast," "normal," "right turn," "halt." I stopped, looking to my left. Sim was nowhere to be seen. He was standing next to the judge.

She called me back. "Your heeling was beautiful. Too bad your dog wasn't with you."

I smiled and looked at Sim. The look on his face as much as said, "I don't think you should be doing this, Mom." The judge asked me if I wanted to continue with the other exercises even though I was not going to qualify. "I can put you through another exercise or two, but if the dog doesn't do anything, I will excuse you. This is a trial and you're not here to practice." I felt terribly embarrassed, but I wasn't going to make any excuses.

"Let's see what happens," I told her. "If he doesn't do the next couple of exercises, I understand that we will be excused."

I was mortified. This judge must have thought that I hadn't trained the dog. Little did she know all the time and effort Sim and I had put in. I was sure that Sim was "off" because he sensed the way I felt. I didn't feel secure in the ring. I wasn't going to get upset with him this time. I had grown and learned to control my emotions. Sim was only trying to take care of me because he sensed my weakness.

After trying two more exercises, we were excused from the ring. "Maybe after we get a good night's rest, we will both do better tomorrow," I told Frank. Some of the spectators that I had gotten to know over the years of showing in Maine and who knew about my surgery were very supportive.

"We'll be here rooting for you tomorrow, Peg," they told me. That helped to take the sting out of the embarrassment of being excused. A dog and handler are more likely to be excused from the obedience ring for poor behavior. We were excused for no behavior.

The following day we were in the other ring. There was a door to the outside that the judge had opened because it was warm in the building. The sun was shining in through the open door. The way the judge had set up the ring, the dogs would have the sun in their eyes when waiting for their handlers to throw the dumbbell over the high jump. "This is not going to go well, Frank. The sun is so bright both the dog and handler are going to be blinded by it. But the judge is the boss of her ring. We'll see." I wasn't feeling very hopeful at all. As we watched the other teams, several of the dogs either wouldn't jump over the high jump or, if they did, they had a lot of trouble finding their dumbbell on the other side.

Our turn came, and the judge showed us where she wanted us to set up for the heeling exercise. She told us, "Forward."

I told Sim to heel. He came along with me.

"Halt," she said. Sim was sitting next to me.

Maybe this won't be as bad as I worried it would be, I thought to myself.

Once again, however, his heeling fell apart. He was lagging well behind me. We finished the heeling pattern. I knew we weren't going to qualify. The stewards came into the ring for the Figure 8 exercise. Sim didn't do too badly, although he was a bit distracted. The judge set us up for the Drop on Recall. Sim did well. He also did very well with retrieving his dumbbell on the flat. The next exercise was retrieving over the high jump. The sun was shining in brighter than before.

"Are you ready?" asked the judge.

"Yes," I said.

"Throw the dumbbell." I threw it and wasn't sure where it had landed because the sun had blinded me. I was looking into blackness.

"Send your dog," she said.

"Sim, over!" I told him. I wasn't sure whether or not he would jump over the high jump, nor did I know whether he would be able to see the dumbbell when he got to the other side. He jumped. I stood there, not able to see what he was doing. Before I knew it, he had jumped back over and sat in front of me with the dumbbell in his mouth.

"Take it," the judge commanded.

"Give," I told Sim.

"Finish," the judge said.

I gave Sim the signal to return to Heel position. He did promptly and then gave me a couple of his "How's that, Mom?" sneezes. My spirits lifted. He had executed the exercise perfectly in a very difficult situation. The last exercise was the broad jump. He flew over it, sat in front of me, and "finished" when I signaled him to. Loud applause came from the crowd. The judge came over to me and said, "Too bad about his heeling. Otherwise he did very well."

I thanked her and ran Sim out of the ring. I gave him several little pieces of hotdog and told him how proud I was of him. He wagged his tail, looked bright-eyed, and gave me a few sneezes. Frank said that he had been talking to the Trial Secretary while we were working. She felt that Sim had done well and let Frank know that there was another trial coming up in Bangor, Maine, in two weeks. She told him that she could give us the entry forms for that trial, and that Rally was also going to be offered.

The judge from the day before had finished her assignments and was walking by us. "How did you make out today?" she asked.

"You won't believe it. He was like a different dog once we finished the heeling portion. He didn't qualify because of the heeling, but he did everything else beautifully."

She gave me a knowing smile. "You just never know what's going to happen when you walk into the ring. There are so many different things that can change a dog's attitude for better or worse, and they are all unpredictable. Something that may be a negative today can end up being a positive tomorrow."

I agreed heartily with her. "It's one of my biggest challenges as an exhibitor and trainer. We're always looking for the right answer, and sometimes it is extremely elusive."

"I know," she said. "You should see me in the ring with my dogs. Sometimes it isn't pretty."

After my conversation with her, I didn't feel as badly about being excused. She seemed to have more of an understanding of the situation than she appeared to the day before. I always have mixed emotions about obedience trials. They can be a very humbling experience, or they can be a very rewarding experience. But I have learned something every time, either from Sim or from watching the other teams. As long as the good relationship between dog and handler is always the most important element, everything else is, for better or worse, an educational experience. I was looking forward to the upcoming trials in Bangor.

Chapter 46

Still round the corner there may wait,
A new road, or a secret gate.

—J. R. R. Tolkien

I was excited about this trial for several reasons. I was hoping and praying that Sim would qualify and get that elusive third leg for his Companion Dog Excellent title. If he qualified in Rally Advanced with Frank, he would win his third leg in that class and be awarded the Rally Advanced title. I also thought that many of the "hard boot" people whose methods I strongly disagreed with would not be at this trial. From what I had seen over the years of showing Sim, it appeared that Portland, Maine, was as far as they would travel. I'm sure there would be other "hard boot" people in Bangor, but as I didn't know who they were, I knew I would be more relaxed. More than likely, I would never see them again. If Sim got his CDX title, I didn't know if I would ever show him in the Utility Class, which is the most advanced of the obedience classes.

If you think of each of the obedience titles and wanted to compare them to college degrees, Companion Dog would be equal to a Bachelor of Arts or Science degree. Companion Dog Excellent would be equal to a Master's degree. Utility would be equal to a PhD. I really did not have any false hopes in his earning his Utility title. I was very proud of his accomplishments to date. If he earned his Companion Dog Excellent title, it would show everyone what I knew. He is a wonderful, smart dog that overcame a horrible start. He was already a Companion Dog Excellent to me.

Even though I had to work Sim slow and easy because of my recouping, he seemed to be very enthusiastic. I was no longer giving him any extra supplements either. He was eating his regular canned duck and potato food and seemed to be doing well with it. Frank took Sim to practice Rally on a couple of Monday nights and told me that he appeared to be coming into good form for the show.

The ride to Bangor took about five hours. We had to stop about halfway so that I could stretch my legs. Sitting in one position made my back ache. When we stopped at the rest area, Frank wanted to go to the men's room located in a pavilion that also served food. I put Sim's leash on him and walked him around the area. There were two pillars that lined up just perfectly so that I could practice Figure 8's. I began heeling Sim, encouraging him around the posts with a little piece of hot dog. After a couple of revolutions, I stopped. Sim sat wagging his tail and looking at me. I praised him lavishly and gave him his special treat.

A man, dressed completely in meticulously matched black shirt and slacks, approached me. He appeared to be in his fifties. Sim positioned himself in front of me to keep the stranger at what Sim felt was a safe distance. The man knelt down to pet Sim. Sim appreciated it but remained reserved. The man complimented me on what a great dog Sim was and how impressive he looked working with me. I explained that we were on our way to an obedience trial and mentioned the class that Sim was competing in. I gave him a very brief history of Sim and that I was a trainer. The man told me that he had a Beagle and asked me for some advice. The conversation was very pleasant, and the man was very respectful to both Sim and me.

I saw Frank coming back from the pavilion. He stopped several feet away from me and watched us. The man in black thanked me for the advice and then knelt down next to Sim to give a parting pat. At that point, something in the side of his belt caught my eye because of the way the sun made it gleam. It appeared to be a silver handgun. He wished us luck and headed toward the pavilion. He passed Frank as Frank headed toward us.

"Why didn't you come over while I was talking to that man?" I asked him.

"You looked comfortable and he seemed polite. Sim looked like he had everything under control."

"When he walked by, did you notice the gun?" I asked.

"Yes, I did. By the way he is dressed, he looks as if he is in some area of law enforcement but in such a way as not to stand out."

I handed Sim's leash to Frank. "It's my turn to go up to the pavilion."

As I walked toward the building, I wondered if I would run into the man in black again. Even though it was just a very brief interaction, it had a surprising impact on me. There was something very calming about his manner. And even though I had no idea who he was, his praise of Sim and my work with him gave me confidence. Of course, I didn't know how things were going to work out, but for the first time ever before a trial, I felt relaxed.

I remained relaxed for the rest of the trip. I slept well that night and still was not too keyed up the next morning. I kept thinking of the man in black, what an odd experience it was, and the calm that I felt after our interaction. We packed up the car, stopped for breakfast, and headed for the show site. I shared a little piece of the ham, egg, and cheese in my breakfast sandwich with Sim. He thoroughly enjoyed it. He was very happy and bouncy.

"Maybe today will be the charm, Frank."

"I hope so. I know how happy it would make you."

"Well, you may earn an advanced title or two today. We both have a lot to look forward to," I said to Sim.

The trial was held in a school gym/auditorium. We decided to leave the equipment in the car and take a look at the facility first. There were a few people from the earlier show in Maine, including the Trial Secretary who told us about this event. We exchanged greetings.

"I'm so glad you made it. I always love to watch Mr. Sims work."

Frank said that he was going out to the car to get the rest of our equipment, and I began walking Sim around the facility so that he could get used to it. I ran into Ed Phipps, who gave me a warm smile and said, "Hello."

Frank returned in a few minutes. We began setting up Sim's crate and our folding chairs.

"How are you feeling, both physically and mentally?" Frank asked.

"I'll just keep thinking about the man in black. I think he is a gun-toting guardian angel."

"That's my girl," Frank said. "Just keep your sense of humor and you'll be fine."

When it was time for us to enter the ring, I handed my leash and dumbbell to the steward. Ed showed me where to set up for the heeling exercise. I took a deep breath and visualized the man in black. It immediately had a calming effect on me. I was ready for whatever happened.

"Are you ready?" Ed asked.

"Ready," I answered.

"Forward," he told me.

"Sim, heel," I said, and off we went. He was with me every step of the way, eagerly staying with me, stopping when I stopped, changing pace with me, making the turns crisply. *Great. He's on today*, I thought.

The stewards came into the ring for the Figure 8 exercise. I set Sim up.

"Are you ready?" Ed asked.

"Ready," I said.

Again, he stayed right with me.

"Exercise finished," Ed said.

I praised Sim as I took him to begin the Drop on Recall exercise. I was very encouraged. Usually, once we got past the heeling exercises that Sim didn't enjoy, he did well with all the other ones. Ed came over and smiled.

"This is the Drop on Recall exercise. I'll give you a hand signal to call, drop, call, and finish." I nodded. "Are you ready?"

"Yes," I said.

"Leave your dog."

I told Sim to "wait," and walked to the end of the mat. I turned to face him. The first thing I saw was Ed's expression and deflated body language. As I left, Sim took about three steps to follow me. This is an immediate disqualification. If he had stood up and not moved, it would have only been a few points off the exercise. We continued with the exercise, and Sim did a great job. As Ed approached me with the dumbbell for the retrieve exercise, I could see the disappointment in his face. I continued to act upbeat, and Sim aced this exercise as well. The retrieve over the high jump was a sight to behold. He sailed over the jump when I sent him and returned quickly, holding the dumbbell in his mouth until I took it. He executed the broad jump with just as much enthusiasm. When Ed said "Exercise finished," the crowd gave their approval with loud applause and cheers.

Ed said, "I thought you had it today. He looks so good. Healthy as well. This is the best I've ever seen him work. Who would figure that he would make a mistake on the Drop on Recall exercise? He always did well with it."

"Oh well, Ed. It's just part of the game. There's always tomorrow. Frank will see you in the Rally ring later on."

"Maybe things will work out better there for Sim," Ed said.

"Thanks, Ed." I was touched by the fact that he felt so badly that Sim didn't make it. Sim and I had shown with Ed a few times, and most of those times, Sim was either very distracted and did little or did well on everything but his heeling. And if everything else went fairly well, he would go down on his Sit. I always tried to stay upbeat with Sim while we were in the ring together, no matter what happened. I had learned from Sim that getting emotionally tense and stressed did nothing for either one of us. Sim always tried to do his best, whatever his best was for that day.

We broke for lunch. The club sponsoring the event had set up a food concession. This was convenient, and we didn't have to drive anywhere to pick up something to eat. We got some lunch and took it back to our seats. Sim gladly went into his crate to rest.

"Don't get too comfortable, Sim. You have to work with Frank in a little while." Sim looked at me then put his head down on his stuffed squirrel that was in the crate with him and started to nap.

"He's relaxed here, Frank. That's a good sign. I think the two of you will do well."

"I hope so. It sure would be nice to get that title and start him in Rally Excellent."

The lunch break was over, and Ed Phipps began setting up the Rally ring. He and the stewards set up the stations for the Rally classes. The Rally Excellent class was going first, followed by the Rally Advanced class.

The Excellent class finished and the placement awards were given out. The stewards were removing a few of the stations so that it was ready for the Advanced class. Ed walked through the ring to check the steward's work. He appeared satisfied and was ready to start the class. The entrants, without their dogs, had the opportunity to do a walk-through of the course. Frank had taken Sim out of his crate and had walked him around a little. He handed me the leash and headed over to the ring. I slowly walked Sim around, working him lightly and rewarding him with small bits of hotdog.

Frank came back and said that the layout was a little tricky. He knew he had to stay fully focused on both Sim and the course.

"Good luck and drive carefully," I told him, giving Sim a good luck pat. Sim looked at me and gave me a knowing look and swallow. "You guys are going to be fine. All you can do is try your best."

Frank and Sim headed for the ring. Sim seemed to be happy and kept his attention on Frank. I headed to the back of the room. I couldn't see the ring very well, but I knew that the reaction of the crowd would help me judge what was happening. I could make out that Frank had entered the ring, and I could see Ed giving him instructions. After that, all I could see was Frank from his chest up, navigating the Rally course. When he finished, I heard a loud cheer come from the crowd.

"They made it!" I said to myself. I was overjoyed. It took a few minutes for Frank and Sim to get to me. "Congratulations. You made it. You got the Rally Advanced title!" Frank and I gave each other a big hug. I lowered myself to Sim's level and gave him some hotdog then a big hug and kiss on the top of his head. His eyes were shining, and he gave me a few little sneezes. "He knows we're very happy. I'm sure he doesn't know why. But what difference does it make?" I asked Frank.

Several people came over and congratulated us. They told me what a great job Frank had done, guiding Sim through all the exercises. He told them that I had done the training; all he had to do was navigate Sim. After all the entries for the class finished, Ed did his paperwork and then called all the qualifiers into the ring.

When the ceremony was over, Frank walked up to me with his qualifying ribbon and a special ribbon for earning the title.

"Great, Frank. That's quite an accomplishment." He handed me the two ribbons to look at. I glanced at them and then immediately showed them to Sim. "Look what you did, Bud. You now have so many ribbons that I'm running out of wall space." He sniffed the ribbons and looked at me. "Of course I have some hotdog for you. If I could, I would buy you a steak for dinner, but we're going to have to stick to your diet. I don't want you to get an upset tummy."

Sim looked at me and swallowed with a resigned look. I couldn't help but laugh. He had become an integral part of my life. I couldn't imagine life without him.

We packed up our equipment. It took us a couple of trips to the car. "I want to go back in and thank Ed," I told Frank.

The crowd had thinned out. Ed was sitting at a table at ringside. He had just finished all his paperwork and looked tired. He looked up and smiled broadly. "Congratulations. Both of your guys did a nice job."

"Thanks, Ed."

He then got a mischievous twinkle in his eyes. "Are you going to make Frank travel home sitting in the trunk?" I burst out laughing.

"Well, I'll have to give that some thought. He does all the driving, though, so I think he'll be in the driver's seat." Ed laughed.

"Maybe your boy will put it all together for you tomorrow. I can't believe that you haven't gotten the Open title yet. You have worked long and hard for it."

"What can I say, Ed. If not tomorrow, there's always next year. Anyway, thanks again and get some rest. You look tired."

We drove back to the motel so that we could feed Sim and then go out for a celebration dinner. Sim seemed very relaxed and was sort of snoozing in the back seat. Every so often, he would sit up to check things out. I would reach back and give him a pat. When we got to the motel, we walked him so he could relieve himself and then went to our room. I fixed his dinner, and he ate up happily. We then put him in his crate.

Sim readily went into his crate and curled up with his stuffed squirrel. I gave him a couple of treats, turned out the lights, and we left. Frank was jubilant at dinner.

"I'm picking up the tab tonight, Frank. You earned it."

"Thanks, Peg, but you really were the one that did all the training so that all I had to do was work him in the ring. I just feel so badly that he made that little mistake that cost you the title in Open."

"You know what, Frank? I'm fine. We'll give it a try tomorrow. If not, we'll see if he can do it next year. I'm just so pleased that he really seems healthy and happy. Even Ed noticed how good he seemed to feel."

"You've worked long and hard to get him well. That part of the toy that he ingested as a puppy really had quite an impact on his health. I thought that once it came up, he would be fine. But you kept being persistent until the vet finally did the scoping. I really admire that."

"It's odd, Frank. It's as though we were supposed to get together. Can you imagine if I hadn't taken him and one of the people I thought might take him did? Or even worse, what if he had gone to the pound? His future probably would have been very short. If he was in pain from that piece of toy in his tummy and someone mishandled him, he might have snapped or even bitten them. That would have been the end right there. Other than his health, he hasn't given us one reason to regret taking him."

"That's for sure," Frank said. Then he laughed and said, "Please remember, the next time someone offers you a free dog, just say no. Sim's been the most expensive free dog I've ever seen!"

Fortunately, we were able to afford whatever medical attention Sim needed.

"That's why I think it was fate that brought us together. I have taught him a lot, but in turn, he has taught me more than I could have ever learned in any kind of animal behavior course."

"Or veterinary course," Frank added.

I began to feel a little emotional. Frank saw my expression and said, "Hey, this is a celebration. Where's your smile?" I couldn't help but smile, thinking again about how well Sim had done.

When we arrived at the show site the next morning, I saw the judge that I was going to show under. She was in the ring setting it up for the Open class. She was middle-aged and seemed pleasant, and I felt that she was competent in what she was doing. This helped me to relax.

I started warming Sim up. He seemed to be happy and eager to work. I walked him around the facility, heeling, having him do a recall, and sharpening up his automatic sit. It was now time for me to enter the ring.

"Good luck," Frank told us. "And drive carefully."

I chuckled. "We'll see," I told him.

I removed Sim's leash and handed it and his dumbbell to the steward. The steward joked with me about how small Sim's dumbbell was compared with some of the other competitors. The judge greeted me and led us to where we were going to start the heeling exercise.

"Are you ready?" she asked.

"Ready," I told her. As we began to heel, Sim was as enthusiastic as he was the day before. He was with me throughout the heeling pattern. *Phew!* I thought to myself, giving him a little praise when we completed the exercise. The stewards entered the ring for the Figure 8 exercise. Once again, Sim did a good job. I began to feel a little more confident. I set Sim up for the Drop on Recall. The judge said that she would give me hand signals for the Come, Drop, Come, and Finish.

"Leave your dog," she instructed.

As I left Sim and told him to "wait," I said it a bit more emphatically than usual. I wanted to be sure that he understood that I didn't want him to start to follow me as he had the day before. I walked to the end of the mat and turned to face him. He hadn't moved out of position. I breathed a sigh of relief. The judge signaled me to call.

"Sim, come." He immediately headed quickly toward me. I was keeping an eye on the judge for the signal to drop him. Sim was getting closer and closer to me. The judge just kept looking at me. All of a sudden, she gave me the signal. Sim was only about three feet away from me, but he dropped when I told him, "Sim, *dowwnn!*"

I wanted to be sure that he didn't get confused and think that I wanted him to come directly to me. She signaled me to call him. "Sim, come." Sim dutifully came and sat at my feet. I could tell from his expression that he was a little confused with what had just happened. It was quite different than the usual way he had learned the exercise. She gave me the signal to "finish." I did, and Sim immediately came around behind me and sat at my left side.

"Exercise finished," the judge said.

"Good boy, Sim," I told him out loud. But under my breath, I said, "That was a close one, Bud."

He looked at me and swallowed, giving me that knowing look as if to say, "And how, Mom?"

I was just hoping that he hadn't been knocked off stride because of what had just happened.

The judge approached us and handed me his dumbbell. He did well with the retrieve and gave me one of his little sneezes as he finished the exercise. I took this to be a positive sign that he had recovered. We then moved to the Retrieve over the High Jump. Again, he did well, flying over the jump, finding his dumbbell, and flying back over the jump to me.

"Great job, Bud. Only the Broad Jump is left to do." Sim looked at me with his eyes bright and his tail wagging. I set him up. The judge asked if I was ready. I told her that I was. I left Sim and positioned myself on the side of the Broad Jump.

"Send your dog," she said.

"Sim, *jump!*" I commanded him enthusiastically. He flew over the Broad Jump, turned as soon as he landed, and returned to me, giving me a couple of little sneezes that meant he was very happy with himself.

The judge said, "Finish."

I signaled him to return to my left side. He did, and I could hear his tail wagging as it brushed against the mat. The crowd, once again, clapped loudly in approval of his performance.

"Nice job," the judge told me. "You really should watch the judge more closely on the Drop on Recall, though."

One thing I learned early on in my competitive career. You never, ever argue with or question a judge. Not that I ever did, but I saw people who tried to change judge's minds to no avail. I thanked her and ran Sim out of the ring.

Frank was very happy, and several people came over to say what a great job Sim had done and what a pleasure it was to watch him work. Now we just had to get through the Sits and Downs.

As the last entrant in the Open class finished, the steward began calling our numbers. We began lining up, all of us a bit tense. We filed into the ring, removing the leash and armband and placing them behind the dogs.

The only thing that was different from Ed's arrangement yesterday was that this judge had us facing in the opposite direction. I thought that she was going to have us taken to the lobby to be out of sight. When the dogs are left on a Sit Stay or Down Stay, the judge always has the handlers leave the ring so that the dogs can watch the handler's backs as they walk away. This, sometimes, helps the dog to maintain position when the handler is out of sight because the dog sees where the handler has gone.

The judge gave us the usual instructions and told us to follow the steward when we left the dogs. The steward, instead of leading us out of the ring and going to her right, made a left turn, which would make us walk behind the dogs to our hiding place. The judge had picked the same area as Ed had the day before but set the dogs up in the wrong direction.

As we all turned left, the handlers began looking at each other as if to say, "This isn't right." But again, you never question the judge, and the steward was only following her orders. As we passed the dogs and started to walk behind them, many of them got up and turned around to watch us. The steward kept on going. By the time we were out of sight, all of the dogs had broken their positions. According to AKC obedience rules, if all the dogs break, the exercise can be repeated.

The judge had the stewards bring us back, and we returned to our dogs. The judge explained how we were going to repeat the exercise, and this time, we would be taken out in the proper direction. All of the dogs were agitated because of what just happened, Sim included. We set up the dogs in a sit again and left our dogs, following the steward. When we reached the lobby, Sim and most of the dogs had broken the sit and were lying down. Several of the handlers were upset. Only two dogs were sitting and stayed in that position for the required three minutes. We returned to our dogs.

The judge explained the instructions for the Down exercise. We put our dogs in a Down Stay and followed the steward out of the ring to the lobby. A few of the handlers started talking about how they were going to "fix the sit" when they got their dogs home. At this point, I had to say something to them.

"First of all, the dogs got confused when we left and walked behind them. When the error was realized, we returned and put them into a Sit again. What are they used to us doing after the Long Sit exercise?"

One of the other handlers said, "Oh yeah, the Sit is followed by the Down."

I could see the realization in her eyes as well as the other handlers.

"It wasn't their fault. We just had a bad experience. No matter how much practice we do with the dogs, something like this could never have been anticipated. We just learned about another way to practice the long stays. We'll just have to remember this, and if we are in this situation again, we all will know enough to ask the question of where we're going to hide when the judge asks, 'Are there any questions?'" They all nodded in agreement. Because two dogs maintained the position on the second try, the exercise was considered valid.

"What luck," Frank said as Sim and I approached him.

"I know. Just when you think you've got it all together, something strange happens. Well, I'm very happy with Sim's performance. Hopefully, he will get the title early next year. I understand that the

Toy Club is going to have an extra trial in March right in Springfield. No traveling required, and it's going to be held in a church downtown, so it should be comfortable for Sim."

We packed up our equipment and headed home. Sim now had his Rally Advanced title, and the initials RA would be added to his name. When a more advanced title is earned, the previous one is dropped. Even so, he had five sets of initials that went with his name when I filled out entry blanks. I was learning to write smaller so that I could fit everything on the line they furnished. Sim was napping on the back seat with his stuffed squirrel under his head as though it was a pillow. He almost looked like he was smiling. I reached back and gave him a gentle pat.

"I'm so proud of you, Bud. You're my best boy." Sim half opened his eyes, gave me a loving look as if to acknowledge my remark, and then settled down again.

"If I can keep his health stable, I think he'll be great next year," I said, thinking out loud.

Frank said, "I've got to hand it to you, Peg. Other people would have given up by now, both on his competitive career and trying to keep him healthy."

"I could never give up on him. He'll let me know when he wants to retire. I know his health is always going to be an issue, but I have learned so much from him and will continue to learn. But I certainly have expanded my knowledge about the care, feeding, and training of a dog. And it's all thanks to Mr. Sims."

I gave Sim a week's rest. We just played and took a lot of pleasure walks. I usually would incorporate a little heeling when we walked, but for this week, I just let him sniff, mark, explore, and have a great time. I wanted to start some of the Utility exercises to keep him from getting bored with the Open exercises. He had learned the Open exercises several years ago and, between practice and actual trials, had executed them what seemed like at least one hundred times or more.

I decided that I would begin teaching him the Go Out exercise and Moving Stand for Examination. The Go Out exercise is part of another exercise named Directed Jumping. The dog has to "go out," when commanded, toward the ring gate, which is about thirty to forty feet away from the team. The dog then has to turn to face the handler and sit when commanded to do so. The dog has to have complete trust in the handler because the handler is sending the dog into "nothingness" as far as the dog is concerned.

The standard way of teaching this exercise is to put a small piece of cheese, hotdog, or another of the dog's favorite treat on a baby gate or fence. Then starting at about three feet away, the handler points to the gate or fence and tells the dog to "go out." In other words, when the dog arrives at the gate or fence, he finds the special treat. I set up a baby gate in the hallway and attached a small piece of hotdog to it, about eye level to Sim.

A very wise person, although anonymous, once said, "Did you ever notice that when you point to something with your finger, the dog focuses on your finger?" This is exactly what happened when I first set Sim up and told him, "Go out." He looked at my finger, looked at me, then looked at my finger and gave a little sneeze. I began to laugh. "OK, Bud, let's break this down for you." I attached his leash to his collar and set him up again. This time, when I told him to "go out," pointing in the direction of the gate, I headed down the hall to the baby gate. When I got there, he found the treat on the gate. "That's it, Sim. Way to go!"

I took him back down the hall and told him to "wait" so that I could replace the piece of hot dog on the gate. I returned to him and once again told and signaled him to "go out," heading toward the gate with him. This time, he seemed a little more anxious to go to the gate to get the treat.

"All right, Sim!" I praised him. "You're starting to get it. What a boy!"

He looked at me, eyes bright, tail wagging, and gave me a couple of his sneezes. I repeated the exercise a couple of more times and then started to play with him to help break the stress. Although he seemed to enjoy the work and finding the treat, I didn't want to overdo it.

After we played for a little while, I thought I would try the Moving Stand for Examination. This exercise starts with the dog and handler heeling. While they are moving, the judge commands,

"Stand your dog." The handler signals the dog to stand and then continues forward ten to twelve feet in front of the dog. The handler then turns to face the dog. The judge approaches the dog and thoroughly examines the dog, as if the dog were being shown in the breed ring. This exam is much more inclusive than the Novice Stand for Examination. In the Novice exam, the judge only lightly touches the dog's head, midsection, and lower back.

The concept of the dog standing and staying while heeling is a bit confusing at first. Again, it must be broken down. The dog has been trained to keep moving after the "Heel" command as long as the handler is moving. When the handler stops, the dog has been trained to sit each time, so this behavior must be altered for this exercise. The handler must watch his or her body language as well. Usually, when heeling and then coming to a stop, the handler stands straight and squares his or her shoulders. This is a silent cue to the dog to sit.

I began to heel Sim for a few feet. Then I gave him the signal and told him to "stand" as I continued walking forward. When I turned to face him, he was standing but looking at me as if to say, "Huh?" I returned to him, praised him, and gave him a treat. He was happy to get the praise and treat but still looked a bit confused.

"It's OK, Bud. I'm a bit flummoxed by this one as well. We'll get it, though. I know you'll understand what to do if I get my part right."

The more I trained Sim, the more I viewed it as an intricate dance. Each partner has to fully understand what his or her part is. We, the handlers, have to be sure that we have taught our partner and ourselves well.

There is an exercise that I use to illustrate how we are careful when we are passing something tangible but don't use the same care when we are passing something in a verbal or abstract way. I use a pan of water for this exercise. It is filled about 75 percent. I pass it to my student, who takes it carefully. I ask the student to hand it back to me. They do and make sure that I have a tight grasp on the pan before they let it go. We pass the pan back and forth several times, being careful not to spill any water or drop the whole thing. I point out to them they don't let go of the pan until they are sure that I have it securely in my hands. They agree.

I then tell them that as careful as we are with something tangible, we are not as careful when we verbally impart information, especially to the dog. Are you sure that the dog has a firm grasp of what you want? This deserves some serious thought. I also point out that some dogs are more like a pan of water that is almost overflowing. You have to be even more precise and careful when you're imparting information to them before you "let go."

Chapter 47

We stumble, every one of us. That's why
it's a comfort to go hand in hand.

—Emily Kimbrough

We celebrated the holidays, and I was really looking forward to 2006. Sim was feeling and working well. He enjoyed the more difficult Utility work. When I added some of the Open exercises that he was so used to, he executed them with enthusiasm and his special flair. It was as though the Open exercises were now a form of play rather than work.

Little did I know that in the coming year, the experience I had in the hospital with the removal of the large tumor would be preparing me for what Sim was about to go through.

As 2006 arrived, I had high hopes that Sim would get that elusive last Open leg and then go on to show in the Utility class. I continued teaching Sim the Utility exercises. He was doing well with the Moving Stand, but the Go Out was a more difficult concept for him. If the treat was attached to the gate, he would readily go to it. If there was no treat, he would head to the gate and then look confused. I had to figure out a way to convince him that he would get the reward if he went to the gate, whether it was attached or not. I began sending him out, and when he got to the gate, I would immediately go to him and give him his treat. I had some success with this, but something didn't feel right to me. I had to break it down a bit more for him.

"I've got to think this one over a bit more, Bud. You sort of get it, but I don't think that you are comfortable yet. I'll keep thinking about it. If you get any ideas, let me know." Sim looked at me, wagged his tail, and swallowed. I definitely got the feeling that he would try his best to show me what he needed. I just had to listen and learn as I went along.

The premium for the Toy Show to be held March 10 arrived in early January. I liked the judge. She had been judging obedience for many years and was excellent in understanding Toy breeds. It was going to be held in the Community room of the Trinity church, so it would be a relatively calm atmosphere. I excitedly filled out the entry form. "This could be it, Bud. The site is great, we don't have to travel, and the judge loves you little guys. You've got a great opportunity to get that third Open leg and your Companion Dog Excellent title."

It was the beginning of February, and Sim was due for his annual physical. He would have his full examination, and blood work would be taken to check him for heartworm infection, Lyme disease, and other tick-borne illnesses. The vet would also take blood to be titered to see if his immunity levels were adequate. He would be given a vaccine for Kennel Cough. I had to bring a urine and fecal specimen to be analyzed. The only other item on the list was his rabies vaccine. It is mandated by law in all states, and Massachusetts requires the vaccine to be given every three years. His appointment was made for February 7.

He was in good humor when we went into the vet's office. The vet tech took us into the exam room. She took Sim's temperature, weighed him, and asked me how he was doing. Was he having any issues?

"He's pretty good, although I don't like to say that too loudly. The canned duck and potato diet seems to be keeping his tummy fairly steady." She made a couple of notes on his chart and said that the vet would be in shortly.

When the vet came in, we greeted each other warmly. I had great respect for her expertise and she, in turn, respected my training capabilities. I would refer clients to her, particularly if they had some odd symptoms that their vet couldn't seem to figure out. Her diagnostic abilities were wonderful. She often referred clients to me whose dogs had behavior problems.

One thing that I learned early on was that if a dog was not feeling well, poor behavior was a symptom. I found this to be the case about 80 percent of the time. Once the physical problems were resolved, the behavior problems often resolved as well. I never jumped to the conclusion, as some trainers do, that the dog was stubborn, lazy, stupid, or just plain bad and would try to solve the problems with that as their paradigm. I would find that the dog wasn't feeling well either while I was putting him or her through my temperament test or as I started to do exercises with them.

The vet listened to Sim's heart and poked and pressed his stomach area. "He's doing well. His stomach area is soft and he's not indicating any discomfort or pain in that area. His eyes and ears look good, and I don't see anything unusual with his skin or coat. It all looks to be in good shape."

"Would you check his anal sacs for me, please? He hasn't shown any symptoms, but you know how they sometimes get full."

She agreed and checked the sacs. They were somewhat full and needed emptying. She drew some blood and gave him his rabies shot. I asked her to fill out the required health form for his Therapy Dog renewal.

"Healthy dog," she noted. "He's really in good shape, Peg. I'll let you know about the blood work and urine culture in a few days, but I'm sure it's all fine." I thanked her, paid my bill, and left.

"Good job, Sim," I told him as we drove home. "You're a real trooper. I'm sure that the exam is not one of your favorite things, but you handled it well." He gave me a quick glance and then sat up, looking out the window. I felt relaxed. His physical had gone well. I didn't expect anything untoward to show up in his blood, urine, or fecal sample. Life was good, or so I thought.

In fewer than four days, Sim had a noticeable lack of energy. He began "night walking." I would wake up in the middle of the night to a scratching noise. Sim would be frantically scratching at the bathroom rug.

"What's the matter, Bud? Are you OK?"

I could tell from the look in his eyes that something was not only bothering him but frightening him as well. Upon waking in the morning, he would be shaking. I called the vet and reported what was happening. She said that it was bizarre but would make a note on his chart. His lack of energy and the other odd behaviors continued but seemed to lessen a bit.

The day of the show arrived. His demeanor was up and down. I took him to the show thinking that maybe when he went into the ring, it might perk him up. He would be doing exercises that he enjoyed other than the heeling, and the atmosphere should not be too stressful. "A little competition might do him some good," I told Frank.

As soon as he got into the ring, he shut down. He showed extreme stress and physical discomfort. When we left the ring, Frank and I took him outside for some fresh air. I felt terrible that I had pushed him to do something that he was physically unable to do. "I'll have to call the vet on Monday. We've got to find out what's wrong with our boy. It's obvious that something is very wrong."

As some of the symptoms subsided somewhat, others would emerge. I began seeing Sim aggressively licking his front legs and scratching his breastbone. The vet said to give him hydroxyzine for allergies. It made sense to me because we were coming into early spring. This treatment had little or no impact. He began exhibiting an odd gait and some minor tripping when he walked as well as the constant licking of his front legs. I thought that he might be developing arthritis. After all, he was over ten years old now.

It was mid-April. I called the vet about this behavior. She told me to give Sim Metacam for four days. Metacam is a non-steroidal anti-inflammatory drug. This class of drug for both humans and animals is known as NSAIDS. They are stronger than aspirin but have no steroids involved. They usually work well but can cause stomach upset and possible bleeding. They have to be used with caution. Given Sim's history, I was a bit worried but felt that the risk might be worth the reward. I was to try this for four days to see if there would be any improvement. If he was not noticeably better, I was to try it for two weeks. Then I was to discontinue it and see if the symptoms reoccurred. If his symptoms came back, Sim might have to take it on an "as needed" basis. I tried the four-day test. There were limited results. As soon as I discontinued it, Sim became depressed and the licking of his front legs increased. Because of these symptoms, I began giving him Metacam daily. He seemed better and was able to resume training but acted as though something was still bothering him.

About two weeks before the Memorial weekend Toy Show, I made an appointment with the vet. I wanted Sim to have a quick checkup to be sure that he was well enough to show. I took a sample of his urine with me because of dosing him daily with Metacam. The vet wanted to analyze it to be sure that the Metacam was not having any ill effects on his kidneys or liver. I received a call two days later that she wanted to take a sterile sample of urine. When a sterile sample is taken, a catheter is inserted into the dog and the urine is taken directly from the bladder. The reason why she wanted to do this was because Sim had an elevated white cell count. By taking a sterile sample, it rules out the fact that the sample I brought in was tainted, and he may have an infection. The sterile sample was then cultured for two days. It showed two different strains of *E. coli* bacteria.

I was quite puzzled. How did Sim get *E. coli?* He never was fed raw food. He was always walked on a leash and watched closely so that he didn't have the opportunity to pick up something that he shouldn't. The vet had no answers for me. She seemed to be as puzzled as I was. She put him on an antibiotic to clear up the infection. This was just about a week before the Toy Show. I asked if she thought he would be healthy enough to compete in the show. She thought that he would be markedly better and that I should feel comfortable taking him. He didn't seem to be tolerating the antibiotic very well. His appetite was not as good as usual, and he was showing some intestinal discomfort. However, the licking of his front legs and the scratching of his breastbone stopped.

We arrived at the Toy Show. Sim didn't seem well enough to participate. Even though I had paid the entry fees for both the Open Classes and Rally classes, I knew I had to forfeit showing him. With the way he felt, it would have been unfair, if not cruel, to ask him to do anything that would stress him. I spoke to several of the people there. When I told them what was the matter, they wholeheartedly agreed with me. One person told me, "Take him home and let him rest. That antibiotic is very strong. Maybe if you add some yogurt to his meal, it might be helpful. The antibiotic is killing all bacteria in his system, both good and bad. The yogurt will help replace the good bacteria in his intestinal tract, and that might help him to feel better and improve his appetite." I thanked her and said I would try it as soon as we got home. Poor Sim. He was so proud and dignified that you could see he kept trying to be himself but just couldn't get past the discomfort.

Three days after the antibiotic was finished, the vet wanted me to bring Sim back so that she could take another sterile urine sample and see if the *E. coli* had cleared up. The sample was sent out to be cultured. I received a call in a couple of days that the *E. coli* infection had cleared up, but there was an elevation of his protein level. The vet wanted to double-check to make sure that Sim didn't have Lyme disease. I brought Sim in to the vet's office to have blood drawn to check for Lyme. I insisted that if the Lyme test came back negative, which I thought it probably would, I wanted a complete blood panel run to see if we could find the root of Sim's problems.

As I suspected, the Lyme test came back negative, but the blood panel showed that one of his liver enzyme levels was elevated. The vet put him on a course of Ampicillin and a medication called Denosyl to help support his liver function. I was told to bring him back in a week for another blood panel to check his liver enzyme levels. The liver enzyme level had dropped somewhat but was still elevated. We discontinued the Ampicillin because it was not agreeing with him, but we continued the Denosyl for another ten days. Sim was not getting any relief, and I was beginning to become more worried.

In July, he began having bloody diarrhea. "Sim, I don't know what is going on with you, but I promise I will help you to feel better soon," I told him, giving him a hug.

I felt helpless, and I wasn't getting any answers as to why Sim was having so much trouble. The vet started him on Metronidazole for his intestinal upset. She also suggested that I make an appointment with the internist at Brookside Road Animal Hospital. I called for the appointment as soon as I got home. There was a two-week wait. My patience was beginning to wear thin. It seemed obvious to me that his decline had begun with the rabies shot.

Chapter 48

Frustration is a feeling of tension that occurs when
efforts to reach some goal are blocked.

—Anonymous

I told Frank that if things didn't start to turn around soon, I was
considering taking Sim into Boston to Angell Memorial Animal
Hospital. I had researched the facility by looking on their website
and found that they had many diagnostic tools that were not locally
available. Frank felt that I was getting too emotionally involved and
that we should let the local doctors handle the problem. I wasn't comfortable with this resolution but was so concerned about Sim that I
didn't want to get into an argument with my husband. And I didn't
know what I really wanted done at Angell. I was fairly certain that a
general workup would be very expensive and didn't want to put Sim
through unnecessary stress, undergoing a battery of tests that might
not show anything. But I knew that something was very wrong with
him. I felt as though I was trying to work my way through a maze
blindfolded.

At the appointment with the internist, I went over Sim's medical
history. My vet had also faxed his records to him as well. He advised
that he should take a blood sample and send it to a laboratory in
Texas. They specialized in certain digestive diseases. It was going to
take about a week for the results to come back. When they came
back, the report stated that Sim had "bacterial overgrowth consistent
with inflammatory bowel disease." He was put on Doxicyclene for

twenty-one days. His bowel movements had returned to normal, but Sim seemed somewhat lethargic and had low tolerance for physical activity. He also seemed to be having a lot of periodic stomach discomfort. He would get restless, sprawl on his stomach for a while. When he felt relief, he would relax and turn on his side. I called the internist to report this, and he suggested that I give Sim Pepcid. I told him that we had tried both Pepcid and Tagamet several years ago, prior to having him scoped. He had not tolerated either medication. In fact, it seemed to make his symptoms worse. The internist sounded frustrated with me and told me to call my vet and see if she had any other suggestions. When I called her and explained what was going on, she said to work with the Doxicyclene and hopefully things would straighten out. She didn't want to add any other medications because Sim was so sensitive, and she didn't want to risk putting his system out of balance any more than it was. I asked her if another blood test was necessary when we finished the antibiotic. She said she would call the internist and let me know.

The next few days, Sim seemed to show no improvement. He had bouts of upset stomach, lethargy, and began licking his front legs again. Now I was sure there was something seriously wrong. I looked in my records and found the phone number of the internist that had scoped Sim in 2003. I called her and told her what was going on. She agreed with me that the rabies vaccine could be causing the problems I was seeing because she felt he had a compromised immune system. When I asked about his immune system, she felt that the imbedded toy and the ensuing lesion had weakened it. I felt helpless.

Ever since I had gotten Sim on Halloween of 1997, I had taken good care of him. I kept trying my best to improve his health. Now it seemed that something out of my control was taking over. I still kept wondering if we should take Sim to Angell for a CAT scan, ultrasound, and possible MRI. I didn't know what exactly he needed, but I knew he needed help with something that hadn't been identified.

It was now mid-September, and Sim had been ailing since early February. He gradually seemed to be getting better but not on a consistent basis. The licking of his front legs and scratching of his breastbone continued. His energy level seemed to be improving, but he lacked stamina. Sim was used to walking about a mile on his walk, both in the morning and in the afternoon. Now, on the afternoon walk, he would start out with energy but would slowly start to show discomfort. Sometimes he would just lie down wherever he was, and I had to carry him for a distance, possibly all the way home.

I decided to call my vet again and let her know how Sim was doing. She must have been having a bad day because when I told her what was going on, she began to raise her voice in annoyance, saying that I was constantly calling her. She had no idea what was wrong with Sim, and she had done everything she felt was appropriate. Maybe I should just give it more time. I was shocked. I thought she and I had a good working relationship. Whenever I felt something was wrong with Sim, it usually was. I had always respected her professionalism and, until now, I thought that she respected mine as well. It was time to get another opinion.

This is a very important point that must be made. No matter how good a veterinarian or doctor is, they all make mistakes or don't know what other avenues to explore when the patient's symptoms make no sense to them. Just because certain tests may come back as negative, it doesn't mean that nothing is wrong. This is when we have to decide what is best for our pet. If you truly feel you have worked honestly with your vet, carefully following the protocols that have been recommended, and your pet still does not show improvement, then it's time for a second opinion. It doesn't mean that the person you have been working with is not good; it merely means that another set of eyes might pick up something that has been overlooked.

I was very upset when I hung up the phone. I picked Sim up and set him on my lap and gave him a hug. I could see in his eyes that he wasn't feeling very well. "Sim, it's time to have someone else take a look at you. Let's see what I can come up with." He looked at me and swallowed. I saw a little of the old spark in his eyes. It was as though he understood how hard I was trying to help him.

The next day, I was speaking with my friend, Sue. She had been checking in to see how Sim was doing. When I told her what happened with the vet, she suggested that I call her vet, Dr. Crouser, at Brookside Road Animal Hospital. He was one of the original founders of the practice. She said that he had a special interest in older dogs. He was very caring and very thorough. She had been a client of his for about twenty-five years and had great faith in him. Sue said that I should make an appointment with Dr. Crouser as soon as possible.

I called Brookside Road Animal Hospital to make an appointment with Dr. Crouser. He spoke with me and said that he would be glad to give me a second opinion. He said that he would be getting Sim's records from the other vet so that he could look everything over and see if he could figure anything out from his history.

"Well, Sim, I'm taking you to a new vet in a couple of days. His name is Dr. Crouser, and he is supposed to be very good. I hope that he can help you to feel better. We've got to start peeling the onion again, Bud." He looked at me with trust in his eyes. It was almost as if he was saying, "If you say so, Mom."

The trust in his expression was very evident. After all this time and all the trials and tribulations we had been through, he finally was coming to me instead of going away from me in his time of need. I wasn't happy with the circumstances of this breakthrough, but I was pleased that we had reached this point of real trust in our relationship.

Just before my appointment with Dr. Crouser, I decided to do some research myself. Sim's problems seemed to occur right after he had been given the rabies vaccine. With the good care that he got, it made no sense to me that he would develop a double *E. coli* infection. We always wiped him down after a walk, whether he peed, pooped, or both. We also wiped his paws because of pollen in the spring, summer, and fall, and because of any salt and/or sand that might have been used during the winter. He was never fed any raw meat, and I was very particular about his treats. I did not allow him to have any rawhide chews, hooves, or pig's ears. He was groomed on a regular basis, and in between formal groomings, he was combed and brushed almost every other day. If necessary, I used a waterless shampoo to freshen him up.

The *E. coli* infection was quite a puzzle to me. I started to do some research on the Internet. I am always very careful about the sites I look at because there is a lot of misinformation as well as good information on the Internet. There are many different opinions on a vast variety of subjects. I trust the professional sites as opposed to chat rooms, where much of the information is merely hearsay.

I typed in "Adverse Side Effects to Rabies Vaccination in Canines." Several informative sites came up. I was surprised to learn from these sites that *E. coli* is in the rabies vaccine. The bacteria is sterilized or purified. Then a certain portion of the purified material is added to the "killed" or modified rabies vaccine when a rabies vaccine is processed. This helps to propagate the virus and stimulate the immune response of the animal to the vaccine. I couldn't believe my eyes. I wasn't sure but certainly thought that it was a strong possibility that this was how Sim was exposed to the *E. coli*. I added this information to my notes that I had written to go over with Dr. Crouser during Sim's visit.

As I drove Sim to his appointment with Dr. Crouser, I carefully thought over how I was going to handle the situation. My first concern was to get Sim better. Being a displaced New Yorker, when I am trying to resolve a situation, I can admittedly be a bit pushy. I had never met Dr. Crouser even though I rented space at Brookside Road Animal Hospital on Sundays for my training classes. Obviously, that was one of his days off and our paths had never crossed. I didn't want him to think that I was being disrespectful in any way. I was taking Sim to him because I valued his opinion. However, I was very concerned with Sim's condition. His health was not what it should be. Sometimes he appeared to be on the upswing, and then he would regress again. I knew Sim so well that I could "read" the subtle signs and knew when he didn't feel well, even if it wasn't clearly evident to anyone else.

As I parked the car, I had rehearsed how I was going to interact and get all my questions asked without being abrasive. When I got Sim out of the car, he seemed pretty comfortable, sniffed, and marked a few places. While we sat waiting, Sim looked at the other dog that was there and sniffed at a crate that held a cat. He seemed relaxed and quickly charmed the other clients.

Kelly, Dr. Crouser's technician, came over to us. We followed her to the scale. Sim dutifully stood on the scale and then sat.

"What a good boy," she said. "That was the easiest weigh-in I've done in a long time." We followed her into the exam room. She took Sim's temperature, which was normal. She then asked me a few questions as to what was going on with him. I explained that I was there to get a second opinion from Dr. Crouser and that he had the other vet send him Sim's records. She said that Dr. Crouser would be with us in a few minutes. I sat on the bench and looked at Sim as he explored the room. He was interested in all the different scents, but I could see that he was not feeling completely well, tripping slightly as he explored the area. *Maybe I'm just worrying too much*, I thought. *Maybe I'm so attached to him that the slightest little bit of discomfort that he may show becomes exaggerated to me.*

With that, Dr. Crouser walked in. He was a trim, nicely dressed man of medium build. When he greeted me, he spoke with a deep, rich baritone voice. He had a thick shock of dark hair, a well-trimmed mustache, and glasses that magnified twinkling eyes. Immediately, I felt at ease with him.

"Hello, Mrs. Lovelock." He shook my hand with a firm grasp.

"Hi, Mr. Sims," he said as he squatted down to pet him.

Sim responded with a wagging tail and bright eyes. He allowed Dr. Crouser to examine him on the floor. Then we put him up on the exam table. Dr. Crouser talked to Sim as he checked his teeth, eyes, and ears. As he ran his large hands gently over Sim from head to tail, he said how he had reviewed Sim's chart. We discussed his up and down appetite and digestive upsets. I told him that Sim was eating a canned duck and potato diet, and I showed him the label so he could see the ingredients. He felt that it was a good diet, and if Sim did all right with it most of the time, then he didn't want to change anything right now. He said he was going to take some blood to check a few things. He showed me where Sim had a bit of a yeast infection in his left ear. Dr. Crouser took samples from each of Sim's ears and put it on a glass slide.

"Give me a minute. I want to get a good look at what's in his ear, but I'm pretty sure it's yeast."

When he returned, he confirmed the yeast infection and had a tube of medication. "I'll show you how to apply this medication to Mr. Sim's ears, and I'd like you to treat him with it once a day." He said that he felt Sim was basically healthy, particularly for a dog that was almost eleven years old, but would let me know if anything showed up in the blood work.

"I'll call you as soon as I get the results." Dr. Crouser shook my hand again as I left. I could tell that he already had a special interest in Sim. It was difficult, but I was able to hide my sense of urgency.

As I drove home, I talked to Sim. "Well, Bud, I did pretty well. I really wanted to hammer home my concern and push Dr. Crouser to do every test that would be appropriate to find out why you're not feeling up to par. I didn't because I like him, and I didn't want him to dismiss us and send us back to the other vet. At least not until we get to the bottom of what is bothering you, and maybe not at all." Sim sat next to me, looking at me intently instead of looking out the car window. "I hope that he will take us on a permanent basis. I feel confident in his expertise. I will just have to be patient and let him get to know you. When he does get to know you well, he will see what I see and just maybe he will know what to do to treat you."

Sim looked at me, swallowed, and settled down in the passenger seat. I know he didn't understand what I was saying, but I'm sure he sensed my concern and love for him. I pulled into the garage and lifted Sim out of the car. He seemed happy to be home. We went in, and I sat in the antique rocking chair that was in the family room. I scooped Sim into my lap. "I know you're getting up there, Bud, but aren't we all? When I look at you now, I see a large timer with the grains of sand running down to the bottom. They are beginning to move at a moderate rate, just a bit quicker than a year ago. You still have a whole lot of sand left, though, and I will do whatever I can to keep things moving slowly."

I gave him a big hug and wiped the tears from my eyes. Sim gave me one of his comforting kisses and jumped off my lap. He ran over to his toy box, carefully searching for a specific toy. He pulled different toys out and scattered them around the room. He was definitely looking for just the right toy. His head disappeared into the toy box again. His tail began to wag, and he came up with the toy that looked like smiling lips. The way he held the toy in his mouth made the lips look like they were part of him. He began squeaking the toy loudly and looking at me. I started to laugh. As soon as I did, Sim began running around with the "Catch me if you can" attitude.

"You're too much, Bud. I think you're letting me know that we're in this together and we're not giving up without one heck of a fight." He dropped the toy and gave me a couple of his little sneezes. "I take that as a 'yes.' I will do whatever it takes, for however long it takes until you let me know that we've exhausted every possibility." Sim ran into the kitchen and went to his dish. "OK. Enough of this serious stuff. I'll make your dinner. What do you think, Bud?" He looked at me and then trained his gaze on the refrigerator. I got his dinner ready and fed him. *All's well with the world for now*, I thought.

That was very short-lived. The phone rang, and it was my neighbor, Nancy.

"I have some bad news and I need your help," she said. "It seems that Jamie has gone blind. We began noticing that something was wrong with her when she stopped being able to catch popcorn. We usually have a bowl of popcorn at night when we watch TV. The dogs sit in front of us, anxiously waiting for the game to begin. Jamie was always better and faster than Bailey. But lately, she hasn't caught one piece. I took her to the vet and she confirmed my suspicions. Can you help me to train her so that she can cope with her condition?"

"I'm so sorry to hear that, Nancy. Let me think it over and look up some information and then I'll get back to you."

I was trying to stay upbeat in the face of Sim's problems, but this news felt like a huge weight on my shoulders. I had been close to Jamie and Bailey from the time they were little puppies. It didn't seem possible that they were now ten years old and age was beginning to take its toll on them as well. They were the reason I now had my dog training business.

I referred to a couple of my training books. The information that I found was limited, so I went to veterinary websites to see what I could find. I ordered a couple of books that looked to be helpful. They arrived within a few days.

I called Nancy and told her that as soon as the books came in and I had a chance to study them, I would try some of the methods with Jamie. In the meantime, I told her that I would come over and look to see what environmental changes would have to be made. I was concerned about Jamie's safety. Nancy had an in-ground pool in her backyard. I instinctively knew that the area had to be secured so that Jamie would not wander into it and fall into the pool.

Nancy met me at the front door, along with Jamie and Bailey. They both greeted me enthusiastically. I took a close look at Jamie.

"If you hadn't told me that she was blind, I would never believe it, Nancy."

"I know. She has no cloudiness or anything that would even give any indication that she can't see. And she looks right at me, or so it seems."

I kept my feelings in check. I was very sad to see this once bouncy, independent animal now disabled.

"Well, let's get to work. I have a couple of ideas. First of all, I think we should put a bell on Bailey so that Jamie can follow her by hearing where she is. Bailey has always been the one with the strong maternal instinct from the time they were pups. She has always looked out for Jamie. I think she will step up and help Jamie. The next important order of business is to be sure that you don't move any furniture. Jamie still has a picture in her head as to where everything is. I know you probably think you should move things out of her way, but this will only serve to confuse her."

"Really," Nancy said. "That surprises me. I'm glad you told me because I was getting ready to move everything so that she wouldn't bump into anything."

"Is she having any problems with that now?" I asked.

"Now that you mention it, no. She seems to be able to get around the house just fine."

I wanted to take a good look at the pool to try to figure out the best way to secure it for Jamie. I looked at the path that the dogs always took. They went down four steps from the family room to the patio. If they turned to the right, they would go into the lawn area. If they went straight ahead, they would be headed for the pool.

"I think we have to come up with some sort of barricade at the bottom of the steps so that both dogs can't head toward the pool. We'll have to set it up in such a way that they can only go to the right."

"I'll have to think that one over. What do you think about blocking it off with a baby gate?"

"Good idea, Nance. You may have to buy a few of them to not only block off the pool area but also set them up so that Jamie and Bailey will be directed to the yard area."

I looked over the books when they arrived. They were helpful but very general. The most important idea that I learned from both of them was that I had to teach Jamie commands that would keep her safe. She would have to learn what the words "right turn" and "careful" meant. I called Nancy to tell her I was on my way over. I grabbed a bunch of hotdogs and headed next door.

"OK, Nance. It may sound crazy, but I'm going to teach you how to teach Jamie some words so that it will help her to navigate the backyard safely."

Nancy began to chuckle. "This is going to be very interesting," she said.

"You can do it, Nance. You're a teacher, remember?"

"Yes. But you're the one that speaks dog."

"Not really. And this is all new territory for me. I just hope I can make this work."

I put Jamie's leash on her and guided her to the family room sliding door. I opened it and told her to wait. I reached into my pocket for a piece of hotdog and let her sniff it. Holding the hotdog in front of her nose, I began walking her down each step, counting out loud as I did.

"One, two, three, four. Good girl, Jamie. Let's go back in now. Up, one, two, three, four."

I did this several times with her. She seemed to be getting the idea. As she got more confident with it, I used the word *careful* before going down the stairs. Jamie seemed to be enjoying the work, but I could tell she was getting tired. It wasn't the physical exertion that was tiring her; it was the mental gymnastics that she had to do.

"That's it for today, Nance. I think we've made some progress. Just keep practicing. She's getting it, and you seem to be picking it up as well. I'll come back tomorrow and we'll start working on teaching her about the right turn. I think that should go fairly well because she will be following Bailey. My main concern was that she could get up and down the stairs safely. I'll leave the books with you so you'll have them to refer to."

"This session has been terrific. How much do I owe you, Peg?"

"Don't be silly. I'm learning and getting experience. I just feel badly that Jamie has this problem."

In a matter of about two weeks, Jamie was able to safely navigate the backyard area. Bailey was always at her side, acting as her eyes and being sure that Jamie didn't get into any dangerous situations.

Once again, I had the pleasant feeling that all was well with the world for a while.

Chapter 49

A friend is one who joyfully sings with you
when you are on the mountain top and silently
walks beside you through the valley.

—William A. Ward

The day after our visit with Dr. Crouser, he called me and said that Sim's blood work looked good, nothing at all remarkable. He said to call him next week to let him know how Sim was doing. *Good*, I thought. *Sim will become one of his patients.*

I kept a close eye on Sim. He still was up and down, some days being playful, working well, and having a lot of energy. Other days he would be lethargic, and his appetite would wax and wane. Morning seemed to be his worst time of day. He sometimes would tremble a little bit when he first woke up. It was becoming more frequent than I was comfortable with. His appetite in the morning also became hit or miss. Sometimes he would readily eat up his breakfast; other times he didn't want to eat until later in the day.

I added the slightest bit of vegetables to Sim's meals. He seemed to enjoy them, and his system seemed to tolerate them. He still was not making any progress, however. Again, he had his good days and bad days, but the good days were not as good as they had been. After a while, his stomach upsets became more frequent. I discontinued the vegetables to see if they were beginning to go against him. There didn't seem to be much of a difference. I called Dr. Crouser to let him know how things were. He said to make an appointment because he thought he should take a look at "Simmy." Even though I was worried, I had to smile at the nickname Dr. Crouser had given Sim.

Dr. Crouser could see that I was very concerned. He examined Sim, especially around his stomach area. He said that it was soft and pliable. He thought that it was Sim's allergies flaring.

"Why don't we try a different medication for his allergies? Maybe he's becoming resistant to the hydroxyzine. Let's try Chlor-Trimeton. Let's get the allergies under control and see if that doesn't make him feel better."

I was always a bit nervous trying a new medication but knew that I had to give this a try. I took Sim home.

"I'll be right back. You wait and guard the house for me, Sim. I'm going to get you some new medicine for your allergies." He stood by the door and watched me leave, as he almost always did. This time, however, Sim had a look of worry. I noted that, and felt a twinge of sadness for him.

As soon as I got back, I gave him a dose as per Dr. Crouser's instructions. No sooner did Sim swallow the pill, than it came right back up. I looked at him.

"Sim, I never saw anything come up so fast in all my life." I was now worried about the medication. "Let me call Dr. Crouser and see what he has to say." I called the animal hospital. Dr. Crouser had left, but his assistant suggested that I give Sim half a tablet and see what happens.

I decided to wait until the next day. This way, if Sim had a problem with it again, Dr. Crouser would be there to answer my questions. I fed him his dinner, which he ate up for me. After he ate, he seemed a bit restless but eventually seemed to be able to rest. I thought it probably was from the pill upsetting his system.

The next day, I tried half a tablet of the antihistamine. This time it stayed down a bit longer, but then Sim began to wretch and the pill came up.

"Guess this isn't working for you, Bud. I'll call Dr. Crouser and let him know what's up."

I called and left him a message. In the meantime, Sim seemed restless again and couldn't find a comfortable spot for quite a while.

I was getting more and more concerned. When Dr. Crouser called, I told him what was going on. He said to stop the Chlor-Trimeton for now. He seemed a bit puzzled about how Sim whoopsed up the first tablet so quickly.

"Call me in a few days and let me know how he's doing."

"Well, Sim, we're peeling the onion again. I'm doing the best that I know how for you, Bud."

He looked at me, and I could see the stress beginning to show on his face and in his eyes. I also could feel the frustration building in me.

"Damn, I just want to make him feel better. Why is it this difficult?"

However, what I was quickly learning was that even though I had great respect for Dr. Crouser, I knew my dog better than anyone. When his discomfort was obvious to me, it wasn't necessarily as obvious to anyone else. I realized that I had to manage Sim's medical care as well as the relationship I had with his attending vets. They are the "experts," but I was the only person who could point out Sim's oddities, medications, or treatments that disagreed with him, and his expressions that told me very clearly whether he was feeling good or feeling poorly. His communication with me might be very subtle, but I knew all his expressions and what they meant. When he felt well, there was a look in his eyes that was soft and happy, without any stress. When he had the slightest bit of discomfort, the look in his eyes would change, and I could see, even if it was ever so slight, the worry, stress, and even fear begin to build in his expression.

After breakfast the following day, Sim whoopsed up. It came up very easily with no retching at all. I was confused. This was unusual because I had seen dogs get sick to their stomach, but it was always preceded by retching, meaning that they work their stomach to get the contents up. Sim acted as though something was wrong. He kept lying down, then moving, and then lying down again, sprawling on his stomach. His discomfort was very evident.

I called Dr. Crouser and left a message. He got back to me and said that since Sim was showing symptoms, to come right over so he could see what was happening. I picked Sim up and put him in the car. He stayed on his stomach and was shaking all the way to the vet's. I tried to talk to him to help him relax, but he really was in a bad state. We pulled into the parking lot. I parked the car and ran around to the passenger side to carry him out of the car. When I opened the car door, he was standing up, bright-eyed, wagging his tail.

"What's going on, Sim? You were a basket case all the way here, and now you look fine."

I put him on the ground, and he trotted along, sniffing and marking, as usual. We walked into the exam room and waited for Dr. Crouser. When he walked in, Sim jauntily walked over to him and gave him a happy greeting.

"I don't get it. He was awful at home, and as soon as we got here, he miraculously recovered. I wouldn't make up a story, Dr. Crouser. I can't believe the difference in him."

"Well," Dr. Crouser said, "let's take him outside and walk him in the parking lot. I want to see if anything appears to be sore."

We took him out, and I began walking him, then running with him with Dr. Crouser directing me. Sim moved without any sign of discomfort. I could feel my face getting red with embarrassment. I stopped, and Dr. Crouser came up to me, trying to hide a smile, but I could clearly see the twinkle in his eyes.

"He looks fine to me," he said.

"I know. I can't get over it," I told him. With that, Sim went over to a telephone pole that was on a steep incline. He lifted his leg so high that he was just about standing on his head.

"Doesn't seem to have any mobility problems," Dr. Crouser said, his dry sense of humor in full gear.

"I'm sorry that we took up your time, and I really appreciate it. But something was very wrong earlier."

"That's OK. Just keep me posted if he acts that way again."

All the way home, Sim was sitting up, happily watching the scenery go by. "I'm glad you're feeling so much better, Bud, but I just hope that Dr. Crouser doesn't think I'm nuts and I'm the one with the problem, not you. He may start thinking that I'm a Munchausen Mom." Sim looked at me and swallowed, having no idea what I was referring to. "You know, Sim. Women who deliberately make their child ill and then take them to the doctor acting as if they have no idea what is wrong. It's just done to get attention for themselves. Sim looked at me again and swallowed. "It's OK, Bud. I understand what I'm talking about. I just hope that Dr. Crouser has gotten to know me well enough to understand that I'm really very concerned about you."

When Frank got home, I told him what had happened. He laughed heartily.

"I know it's a very funny story now, but not when it was happening to me," I told him.

"You worry about Sim too much. Dr. Crouser is probably right that it's just his allergies kicking up. He'll be fine." Frank sounded confident in his appraisal of the situation. I, on the other hand, was worried sick. I surely wanted Sim to get better, but I didn't want to lose my credibility with Dr. Crouser. We had no explanation for Sim's distress, so it probably was going to recur.

I was calling Dr. Crouser almost on a daily basis. Sim's health was declining, and he was having more frequent stomach upset. He had another episode of appearing to be in great distress. Dr. Crouser again said to bring him right in. I raced him over to the vet's office. He was, again, lying on his stomach next to me, shaking all the way. However, when I parked the car, we had an exact rerun of the last visit. He seemed to recover and act as though nothing was wrong. Dr. Crouser examined him thoroughly again and found nothing. Once more, I was a bit embarrassed and puzzled as to what was going on. Dr. Crouser remained patient and just told me to keep in touch.

A few days later, on Friday, Sim would not eat or drink anything. He was very lethargic and restless. I waited for as long as I could stand to wait before calling Dr. Crouser. I finally called him late in the afternoon. He told me to bring him in. This time, he did perk up a little when we got there, but it was quite different from the last two visits.

As soon as Dr. Crouser saw Sim, he could tell there was a difference. He thoroughly examined him, paying particular attention to his stomach area. He said it felt soft and pliable, and Sim gave no indication of discomfort in that area. Both Dr. Crouser and I were a bit perplexed.

"Dr. Crouser, would you mind doing two things before we leave? I have found that sometimes Sim will have one of these episodes after lying on his back and getting a tummy rub."

"Sure," Dr. Crouser said. We got Sim to roll on his back on the exam table. Dr. Crouser gave him a good tummy rub and then let him turn over. Nothing unusual happened.

"He hasn't eaten anything all day. Would you mind giving him a treat?"

Dr. Crouser was more than willing to oblige me. I reached in my pocket and took out a piece of hot dog. He decided that he wanted to give something completely different than what he was used to. This was to see if he would take something that might be a bit more interesting. Dr. Crouser placed a small dog cookie on the floor, about three feet away from Sim. He told me to let him go to the treat. Sim headed toward it enthusiastically, and then, for no apparent reason, his legs went out from under him. He was sprawled on his tummy, licking his lips as though he was very nauseous.

"Oh!" Dr. Crouser said. "I'll be right back."

He left the room for a very short time.

When he returned, he had two different types of treats. He made two piles on the floor and then told me to send Sim to the first pile. As before, Sim started for the pile of treats and then collapsed, acting very nauseous. I heard Dr. Crouser heave a heavy sign.

"Send him to the other pile. Let's see what happens." The result was exactly the same as the first two times. Dr. Crouser looked concerned. "Let's put him on some Carafate to soothe his stomach. Call me on Monday and let me know how he did over the weekend."

"Now you're beginning to see a little of what I've been seeing. I hope this helps to give us some answers."

Dr. Crouser gave me a reassuring pat on the arm. "I'm going to be very interested in how he is over the next few days. We may have to do a barium study to see what's going on. Do you think Santa could bring Simmy a raised food dish? I think it might help his digestion."

"I will order one for him as soon as I get home. Is there anything in particular that I should look for?"

"Just be sure that you can adjust it. The dish should come just under his chin." Dr. Crouser took his hand and made an imaginary line on Sim's neck."

"OK, Dr. Crouser. As far as Monday is concerned, you have my permission to do whatever it takes. If that means an ultrasound, x-rays, or any other diagnostic test, I'm fine with it."

Sim seemed to respond positively to the first couple of doses of the Carafate. I thought we were on to something. However, by Saturday evening, he appeared to be backsliding. When I called Dr. Crouser on Monday and told him how things were going, he said he wanted to schedule Sim for the barium study the next day. I was somewhat relieved. I was hoping that maybe we were going to get to the "center of the onion" for Sim. Maybe, just maybe, this time we would get some answers and give him some long-term relief.

His appointment was set for 8:00 a.m. As I drove him to the hospital, I told him to be a good boy for Dr. Crouser. Whatever they did to him was to get to the bottom of what was bothering him. Sim looked at me and swallowed. He put his head on the console between us. "It's going to be fine, Bud. I really hope that Dr. Crouser finds something wrong with you that he can fix, but nothing that's too serious."

We pulled into the parking space, and I got out and lifted Sim out of the passenger seat. He walked along, sniffing where other dogs had been but seemed a bit more reserved today. When I got to the desk, the receptionist called for Dr. Crouser. It wasn't very long before he came out. He gave me a cheerful "Good morning" and asked how "Simmy" was doing. I told him that he seemed a bit more reserved today.

"Don't worry, Mrs. Lovelock, we'll take good care of him while he's here."

"I know, Dr. Crouser. I just hope we get to the bottom of what's bothering him."

"I'll call you as soon as I know something."

"Great. I'll be home waiting."

Dr. Crouser took Sim's leash, and the two of them walked to the doorway that led to the testing area. Sim was trotting next to Dr. Crouser as though he thoroughly trusted him. And I could see that Dr. Crouser was particularly attached to Sim. I swallowed the lump in my throat because it was such a touching scene. "He's going to be fine," I told myself. "He couldn't be in better, more caring hands."

Even though I kept busy, the morning dragged on. I kept looking at the clock every ten minutes. As it drew closer to noon, I began to feel a bit worried. The phone rang, and I jumped.

"Hello," I said, hoping it was Dr. Crouser.

"Mrs. Lovelock, Dr. Crouser. Simmy's doing well although he doesn't like the barium, and it's been a bit of a struggle to get him to drink it. I took some pictures, and there appears to be a foreign object in his intestines." I had to catch my breath for a minute.

"I don't understand, Dr. Crouser. Sim hasn't gotten into anything that I know of, and all his toys are in great condition."

"Well, I'm going to show the x-rays to Dr. Houghton. Simmy will be here for a while longer. I'll call you when I finish."

"Thanks, Dr. Crouser. Talk to you later."

On one hand, I felt upset. On the other hand, I felt relieved that he had found something. It was a mystery as to what he had found because Sim was always leash-walked, and we made sure that he didn't pick up anything he shouldn't. He had a houseful of toys because he never destroyed anything that was given to him. I was 99 percent sure that he didn't have a "foreign object" lodged in his gut again. But what could it be? I was at a total loss.

I called Frank and gave him the news. He was as puzzled as I was.

"We'll just have to wait until Dr. Crouser calls back. I'll call you when I get more information."

If the morning went slowly, the afternoon went even more slowly. It was about a week before Christmas, so I had plenty to keep me busy. I wrapped gifts, did some finishing touches on my decorating, and took several phone calls from friends who wondered what we had found out about Sim. I told everyone that I would call them back later when I got some news.

It was after 5:00 p.m., and I still hadn't heard anything. I was getting worried. What could be taking so long?

At 5:45 p.m., the phone rang. It was Dr. Crouser. He asked me if both Frank and I could come in to go over the results of what he found. My heart sank to my shoes, but I didn't want to ask him anything over the phone. If it was very bad news, I wanted to hear it face-to-face with him. I called Frank and told him that I was on my way to have a consult with Dr. Crouser and that he wanted him there as well.

"What do you think is going on, Peg?"

"I have no idea. I'm very worried about that foreign object Dr. Crouser talked about earlier."

As I was driving, all sorts of things were going through my mind, from best case scenario to worst case scenario. I also was saying some prayers both for Sim and for me, that I would be able to handle or make the right decision for him once I heard the results of his test. I pulled into the parking spot and got out of the car. Frank pulled into the space next to me.

"Great timing," I said.

We held hands and went into the hospital. The receptionist called for Dr. Crouser. He ushered us into an exam room.

"Simmy really didn't like the barium at all. He's being cleaned up now, and I'll get him for you as soon as we go over the x-rays."

Frank and I both laughed nervously. Dr. Crouser turned the lights out and began putting the first x-ray up on the lighted screen so we could see it.

"This is when the barium began traveling to his stomach. As you can see, everything looks fine. I also timed the motility as the barium moved along at a normal rate." He took down that x-ray and put another one up on the screen. "This is when the barium began entering the stomach. So far, so good."

Frank was looking intently as Dr. Crouser described in detail what was going on. I, on the other hand, was ready to jump out of my skin. I just wanted him to get to what the problem was.

This is like watching a neighbor's slide show of his recent Alaskan Cruise, I thought. *First, we get on the ship, see? Now we're waving as the ship leaves the dock.* I was getting edgier by the minute. *I've got to focus on what he's telling us. He's only being very thorough, so I must be patient.*

"Now, on this film, I saw the problem. See this dark area right here?" Dr. Crouser said, pointing to a spot just below Sim's stomach. "After I spoke with you, I took this x-ray to Dr. Houghton and asked him to take a look at it to get his opinion. He told me to take a few different angles of it to see if we could figure out what it was. What we have concluded is that it is an intussusception. This part of Simmy's intestine is being pushed into the other part of his intestine, much like a collapsing telescope."

He took a piece of paper and pen and drew a diagram for us so that we could better understand what was happening. He opened the drawer of the cabinet in the room and took out a thin piece of vinyl tubing. He tried to demonstrate what a collapsing intestine might look like.

"He's going to need surgery. Depending on Dr. Houghton's schedule, hopefully we can get it done this week. We won't know until we get in there whether or not some of Simmy's intestines will have to be removed. I'm hoping that Dr. Houghton can just stitch back the collapsed portion. It will be easier on Sim and make the recovery quicker without the complications that could occur if we have to remove anything."

My head was spinning. "How does something like this happen?"

Dr. Crouser said, "Honestly, it's hard to say. Some dogs with inflammatory bowel disease develop this. Whatever the case, it explains why he looked so bad at home and by the time you got him here he seemed fine. The intestine would collapse on itself and then release. It's good that we found it now. At some point, the intestine would have telescoped and not released. Infection would then have set in very, very quickly and we would have lost him."

Frank rubbed my back a little. I think both he and Dr. Crouser could see the strain on my face.

"I'm so glad we have an answer and the problem is fixable."

Dr. Crouser smiled. "We'll do our best. Call Dr. Houghton's office tomorrow. In the meantime, I'll consult with him. You could wait until after Christmas if you want, but I would get it done as soon as possible."

"As soon as Dr. Houghton can give me a date, I'll have him taken care of," I said.

"Let me go get Simmy. He has no restrictions until you speak with Dr. Houghton. He'll give you pre-op instructions. Do either of you have any other questions?"

"One thing, Dr. Crouser. If Sim has a bowel movement tonight, will it glow in the dark?" Frank asked.

I rolled my eyes while we all laughed. Leave it to Frank to come up with some humor to break the tension.

"I don't think so," Dr. Crouser said with his eye twinkling. "But it may be very light in color and look like chalk as he gets rid of the barium."

I called Dr. Houghton the next morning. He was in surgery, so I left a message with his secretary.

"Here we go again, Sim. Hurry up and wait."

A short time later, Dr. Houghton called me back. "We'll schedule him for Friday morning. I won't know until I can see what's going on if I'll have to remove part of his bowel. I'm hoping I can just tack both sides where the intussusception is. It will make the recovery easier. It won't be as traumatic to his system. Don't worry. He's going to be fine. It's a good thing we found it now. If we hadn't, we could have lost him."

"That's what Dr. Crouser told me. I'm thankful that we've had this outcome," I told him. "I have a question for you. Sim has not been healthy since he got his rabies vaccine in February. Could this be caused by that shot because of his compromised immune system?"

"Sounds reasonable to me," Dr. Houghton answered.

"Thanks, Dr. Houghton. We'll see you in the morning." I hung up the phone and felt a combination of relief that the problem was going to be addressed but worried about the whole idea of putting Sim through the surgery.

"Come here, Bud. I have to tell you what's going on."

Sim came over to me and I picked him up and set him on my lap. I let him find what the most comfortable position for him was.

He snuggled into the crook of my arm, as though he was sitting up like a person. He looked at me as though he knew we had something serious to discuss. "This is what's up, Bud. You have something in your intestines that has to be repaired. It's what has been making you feel so bad and have pain sometimes. Dr. Houghton is going to unzip you and take care of your problem."

I took my finger and traced a line from the bottom of his ribcage into his groin area. He watched me intently and swallowed. "You and I will have matching scars, Bud." I gave him a hug. "I'm worried, but I trust Dr. Houghton and Dr. Crouser. They will do everything for you. You will be there for a few days, but Frank and I will come and visit you as soon as we get permission. And Christmas will be here in a few days. Having you back home will make it very special." He snuggled his head under my chin and gave me one of his little kisses. It was if he was trying to tell me he really didn't understand what I was talking about, but he would go along with whatever it was because he trusted me.

Friday had to be one of the longest days of my life. I kept thinking about Sim, praying that everything would go smoothly. Late in the day, Dr. Houghton called.

"The surgery went well. I was able to just tack the intestine on each side to hold it in place. I also did an exploratory while I was in there and took quite a few biopsies. Nothing looked suspicious, but I just wanted to be cautious. However, I found where his spleen had sustained a trauma as though he had been hit by a car."

I felt as though I had the wind totally knocked out of me.

"Not on my watch, Dr. Houghton. Sim is a trained obedience and therapy dog. He never is walked without being on a leash. The only time he is free is in our backyard and that is fully fenced in. He has never gotten away from us. When I got him, I had his records sent to your hospital so that they would be available when he had his wellness exam. There was nothing unusual in his records, just neutering and usual vaccinations. There was nothing that indicated that he had any emergency treatment for a ruptured spleen. I took him because his owner no longer wanted him. I knew from some of the things she told me that he was in an abusive relationship, but I never dreamed that it was this bad."

Dr. Houghton said, "He's a tough little guy and was very lucky to become part of your family. I was able to tell that his spleen had been ruptured when he was very young because of the amount of scar tissue."

"My gosh," I said. "He must have been in agony when this happened. How could he survive this without medical intervention?"

Dr. Houghton let out a heavy sigh. "He certainly was in agony. When the spleen is ruptured, the stomach fills with blood. It's amazing that he survived. Because there was no treatment noted in his chart, my best guess is that he was either thrown against a heavy piece of furniture, thrown down a flight of stairs, or cornered and kicked. It's like 'beaten woman syndrome.' A woman might seek treatment but will not say that she was beaten. She would offer a different reason for her bruises such as falling or bumping into a door. What could Sim's previous owner have told a vet when asked? It would have been fairly obvious how he sustained the injury. But that's in the past. I can't give you a prognosis until the biopsies come back. I want him to stay here for a few days. I'll call you tomorrow with an update on his condition, and if all goes well, he may be able to go home on Sunday."

"Thanks, Dr. Houghton. By the way, I left portions of his food when I dropped him off. He's on a restricted duck and potato diet. However, I found that when all else fails, he will eat a scrambled egg, so I left a container of egg with his other food."

"OK. I'll remind the girls. He won't be eating anything today, though. He'll be doing a lot of sleeping. We have him on a lot of pain medicine."

As soon as I hung up the phone, the tears welled up in my eyes. I just couldn't imagine anyone mistreating any animal to that extent. And Sim was such an intelligent, loving dog that it broke my heart to think that he had gone through such hell. *The longer I have him, the longer it appears that it was destiny*, I thought to myself.

I filled Frank in on the conversation when he got home from work. He was as shocked and angry as I was, but we were very, very thankful that Sim had come through the surgery and appeared to be doing as well as could be expected. Frank was concerned about the biopsies and not knowing fully what was going on. I told him that we would hear from Dr. Houghton as soon as he got the results. The most important thing now is Sim's post-operative care.

"I'm a little nervous about taking care of him. He's been through so much I just want to keep him as comfortable as I can."

"Don't worry, Peg. You've done a great job so far. And if it wasn't for your persistence, he still would have a serious problem. You'll just know what to do when he comes home."

"Well, I'm sure that there will be all kinds of instructions for me to follow. I'm hoping that none of the medications he has to take go against him because his system is so sensitive."

"I sure hope we can visit tomorrow. I miss the little guy already, and he's only been gone for a few hours. It's incredible how much a part of our life he has become."

"I don't even want to think of what it would be like without him."

We ate dinner, reminiscing about Sim and some of the funny things he had done in the time we had him. We also talked about his ups and downs in the obedience ring. "He's certainly made life interesting. He's also kept me on my toes. Or should I say, Sim has increased my knowledge because of his way of learning things and how I had to figure out the best way to work with him. Then given his physical problems and sensitivities, I've had to learn about nutrition on an advanced level, and the side effects of a lot of medications. Sim has truly been my mentor."

"He sure has," Frank agreed, "and he's also taught me a thing or two. It's a very humbling experience working with him in the Rally ring. Just when you think everything is going to go along smoothly, he throws you a curve. But once we figure out what happened, it makes perfect sense." I smiled at Frank's musings.

"Been there, done that," I told him. We both laughed, which helped to break the anxiety that we were feeling.

As soon as I got up on Saturday after a rather less than restful night, I called to check on Sim. I was told that he was doing well but still hadn't eaten. They were trying different things to entice him and get his appetite going, but to no avail.

When I hung up the phone, I said to Frank, "When we leave Mass, I want to go to the supermarket. I think I should pick up some Pedia-sure for Sim. It comes in vanilla flavor, and I can put it in a syringe if he doesn't lap it up for me."

"Do you think he'll like it? And there's nothing in it that should upset his stomach, is there?" Frank's tone was a bit sharp and edgy. He was as concerned as I was, and I wasn't as amiable as I usually am. I knew that I had to compose myself before answering because I didn't want to sound annoyed.

"Well, we'll see. Maybe he won't like it, but it's for babies, so it should be safe. And I like the idea that it is fortified with vitamins. I just think that if we can prime the pump and get his appetite going, he'll take care of the rest."

"Oh, I see. Let's try it. Your instincts are usually right on the money with Sim."

"After dinner, we'll go see him. Maybe seeing us will relax him enough to eat."

I had purchased a boneless prime rib roast for Christmas dinner. "I'm going to hack off a piece of that sucker and take it with us. If Sim doesn't eat that, then he really doesn't feel too well."

As we drove to the hospital, we discussed what we might expect when we saw Sim. We wondered if he would recognize us, what his demeanor would be, if he would eat for us. On one hand, we were relieved that the surgery went well. On the other hand, we were concerned about what the long-term effects would be and if he would fully recover.

We pulled up, parked the car, and quickly walked to the Emergency/Specialty entrance. The receptionist called for a tech and to say there were visitors for Mr. Sims. Kelly, Dr. Crouser's assistant, guided us to an exam room and said that she would be back shortly with Sim. Although it was only a few minutes, it seemed to take forever. Finally, the door opened, and Kelly had Sim in her arms.

Oh my, I thought. He looked disheveled because he hadn't been brushed. His eyes were glassy, bloodshot, and had an eerie, greenish cast to them. Kelly placed him gently on the exam table where she had put a blanket so he wouldn't slip.

I stoked him and softly spoke to him. At first, he seemed unaware of our presence. Eventually he appeared to, on some level, know that we were there.

"I guess it's all the pain killers and anesthesia," I said, really just thinking out loud. I was trying to keep my emotions in check so that Sim didn't pick up on my concern.

"Hey, Bud, how's my boy doing?" He was pacing on the blanket from one end of the table where I was standing to the other, where Frank was standing. Every so often, the expression in his eyes changed and he seemed to recognize us. Then he would revert back to the odd behavior. Frank and I both kept softly speaking to him in a manner that we usually did, acting as if everything was fine.

I reached into my pocket and unwrapped the piece of prime rib roast. I had cut it into small pieces so it would be easy for Sim to eat. I held out my hand and offered him a piece. He either ignored it or was not aware that it was there. This surprised me because of the oft-touted dog's wonderful sense of smell. I looked at Frank and said, "Maybe all the meds have also altered his ability to smell this meat." Sim made another lap around the top of the table, stopping as Frank talked and petted him, and then came to me. I offered him the meat again. This time he took it but didn't quite seem to know what to do with it. He rolled it around in his mouth. Finally, he chewed it up and swallowed it. It was not with the gusto that I had been hoping for, however.

"Well, at least he took a little bit," Frank said, trying to reassure me. We visited for about thirty minutes. I gave him a kiss on top of the head and told him that we would be picking him up tomorrow. I breathed in deeply, hoping to get his usual aroma. Instead, he smelled very medicinal. I said to him that he'd be home before he knew it. Sim just gave me a confused look. Kelly, the tech, told us not to worry.

"It's all that he's been through. He'll look better when you come for him tomorrow."

The next day was Christmas Eve. I called the hospital in the morning, and they said we could come any time after noon. At noon, we were on our way. When we got there, the tech went over all the post-surgical instructions. I barely heard what she said. I just wanted to get Sim home. I knew she was going to give us the instruction sheet, and I also knew that I could call if I had a problem or question. She said she would be right back with Sim. She came back fairly quickly with Sim in her arms. She told us that he was a little woozy because of the opiate patch for pain that we should leave on for the next three days. She also said Dr. Houghton would be calling me with the results of the biopsies and that I should call Dr. Crouser to make an appointment for a checkup and to have Sim's stitches removed.

Frank took Sim outside while I waited at the desk to pay the bill.

When I reached the car, Frank had a huge grin on his face. Sim had peed and pooped for him. Isn't it amazing what makes you happy at certain times? "That's one of the best Christmas gifts I could get," Frank said, beaming.

"Actually, I was hoping for a ten-carat diamond, but I guess I'll have to settle for a fourteen-carat poop."

I got into the car, and Frank carefully placed Sim in my lap. Sim seemed to know that all was right with the world because he curled up in my lap and let out a very contented-sounding sigh. He stayed that way all the way home, snoring occasionally. As we drove down our street and reached our driveway, Sim woke up and stretched then sat up in my lap. This was the most animated I had seen him since I dropped him off for surgery on Friday. He started, although weakly, what I call his happy chortle.

He was as happy to be home as we were to have him there. Frank carried him into the house, placing Sim on the floor in the family room. Sim was still a bit woozy on his legs but looked around. He walked over to his toy box and very carefully pulled out the stuffed squirrel, one of his favorite toys. However, the squirrel seemed too much for him after just a couple of squeaks. He dropped it and looked up at me. I picked him up, placing him in the kitchen. He slowly began to walk around, inspecting each room. He gradually made his way down the hall to the guest bedroom. He stood at the foot of the bed, looking under it. I gave him a pat and told him I would be back shortly to check on him.

After I gave him some time to get used to being home, I went back into the bedroom to check on him. He was under the bed on his side and seemed comfortable.

"How about I get you something to eat, Bud?" Sim looked at me but did not indicate that the word *eat* was something he was interested in. He still had a spacey look in his eyes. I felt that if I could get some nourishment into him, it would help to absorb all the meds and make him feel better.

"Well, I've got to get something into you to prime your pump so that you feel like eating. Let me go get you some Pedia-sure to get you started. I poured a small amount of it into a dish and brought it to him. "Here, Sim. Try this. I think you'll like it."

He sniffed it and turned his head away.

"OK. I don't like having to give it to you with a syringe, but I've got to get your appetite going."

I returned to the kitchen and took out a small syringe from the cabinet. I carefully filled it with just a bit of the liquid and returned to Sim.

"This may be a little uncomfortable, but it's the only way I can get it into you."

I crawled partially under the bed and took his head gently in one hand while putting the tip of the syringe in his mouth with the other. I gradually pushed the plunger on the syringe so that he wouldn't choke on the liquid. He wasn't too pleased, but once he got the taste of vanilla in his mouth, he became more accepting of it. He swallowed and gave me a quizzical look.

"How about just a little bit more?" This time he swallowed it and then licked the end of the syringe. Frank had quietly entered the room and was watching. I looked up.

"This just might work. I'm going to offer him the dish now and see if he will lick it." Sure enough, he licked some.

"Nice going!" Frank said.

"Hopefully, this will get his appetite going and I can give him some of his canned food in small portions when we get home from Mass."

Frank agreed. "How is he going to be while we're at Mass?" Frank asked me.

"We'll just put him in his crate. He feels very safe in it, and with the mattress and soft blanket, he should be fine. We won't be gone that long. I know it's a bit worrisome, but he'll be fine. He'll probably enjoy being alone for a short while without us hovering over him every minute."

"True," Frank said as we both laughed. Sim always knew how to rise to the occasion, and even though he enjoyed the attention, I could tell that he was getting a bit too much for his liking. The meds were still making him sleepy, so after the small meal, I was sure he would sleep while we were gone.

After Mass, we wished several people a Merry Christmas and immediately headed home. I held my breath as we opened the door and I started down the hall to our bedroom. Logically, I knew Sim was OK, but emotionally, I was worried. I walked over to his crate.

"Merry Christmas, Bud. How are you doing?" Sim looked up at me with eyes that were brighter and more alert. He gave me the Shih Tzu swallow.

"Yay! That's my boy!" I told him as I opened the crate. He got up, stretched, and slowly started to walk out of the crate.

"Go easy, Bud. There's no rush." He stood on the rug and gave himself a shake that started at his head and finished with a strong shake of his tail.

"Hey, Frank, I think our boy is going to be OK. I'm going to put a little portion of his food down for him. It looks like he's gotten over the first hurdle." I measured out a small amount of canned food, warming it slightly. Even though he hadn't gotten his "sea legs" back, he stood at his dish and ate with great enjoyment. "Good job, Sim," I told him as I gently wiped his face.

I brought in the new nest bed from the living room into the dining area so that he would be comfortable as we ate our dinner. He loved this new bed and stepped into it readily. He did his usual nest-ing routine, scratching at the bottom of the bed with two or three swipes of the right paw and then two or three swipes of the left paw. When he got it to his liking, he settled down, keeping an eye on us while we ate. He dozed but didn't want to miss the possible treat that one of us might give him.

"We're going to have a nice Christmas, Frank. Sim's got some recovering to do, but I really think that he's going to be fine." With that, Sim brought his head up and looked at me with a very serene expression on his face.

"I think he's agreeing with you, Peg."

"I think so too, Frank. How can one little dog turn your life upside down emotionally?"

"I know what you mean, Peg. He's just got such a great personality that he's like a person in some respects. He's a huge part of our lives. We loved our other dogs, but our relationship with Sim is very different. Maybe it's because you rescued him. He appreciates having a good life now, and there is such a strong bond. In the time that we've had him, we've been through an awful lot of different situations with him. There has been his on-going physical problems and his obedience and training career. You have developed a greater understanding of dog behavior because of becoming a trainer. Maybe that makes the bond stronger. I don't know what it is, but it is very special."

"It sure is, and I just dread the day that it comes to an end. This episode with him has brought home to me how fragile he is physically. Hopefully, this surgery will help to give him several more years where he will be healthy and be able to enjoy his life."

The holidays brought a lot of visitors. I think they came to see Sim rather than to visit with Frank and me. Of course, he was more interesting, putting them in stiches. Sim greeted each one with as much enthusiasm as he could muster and readily rolled over on his back to expose his nicely healing incision. The more strength he regained, the more vigorously he showed off his belly. We all thought that we had finally found what had been bothering him all these months and that he was on the way to a full recovery. I was silently hoping that after he made a full recovery, we could pick up where we left off with his obedience career.

Chapter 50

Love is the seed of all hope.
It is the enticement to trust,
to risk, to try, to go on.

—Gloria Gaither

The week after we celebrated the New Year, we had an appointment with Dr. Crouser to have Sim's stitches removed. Dr. Crouser examined him and was very pleased with Sim's progress. He removed the stitches and said that the incision looked healthy. I thanked Dr. Crouser and said that I hoped I wouldn't see him for a while. Neither one of us knew what 2007 would bring with Sim's health.

"Sim will be due for his physical in February. Should I make an appointment now or wait for a little while?"

Dr. Crouser thought about it and said, "There's no big rush. I've seen him quite a bit, and we've done blood work several times, so I don't see any reason not to wait a while. His teeth need cleaning, but I don't want to put him under until more time has gone by from his surgery." I agreed.

Sim continued to recover, but it was an up and down process. As usual, he would have good days and bad days. A phrase I began using frequently was "he waxes and wanes." Occasionally, I would feel the need to call Dr. Crouser, especially when Sim's appetite or intestinal health seemed out of balance. Dr. Crouser was always very supportive and would have me go back to a short regimen of Carafate to soothe his stomach and metronidazole to address his intestinal tract.

A few days before Easter, Sim woke me in the wee hours of the morning, letting me know he had to go out. I immediately got up, hurriedly dressed, grabbed a flashlight and took him out. He seemed very agitated as we walked up the block. We got about three houses away from home when he assumed "the position." I heard some loud gurgling and then saw bloody diarrhea. He took a few more steps and then there was more blood. We started back home and once again he had to stop. When we got in the house, I cleaned him up and gave him a dose of Carafate. Frank was beginning to stir as it was almost time for him to get up. I told him what had happened and that he should give Sim a Metronidazole when he fed him breakfast.

"I don't know if he'll have to go out again or if he'll even want to eat but give him the medication in any event. I'll have to take him in to see Dr. Crouser. I don't like what I'm seeing."

Frank said he would let me know how Sim was when he was leaving for work. I crawled back into bed to try to get a few snoozes.

Frank gently woke me. "I'm just about ready to leave. I gave Sim his medication. He ate just a little of his breakfast. He wanted to go out again. Pegs, I almost passed out when I saw the blood. He's a trooper, though. He didn't have an accident in the house. He made sure to let me know that he had to go out."

I got ready fairly quickly, put Sim in the car and drove him to the hospital. It was Tuesday, the day that Dr. Crouser does surgeries. I had to go through emergency. Sim's tummy was loudly gurgling, and I could see how uncomfortable he was. The ER doctor came in.

"So this is Mr. Sims," she said, smiling. "I've heard a lot about him but never have had the pleasure of meeting him."

"It's too bad you have to meet him under these circumstances," I told her.

She examined him and could hear how agitated his stomach was. I had brought a sample of the bloody diarrhea. She said that she thought the best for Sim was to admit him for tests and to try to stabilize him. She left the room to make the arrangements.

I heard Dr. Crouser's voice, and he came into the exam room wearing his scrubs. He obviously had just come out of surgery. "What's wrong with Simmy?" he asked me.

I told him, "He's having bloody diarrhea and you can hear his stomach gurgling half way down the hall. The ER doctor is going to admit him for tests and to try to stabilize him."

"Don't worry, we'll take good care of him. As soon as I have some information, I'll call and let you know how he's doing."

"I'm just wondering if his duck and potato diet is beginning to go against him. Maybe it's too rich or his system is having a problem with it."

"We'll take a look at everything and maybe we'll try a different novelty protein diet while he's here to see if it helps."

I gave Sim a hug and told him to behave himself. I don't know if he understood, but he gave me the Shih Tzu swallow and trotted off with Dr. Crouser.

When I got home, I began thinking that I should research some of the new diets that were available. There is a company in California that sells dehydrated dog food. It is all fresh vegetables, fruits, and a special vitamin supplement so that it is balanced. I decided to call them to get more information. The person I spoke with was very helpful. We went over Sim's history of his recent surgery and inflammatory bowel disease to determine which one of their formulas would be the best for him.

"Let me send you some samples of our variety that you add the protein source to. This way you can vary his protein. The protein source is usually what causes the dietary allergy problems. They do well on a food for quite a while and then, for no apparent reason, it goes against them. I'll ship it overnight so that you can look it over before he gets home. I hope it works for you. Call and let me know how he does with it."

I felt very comfortable with the product and the company. They seemed very knowledgeable and interested in my problem.

I called later in the day to see how Sim was doing. They were giving him IV fluids and they said he was stable. They were waiting for test results and would possibly try feeding him a venison and green pea diet.

The next day, the food arrived from California. It didn't look anything like dog food I had been used to. It was dehydrated assorted fruits and vegetables such as cabbage, kelp, and spinach, sweet potato, apple, coconut, and banana. When I looked, I could clearly see the ingredients. I had purchased some ground chicken to add when I started Sim on it. Of course, I had to wait for him to be released and to hear what regimen the vets wanted to try.

I called to check on Sim the next morning. The attending vet told me that he was stable, and they were going to start the venison and pea diet in small doses. I asked if the diarrhea had cleared up. She said that he hadn't had any bowel movement since he was admitted. She thought it could be the medication they were giving him to settle his stomach as well as the fact he hadn't had any solid food yet. They wanted to keep him for another day to test the diet and that he could possibly come home tomorrow.

I did some more research on the dehydrated diet. Everything I read was positive. It was made in a factory that also processed food for human consumption, so it was classified as "Human Grade." It was a very low carbohydrate formula. I was a little concerned about that, but when I did some more research, I learned that grain free, low carbohydrate diets are good for dogs with inflammatory diseases, including seizures, arthritis, and inflammatory bowel disease. The ratio that the food company advocated made up carbohydrate calories with more protein. Of course, I would check with Dr. Crouser as to his thoughts on it, if he thought it would be good for Sim and if he felt it was a complete diet. Once again, Sim had me "peeling the onion." I can't stress enough how important it is that as your pet's steward, you must always go the extra mile. You know your pet better than anyone else. What works well for one does not necessarily work well for another. It is also very important that the sources you use for research are credible. Anyone can publish or say anything. Always check your sources.

I made a call to the hospital that evening and spoke to the ER vet on duty.

"He will be on some meds as well as the new diet when we send him home, and hopefully, he'll make a speedy recovery," she told me.

When I called the next morning, the ER vet told me that I could pick Sim up in the early afternoon. The time dragged, and at one minute after noon, I left the house to pick him up

While I was waiting, I purchased a case of the new canned food and a bag of the kibble. "This should hold us for a while," I told the receptionist as I paid for the food and hospital bill. "I just hope this new diet will agree with him." The tech returned with Sim straining on his leash to see me. I knelt down to greet him. He started his little happy chortle sound, sneezed, and danced around in circles.

"I guess he's feeling a whole lot better than when I brought him in."

I gathered up all the food and meds and headed for the car with Sim leading the way. I put the food in the trunk of the car and walked Sim around the parking area to see if he had to relieve himself. Sure enough, he gave me a great pee, leg held high in the air and aiming as high as he could on the tree.

"Wow, Bud, I guess you really are feeling better." I headed back to the car, but Sim wasn't quite ready. He guided me to a spot near the tree and gave me a small BM. It was small but normal looking. I picked it up in a plastic bag that I always had in my pocket for such occasions. I felt more at ease seeing that everything looked "normal."

"Let's go home, Bud, and I'll give you a little bit of your new food." He looked at me from his spot in the passenger seat and gave me his classic swallow. With just that little communication from him, I felt more at ease.

As we entered our neighborhood, Sim sat up and started his little chortle again. "Bet you're glad to be home. And I'm so glad to have you here." I reached over and gave him a little pat.

As I pulled into the driveway and then the garage, Sim was beside himself; he was so glad to be home. "OK, Bud. Let me come around to your side and help you out of the car. Wait." I held up my hand as I told him to wait. He stayed in the passenger seat. I opened the door for him and told him to "wait" again because I didn't want him to jump out. As I scooped him up, he shifted his body so that it was very easy for me. "Thanks for helping, Bud. I'll let you in, and then I have to get your food out of the trunk."

I unlocked the door, and Sim ran inside, immediately checking his toy box to decide which of his toys he would start playing with. I got the food from the trunk. As I came back into the house, Sim was sitting by the door with his stuffed squirrel, squeaking it happily.

According to the paperwork that I had been given with the instructions on it, Sim hadn't eaten since about 6:00 a.m. "You must be hungry, Bud. I've got to give you your pill to coat your tummy first. Then you can eat." I opened the can of new food and made a small meatball out of some of it, then hid the pill inside of it. Sim readily took it. "Good job, Sim. Give me a couple of minutes to get your meal ready."

He sat politely, waiting patiently for his meal. I measured out about one-third of the amount he would normally get because I didn't want to overfeed him. I put his dish in the holder and told him OK. He walked to his dish and dug in, finishing the amount I gave him.

"That must have tasted good, Bud. Let me wipe your face."

When Frank came home, I gave him the update. "I'll give him another small meal later on. I don't want to give him too much too soon."

The following morning, Frank walked Sim and fed him breakfast and made the appropriate entries to what became known as "Sim's daily chart." Since his surgery, I had begun keeping a daily log, entering when and what Sim ate, toilet habits, medications when necessary, and overall demeanor during the day. This gave me something to refer to if he didn't seem right or if he was having a very good day.

"He seems to enjoy the new diet," Frank told me before he left for work.

Sim was in his usual place on the bed, curled up into the back of my knees.

"He seems comfortable. I think we may be making some progress. Have a good day and drive carefully," I told Frank. I got up and started my day. Sim seemed fairly chipper, but I noticed that his ears looked a little pinker than usual. "Let's have a look at your ears, Bud." Sim gave me the "swallow" as I gently lifted one of his ears and sniffed to see if there was any foul odor indicating the beginning of an ear infection. It smelled fine. "You passed that test, my boy." Sim jumped off the bed, grabbed his orange octopus toy, and started following me around as I got ready to do my morning exercises and stretches.

About noontime, I took Sim for a walk before I fed him lunch. His ears were much less pink, and I was pleased with the way he seemed to be feeling. When we got home, I fed him lunch. He ate up willingly. I wiped his face, and he took off to the living room for his ritual of rubbing his face on the couch or chair. Then he jumped into my chair for his afternoon nap.

I still hadn't heard from Dr. Crouser yet, but I felt I had some positive news to tell him. I went into the living room to check on Sim. Much to my dismay, his eyes were very bloodshot, the inside of his ears were very red, and his skin was almost hot to the touch and inflamed.

"Goodness, Bud. What's going on?" I picked him up, sat down, and placed him in my lap. It was obvious that something was wrong. I heard the slightest bit of a wheezing sound coming from him. "It seems that you are having an allergic reaction. Let's get you an allergy pill."

I took Sim into the kitchen and wrapped his allergy pill in a small piece of cheese. I went over everything that had happened, trying to figure out what had given him the bad reaction.

I took the bag of food and began to read the ingredients. The first few looked fine. As I continued reading, however, I found that one of the ingredients was fish oil. My memory was jogged. Several years before, Sim had a reaction to a special diet and supplement with fish oil in it.

A few minutes later the phone rang. It was Dr. Crouser. I told him what had happened. I heard him take a deep sigh. He never wants to do anything that will be offensive to his clients, both human and animal.

"It's OK," I told him. "I had forgotten about his sensitivity to fish."

"Well, I'm going to make a note in his chart so this doesn't happen again," he told me.

"I guess I'll try the new dehydrated food and see how it goes. The company has sent me a few samples, so I can try it for a couple of days."

Dr. Crouser said. "Just go slow. Fix one tablespoon and see how he does with it. Then do that every hour for a few times. This way, we're not shocking his system with something different."

I made an appointment for Friday. Sim continued eating the new food without any problem and appeared to enjoy it. I mixed ground chicken with it. If I had to rotate or change the protein source, I could.

Dr. Crouser was pleased with Sim's improvement. He gave him a thorough exam, as usual, and said that he seemed to be in good shape and spirits. He said that Sim's stool sample also looked normal. I had him look over the new food. He felt it was nutritionally good and balanced.

"You could add an egg every so often for variety instead of the chicken all the time. But it looks to be a good food and is agreeing with Simmy."

Later that day, I received a call from a training facility in the eastern part of the state. They wanted me to do Canine Good Citizen and therapy dog testing. I agreed and we set the time and date. Sim's health seemed good, and I was curious to see how well he would do in a situation that he enjoyed but was a little stressful.

I told the person who called me that they should have a backup distraction dog in case Sim couldn't work the full day. There were going to be about twenty entrants, and it takes about fifteen to twenty minutes per team to be evaluated. The trainer agreed with me and said that they would have a backup for Sim so that he could take an appropriate break or two. "Thanks. He belongs to the union and sticks to the rules."

The day of the testing, Sim was in fine shape. When we got to the facility and unloaded the car, he was straining on his leash to sniff the new area and leave his "mark" for all to admire. One of the women associated with the facility greeted us and immediately was attracted to Sim.

It was a long day of testing, but Sim did well. He seemed to enjoy getting back to "work." We used the backup dog twice so that Sim could take a potty break.

As the rest of the year went on, I felt that we had made a breakthrough with the food. Sim seemed good, was eating well, and didn't appear to have any intestinal upset.

Two different training facilities in Connecticut and one in Greenfield, Massachusetts, called to have me schedule therapy dog testing. I explained that Sim was the "distraction dog" in the testing, but he had been having some health problems. They would have to have available a Canine Good Citizen–certified dog as backup in case Sim was not feeling well. Each agreed.

Sim did well and, again, enjoyed working. However, he began to work in a pattern. He would test with six dogs and then rest. When Frank tried to get him out of his crate for the seventh dog, Sim would turn his back and refuse to come out. Of course, everyone thought this was quite funny. After the next three dogs were tested, he was ready to work again. I don't know why he did this other than to say that he knew his limits and when to rest. This was another lesson he taught me. Pay attention to your dog's actions. They always mean something, but let them translate for you. Never assume what their actions mean. Someone else may have interpreted Sim's actions as being stubborn or disliking the work. Neither of these were the case. He just knew how to pace himself. He also showed that he wanted to please me and do what I asked but could only, at this stage of his life, do it on his terms.

In October, Dr. Crouser thought that it would be a good idea for Sim to have a cardiogram just to get a baseline. Sim was approaching his twelfth birthday, and Dr. Crouser just wanted to be sure that everything was in good order. Sim came through it with flying colors. The cardiologist was very impressed and said how Sim appeared to be younger than ten years old. He complimented me on the good care that I had given him. He had read Sim's chart and was expecting a dog in very different condition than what he saw.

"He's all set for a year. I'd like to recheck him then. Of course, if there are any problems, I'll see him sooner."

I was relieved with the results. At least Sim's heart was strong and no deterioration showed up. The main issue seemed to be just keeping his tummy under control.

In the early part of 2008, things were going fairly well with Sim. However, every once in a while, he would have slight stomach upset. Nothing major but noticeable. As February approached, I knew I had to make an appointment for Sim's annual physical. I made some notes to take with me so that I could update Dr. Crouser on some small changes that I noticed.

As Dr. Crouser examined Sim, I went over how he was doing. "Basically he's doing well, although we're getting an occasional 'whoops up.'"

"Well, his tummy feels soft, and he didn't react at all when I palpated it. It seems good to me. His weight is good, and his stool looks normal. The only thing that I feel we should do is schedule him to have his teeth cleaned. He has quite a tartar buildup, and I don't want his gums to become inflamed or infected because of the bacteria. Let's see what his blood work looks like, and if all is well, I'll have you schedule an appointment to get those teeth cleaned. I'll call you tomorrow and let you know how everything is."

Dr. Crouser called the next day, and Sim was scheduled to have his teeth cleaned on Tuesday. I dropped him off early that morning. He cheerfully went off with Kelly to be prepped for his procedure.

I left carrying Sim's collar and leash. I said a silent prayer that all would go well. I had great confidence in Dr. Crouser, but the thought of general anesthesia always made me worry a bit.

Dr. Crouser called me in the afternoon. "He came through just fine. I cleaned his teeth well and there were only two little shallow pockets that I cleaned up."

"What do you mean, *little shallow pockets*? Does that mean there was infection?"

"Yes, but very minor. He's so sensitive, and there was so little infection that I'm not even going to give him any antibiotics. I think he'll be fine. Make an appointment so that I can check him in a week to ten days. He's in recovery now, so someone will call you when he's ready to be released. I'll check on him a few more times before I leave."

Early in the evening, we got the call that Sim was ready to go home. Frank and I went to get him. The nurse went over his post-op care and then left us to get Sim. He seemed pretty comfortable although still a bit groggy.

"You can offer him a small amount of food to see if he is hungry. His mouth is probably a little sore from the cleaning, so give him something soft. Don't worry if he doesn't feel like eating. He'll make up for it tomorrow. You can always call us if you have any concerns."

I got into the car, and Frank put Sim on my lap. He curled up, and I could feel him relax and then fall asleep on the ride home. *That's my boy*, I thought as I petted him. He usually seemed to find comfort and safety with me.

I brought him back for his checkup in about a week. Dr. Crouser was pleased with the way Sim's teeth and gums looked. "Hopefully he won't build up a lot of tartar, but because he is on a soft diet, there isn't much we can give him. Try to gently brush his teeth a couple of times a week. Maybe that will help."

Things were going along well. Sim seemed to be getting better and even began to enjoy his training sessions again. I tried to make them short and fun so that he didn't become stressed. I was beginning to think that just maybe I might be able to show him again.

One evening in early April, Sim was playing with one of his toys. His favorite game was to toss the toy around, throw it down, and roll on his back with the toy underneath him. He would whip his head around and grab the toy with his mouth, and the game would start all over again. I was watching him do this when all of a sudden, he stopped rolling on his back, turned over on his tummy, and became very still. This all happened so quickly it was as if he had been shot.

"What's up, Bud?" I asked him.

He looked at me with pain and fear in his eyes. I began to stroke him gently. I reached down and checked his pulse at the inside of his thigh. It was slow and uneven. I began to worry but didn't want to let Sim know that I was getting upset. I got up and called Dr. Crouser and left him a message as to what was going on. I knew he had left for the day and probably wouldn't get back to me until tomorrow.

I went back to check on Sim and took his pulse again. It was a bit stronger and seemed to be returning to a more normal stage. He still had an uncomfortable look in his eyes, but he seemed to be slowly feeling better. I was fully prepared to take him to the emergency room if necessary, but I exercised patience to be sure that trip would be necessary. Little by little, Sim came out of the "episode." I didn't have any idea what had caused it.

Dr. Crouser called me in the morning. I told him that Sim seemed much better, but I was very concerned. Dr. Crouser agreed that there appeared to be reason for concern, so he was going to set up an appointment with Dr. Campbell, the cardiologist. He said he would call me back with the date and time, but it would probably not be for a couple of weeks. He said I should keep an eye on Sim and make an appointment with him if necessary.

Chapter 51

Love…always protects, always trusts, always hopes, always perseveres.

—1 Corinthians 13:6–7 NIV

Sim was not himself over the next couple of weeks, seeming to tire more easily and not wanting to walk his usual route, opting rather for a shorter one. I reported all of this to both Dr. Crouser and to Dr. Campbell when we arrived for our cardio appointment. I waited while Dr. Campbell examined Sim and performed the ultrasound on his heart. About an hour and a half later, he came out with Sim in tow. He told me that everything appeared fine. Sim's heart looked even better than his last ultrasound, and his blood pressure was normal.

"Maybe there is something else going on," I said to him. "Would you please let Dr. Crouser know how your testing turned out and if he might want run some other tests on Sim while I'm here?"

"OK," Dr. Campbell said. "Let me speak with him, and then I'll let you know where we go from here."

I took Sim out to stretch his legs and relieve himself. He seemed pretty perky, considering his stressful morning. We returned to the waiting room. Soon the vet tech ushered us into an exam room, and Dr. Crouser came in. He greeted Sim warmly, as usual, and Sim happily responded. After a brief exam, Dr. Crouser said that he wanted to have me bring Sim in the next day, and he was going to do some x-rays. Maybe that would show up something. He was very pleased, however, that Dr. Campbell found Sim's heart and cardiovascular system to be in very good shape.

I dropped Sim off the next morning. The vet tech told me Dr. Crouser would call me when he had completed the testing and took Sim to begin his day. He happily went with her. I began to think that he knew why he was there, that we were trying to get him help to feel better again. Early in the afternoon, Dr. Crouser called me. The x-rays of Sim's back showed some irregularity and he would fully explain it to me when I got there. I anxiously drove to the appointment.

Dr. Crouser came into the exam room with the x-rays of Sim's back. He showed me where there was a "shadow" between two of Sim's vertebrae.

"This is called disk spondylitis. It is an inflammation caused by infection of the intervertebral disk and adjacent vertebral bodies. It could be caused by a bacterial infection. The problem is that one type of bacteria, called *Brucella*, is highly contagious and can be spread to humans. I'll have to take some blood from Simmy and have it analyzed. You will have to be very careful that he doesn't interact with any other dogs and also be diligent with your hygiene until the results come back. If it is a different bacteria, I want him to go to Puritan's for an MRI and possible CAT scan to find out what is going on. In any case, he'll be put on a long course of antibiotics, but we have to determine what type of infection it is so that the appropriate antibiotic can be prescribed. Clearing up an infection in the spine is very difficult."

Puritan's was a large veterinary diagnostic and teaching hospital.

I took a deep breath. "There's good news and bad news in all of that. What other types of bacteria could it be?"

"Well, most likely it could be a staph, strep, or possible *E. coli* infection. Those will be easier and less worrisome to handle, so I'm hoping that will be the case."

"Dr. Crouser, I know that you always have Sim's best interest at heart and always use great caution with him as a top priority, so there is no disrespect in my question. It is just for my own information. If the infection is not *Brucella* and is one of the other ones, could it have come from bacteria being spread in his system by the dental cleaning and the shallow extractions that he had? I know you didn't want to give him any antibiotic because there was no active infection and he is so sensitive to medication. I'm asking this because I'm trying to make sense of what is going on."

Now it was Dr. Crouser's turn to take a deep breath. "It could be," he said with a lot of concern in his voice.

"Believe me when I say I hold you blameless. Sim has been very difficult to keep healthy because of all of the odd problems he comes up with. So far, I think we have both done a good job with him."

Dr. Crouser smiled. "Thank you for that. It means a lot to me. I'll call you with the results. It will probably take a few days, but I will be in touch as soon as I have any information."

I had made an appointment for Sim to be groomed by a groomer who would come to the house. She had a specially outfitted van that looked like a grooming room. It had a tub, drying table, and all the usual equipment that any pet grooming shop would have. I felt badly leaving Svetlana. She had always been wonderful and very caring with Sim and they had a very special and close relationship, but Sim's health was becoming more and more fragile, and I was trying to keep him as stress-free as possible. My concern was that the drive to Svetlana's, leaving him for a couple of hours, and then the drive home might tip the delicate balance I was trying to keep him in.

Angie Parks, the groomer, had come to me several years ago with one of her dogs for a temperament evaluation and would call me every so often to keep in touch. I called and explained Sim's situation. I liked her plan of how she would work with him, keeping in mind his physical history. She said that she wanted to bathe and trim him on one visit and then return in two weeks to do his nails, ears, and any touch-up trimming that needed to be done. This way he would not undergo a long, possibly stressful grooming session. I agreed that breaking it up would be better for him. We were all set for his first session with her.

After the news from Dr. Crouser, I called Angie and explained what was going on. I realized that we couldn't do anything until the blood work came back. I didn't want to risk her health or the health of any of the other dogs that she would be grooming. She agreed but wasn't overly worried.

"I think it's probably one of the other kinds of infections, knowing how well you take care of him. Of course, anything is possible, but I think everything will be OK. Let me know as soon as you hear something, and I'll come over and groom him when it's advisable."

Within a few days, Dr. Crouser called with the results. "Good news. No Brucella, but you'll have to call Puritan's so that they can do a further diagnosis. I'll give you their phone number. Make the appointment with the neurology department, and I will fax over Simmy's history. I'll be anxious to see what they come up with."

"OK, Dr. Crouser. I'll let you know as soon as I have contacted them. I understand why you want us to go there because you don't have the equipment to do the CAT or MRI. I'm just not really comfortable because I'm sure that I will be working with interns, not the top neurologist. Sim is so unique that I just hope we don't get into any issues because of anyone's lack of experience." Once again, I had to choose my words carefully. I didn't want Dr. Crouser to become annoyed with my protectiveness of Sim. But I was Sim's advocate, and I wasn't about to relinquish that role now.

"Don't worry. I just need the technical information. Hopefully, they will come up with the answer, and I'll be able to take it from here." Once again, I could hear the concern in Dr. Crouser's voice.

I called Puritan's and was connected with the neurology department. I spoke to the receptionist and told her why I was being referred and that Dr. Crouser would be sending them Sim's records as soon as an appointment was set up. She gave us an appointment for September 18 at 9:00 a.m. I called Dr. Crouser and told him that we had the appointment for this coming Friday.

"Great. I didn't think you would get him in that fast. I'll fax them Sim's latest lab work along with some of his history. I'm sure they will send me their results and opinion, but please call me when you get home. I'll be anxious to hear what they have to say to you."

Frank and I arrived at Puritan's, and Sim seemed in good spirits, considering why we had made the trip. We filled out the paperwork that the receptionist gave us and then waited to be seen by the neurologist. Most of the people there had dogs with serious problems. The Spaniel that needed eye surgery, the Mastiff waiting to be seen by the cardiology department, and the Boxer that had been diagnosed with cancer, just to name a few.

Finally, we were called and brought into an exam room. The tech took Sim's vitals and asked us a few questions. I told her that our vet had sent us there for Sim to have either a CAT scan or MRI to get a better diagnosis regarding the disk spondylitis.

Dr. Carmine came into the room. She was a pleasant-looking woman in her early thirties. Again we went over Sim's history and why Dr. Crouser had sent us there. I recounted to her what happened when Sim was rolling on his back and then stopped as though he had been shot. Dr. Carmine said that he was displaying pain even though I could not pinpoint it. She examined Sim and then told us that she wanted to do some x-rays of his back to get a baseline. She also said that she would speak with Internal Medicine because she found a bit of tenderness when she palpated his tummy and also because of his history of GI problems. He would be there for a few hours. We could come back around 3:00 p.m. to pick him up, and she would give us further instructions at that time. She also said that this was the first of probably several visits. He would have to have follow-up visits to keep track of his progress. I asked her about the CAT scan or MRI. She said that there wouldn't be that much of a change in Sim as Dr. Crouser had just done the x-ray on Sim's back. She might do either one of those procedures on our next visit.

Frank and I left, and even though we really weren't hungry, we decided to stop for lunch. My stomach was tied up in knots. The concern I had about not seeing the experienced neurologist seemed to be validated. I told Frank of my concern.

"She's really nice, but Dr. Crouser specifically wanted Sim to have a CAT scan or MRI. He's had discomfort for a while now, and I don't want to see him continue with it. I just want to get the answers and have Dr. Crouser take care of him."

Frank tried to calm my fears. "You know they have their protocols that they have to follow. Dr. Carmine is training to be a neurologist, but she is a vet. She's got to know what she's doing and obviously has experience."

"I know but I don't feel comfortable with this. I'll just have to wait and see. I won't give this a whole lot of time. Either they come up with answers pretty quickly or I'll have to find another resource." My demeanor was making Frank edgy.

"You really have to let them do their job, Peg. They know what they are doing."

"Really? I'm not here to find out about Sim's GI issues. Dr. Crouser knows all about that. I'm here to find out what we have to do to give him relief from this disk spondylitis thing. At least I learned from her that what I saw was his way of showing pain."

At this point, I was on the verge of tears due to frustration and anxiety. Frank's frustration was coming out as annoyance with me.

"We'll just have to wait and see," he said with attitude. That was the last straw for me.

"I did it your way since that damn rabies shot in 2006, and look what has happened to Sim!" I was angry, and my eyes were welling up. We were still in the restaurant, and I tried to choke back tears. This was not the time or place to explode with the reality I knew in my heart. Sim's time with us was getting shorter and shorter. My deepest prayer at this time was to keep him as comfortable and happy as I could for the rest of the time that he would be with me.

"I'm sorry, Frank. I'm just at the end of my rope with this. It seems as though we take two steps forward and then one or two steps backward with Sim's health. Just when I think I've got things under control, something else crops up."

Frank reached over and patted my hand. "It's OK. I promise I'll do whatever you think is necessary from here on in for Sim. I care about him as much as you do. I'm not around him all day as you are, but I'm beginning to understand what you are going through. Let's go for a little ride to kill time before we have to go back for Sim. Maybe it will take your mind off of him for just a little while."

As we drove along, I tried to become interested in the sights. I was slightly diverted from worrying about Sim, but I kept looking at the clock on the dashboard.

"It's a little early, but let's go back now."

Frank agreed. I guess we both thought we would be more at ease waiting for Sim at Puritan's.

We waited about forty-five minutes. A tech came over to us with Sim. He was very happy to see us and seemed comfortable in this new environment. We were taken back to an exam room and told that Dr. Carmine would be in to speak with us soon. When she came in, she told us that in her thorough exam of Sim, she found him to be mentally alert with no cranial nerve deficits. He appeared to be moderately uncomfortable when his lumbar spine was palpated. She couldn't tell, however, if the discomfort was abdominal, spinal, or both. For now, she was going to prescribe Tramadol, a pain control medication. She said that she wanted to see us in two to four weeks to re-x-ray his spine to see if there were any changes.

"What about the CAT scan or MRI that Dr. Crouser wanted done?" I asked.

"We'll see how things look when you bring Mr. Sims back. In the meantime, the Tramadol should make him more comfortable."

I was not pleased with this outcome but went along with what she wanted us to do for now. I didn't feel that we were getting to the root of the problem, and now we had to wait another month. She did not want to give Sim an antibiotic right now because it might skew the next set of x-rays. She suggested that we should make an appointment for him with Internal Medicine along with the appointment with her so that he could be examined by one of the internists.

We agreed. I was hoping that another set of eyes might be of help although I had complete faith in Dr. Crouser's abilities.

"I'll be sending a copy of my report to Dr. Crouser so that he will know exactly what we have found so far. I must commend you for the great care you have given Mr. Sims. After reviewing his medical history, I expected to see a much older-looking, debilitated dog. He looks great. I would have never guessed from looking at him all the physical problems he's been through."

For a while, the Tramadol seemed to give Sim some relief, but he still had an uncomfortable look and demeanor about him. I had been in touch with Dr. Crouser regarding the follow-up that the neurologist wanted in about a month. It made sense to him, but he couldn't figure out why they didn't perform or schedule the CAT scan or MRI as he had requested. I told him that possibly the next time we went back, they would do it.

"It's the only way we can really get a handle on what's going on. They must have certain protocols to follow. We'll see what happens when you go back."

"I'll stay in contact with Dr. Carmine and let her know how Sim is doing. I don't see much of a change other than the Tramadol seems to be giving him some relief, Dr. Crouser. I know I have to wait about four weeks, but I'll call and make an appointment so I can get him in sooner rather than later."

I contacted Angie to come and give Sim his bath and trim. When she came, I told her what had happened at Puritan's and that he was on pain medication.

"I'll be careful with him while I'm grooming him. I won't push him beyond his limit. If I have to come back tomorrow to finish him up, I will."

"I appreciate that, Angie. He has an appointment to go back at the end of the week. I'm frustrated that we haven't made much progress yet."

Angie picked Sim up and carried him out to her van. About an hour and a half later, she brought him back to me. He looked pretty good. It was not the perfect grooming that I had gotten used to with Svetlana. However, Sim seemed happy and not stressed. Angie had given him a small orange stuffed rabbit, and he started tossing it around the living room. We were both pleased to see him perkier than he had been in a while.

I began to notice that every so often, he would have what appeared to be a nervous twitch. I wondered if it had anything to do with the Tramadol. He was prescribed up to three half tablets a day. I used them sparingly and tried to keep him on two halves a day unless he showed a lot of discomfort. The nervous twitch would show up particularly if the lighting in his environment changed quickly. For instance, if it was a sunny day and we were walking in shade and then came into a sunny spot, he would blink rapidly and thrust his head back and forth. The first time it happened, I thought that it was possibly a seizure, but he kept moving, and when he got back in the shade again, he was fine. I called Dr. Crouser and told him about it. He said that it could be that his eyes were not adjusting as quickly as they should because of his age.

The day we took Sim back to Puritan's, he seemed a bit "off." There was nothing I could really put my finger on, but he seemed less perky and there was a dull, pained look in his eyes that he would get when he didn't feel well.

Dr. Carmine took Sim to examine him while we met with the internist, Dr. Mason, to go over Sim's history. We told her about his GI problems and the fresh diet he had been eating since his last acute episode back in April. I also told her about his sensitivities.

With that, Dr. Carmine came back in with Sim. She was very happy with him and had even taken him out for a walk. She felt he seemed more comfortable and that the lesion had not progressed. I mentioned to her about his nervous twitch. She said that nothing happened when she walked him even though the light changed. She asked us to make a film of this behavior so that she could actually see it. She said to bring it next time we brought Sim in to be checked again.

In the meantime, Dr. Mason had Sim up on the examination table and was going over him, pushing and prodding, looking in his ears and mouth, doing a thorough exam. She finished and placed him back on the floor. Sim started to act agitated, and Frank said he would take him out to "potty." They just got out of the exam room when Sim vomited up some bloody mucous. Dr. Mason immediately went out to the hall and looked at what Sim had whoopsed up. She picked some up to examine.

"I think we should have him stay with us today and overnight. I'd like to do an ultrasound to see what the problem is. It is, more than likely, his inflammatory bowel disease acting up."

We agreed. I gave Sim a kiss on the head and told him we would see him tomorrow.

"I knew he wasn't himself this morning, but I didn't know that his tummy was so upset. Maybe this will give us some answers," I said, thinking out loud.

Dr. Mason said she would be in touch with us after the procedure. It would be done tomorrow, but she didn't know what time. It all depended upon the schedule for the ultrasound. Since he wasn't scheduled, she would have to get him in whenever possible. Someone would call us to let us know what time we could pick him up, and she would meet with us to go over what she found.

I was conflicted on the ride home. On one hand, I felt that the ultrasound might show us if Sim's inflammatory bowel disease was getting worse and if that was the real source of his discomfort. On the other hand, I wasn't pleased with the answer from Dr. Carmine regarding the nervous twitch that Sim was occasionally exhibiting.

"I guess we'll have to walk around with a camera so that we can catch Sim's twitch. You would think a neurologist might have some idea and give us a better answer than that. I don't feel as confident as I should with her. Now poor Sim's tummy is riled up. Here we go again. One step forward and one step back. All I want is some answers so Sim can have some peace. It wasn't this bad when I needed serious surgery. They took the ultrasound, found the tumor, and I was taken care of and recovering in less than three weeks. Sim's been at this for a month now, and we still haven't gotten the CAT scan or MRI we originally went there for. I just don't know what the answer is."

Frank was sympathetic to my musings. "I feel much the same way you do. I was hoping that this visit would give us the answers we were looking for, but I guess we'll just have to be patient a bit longer."

"My patience is wearing thin, but I have no choice. I think that is the most frustrating thing. What else can I do? I know something is wrong and getting worse with Sim, and yet I'm at the mercy of the supposed professionals. I'm only a dog trainer without all of the veterinary studies and diplomas. But I know my dog, his moods, when he's feeling well, and when he's not. You can see the difference in his eyes. That's all I need to see to know whether he's feeling tip-top or off. You know how I keep a daily diary for him. Whenever I have an appointment, I bring in all the information that I can. And yet, I'm always met with blank stares."

I knew then and there that I had to dig down deep and muster up even more patience and perseverance.

I had a very restless night. I would doze off for a short time and then wake up worrying about Sim. What would they find with the ultrasound? Had the irritable bowel disease caused cancer? Where was the pain coming from? Was it the lesion in his back, and was that more serious than we knew? Or was the pain coming from a combination of things? I got up and went to the kitchen for some milk to help me sleep. On the table were pages and pages of the daily notes I had taken. *The answer has to be in there*, I thought to myself. *But I just don't know what I'm looking for.* I drank my milk and went back to bed. "I'll go over my notes tomorrow, and maybe something will strike a chord with me that will lead me to the right answer."

We returned the next evening to pick Sim up. I was waiting to meet with Dr. Mason when I was called over to the reception desk. The receptionist told me that Dr. Mason was on the desk phone and wanted to speak to me. I was rather surprised that a facility with the reputation of being one of the best in the country would allow a medical report to be given on the reception area phone. I at least expected to be given the report face-to-face with the doctor. The phone was not in a quiet, private location either. It was at the reception desk where there was a lot of normal activity going on. There were people coming in with their pets or paying their bill and picking up their pets, certainly not an atmosphere conducive to having an in-depth conversation regarding Sim's health. I was very annoyed but had to stifle my feelings for the good of my dog. Why an animal's health report is not handled with the same discretion as a human's makes no sense to me. To the owner, it is just as personal and private.

Dr. Mason told me that Sim's GI tract was very irritated, indicating inflammatory bowel disease. His kidneys showed up as slightly brighter than normal, which could be an indication of early kidney disease. She also said that his liver was a little smaller than normal, which could be a sign of chronic liver disease or could be normal for him. Her main concern was treating his intestinal condition.

Diagnostics for his kidneys and liver could be done at a later time if he showed clinical signs or significant changes in his blood work. A change in diet would be in order, as well as continuing the Tramadol for pain, Carafate to coat his stomach before meals, and Prilosec to help reduce stomach acid and the possibility of gastrointestinal reflux and ulcers. She told me that Dr. Carmine recommended that we re-x-ray Sim's spine in about two weeks to see if the lesion in his vertebrae is becoming worse or remaining constant. If it became worse, then an MRI would be in order.

As we learned later, perhaps if this MRI had been done when Dr. Crouser ordered it, we would have found that Sim was in the beginning stages of a serious neurological disorder that possibly could have been brought under control. It was incurable, but identifying it earlier just might have made the rest of his time with us more comfortable. Here again is a case where I probably should have been more assertive with the "professionals" instead of just accepting what they told me. For better or worse, it was another learning experience and taught me that no matter how experienced someone is, nothing, *nothing*, replaces what we observe about our own pet. We have to learn all the subtle ways that our pets "communicate" with us.

I had a few questions. What change should be made in his diet? She mentioned two prescription diets or to change his food to one with a "novel" protein that he had never been exposed to. I passed no comment, but I didn't care for either one of the "prescription diets." I had learned a long time ago to read labels carefully on anything that I fed Sim. Many of the ingredients in these "prescription diets" were nothing I would eat myself, including cellulose, a.k.a. a wood product. Therefore, I would not feed them to my buddy. I knew I would be scouring the pet food aisle at the pet store to find Sim a novel protein with ingredients that through my experience with him, he could tolerate.

I also asked her why we had to wait for a possible MRI when that was the main reason Dr. Crouser sent us there. She said I would have to speak to Dr. Carmine about that. I mentioned that he had taken both Prilosec and Carafate before and that they had worked for a short time but then gave him a problem. She said to try this protocol again and see what happens. That ended the conversation, and I proceeded to pay the bill.

I was not satisfied with this outcome at all on many levels. I felt that by speaking to me by phone instead of face-to-face, the doctor limited the amount of time she had to spend with me. She should have been more attentive with the amount of money it cost. I had no problem with paying for whatever was necessary to help Sim. In fact, I would have spent double if it would have helped him. However, I was made to feel that any input I might have was unwanted. Well, it is my dog and my money, and his well-being is my highest priority. The other issue that annoyed me was that the MRI was becoming more and more elusive. And other than pain medication, nothing was being done for his back. Monday morning, I would have a long talk with Dr. Crouser about all of this.

Chapter 52

Trust but verify.

—President Ronald Reagan

I began the protocol that I had been given to get Sim's GI tract settled down. The Carafate that I gave him to soothe his stomach, about fifteen minutes before his meal, seemed to be making him worse. He would vomit it up shortly after being dosed. I tried this several times, each time with the same result. I called to speak to the internist and was told someone would call me back. A different vet called me. He suggested that I try Mylanta. I purchased it, but when I read the label, I found that it contained sorbitol, which is not supposed to be given to dogs. It metabolizes in the liver and can have the same effect as alcohol. I tried a smaller amount, however, to see if it would help him. Instead, I got the same result. It made him sick to his stomach.

I called back and was told to try several other liquid antacids to see if one would agree with Sim. None did, and every one of them contained sorbitol. I also found that when I gave Sim the Prilosec, he seemed to have tremendous distress. I would hold him and massage his belly. I also would warm up a heating pad, wrap it in a towel, and hold that to his belly. I could gradually feel the tension leave his body. The Prilosec obviously was going against him as well. To this day, I still don't understand why, but when I told the internist that he had previous problems with it, she still wanted to try it.

I spoke to Dr. Crouser and went over everything with him. He had received the report from the both the neurologist and internist at

Puritan's. I told him that I was not satisfied with how Sim's treatment went. I was glad, however, that he had the ultrasound and that we could address that issue. I told Dr. Crouser that everything I tried to use to coat Sim's tummy went against him, and he had a very bad time with the Prilosec.

"Where do we go from here, Dr. Crouser? Sim is not doing well, and I feel that we need to do something. As far as I am concerned, other than the MRI that Puritan's didn't do, you can handle his case as well, if not better, than they can."

Dr. Crouser tried to reassure me. He said he would give me a small amount of barium. Although it is used for GI x-rays, it has a soothing effect on the GI tract, so maybe it would work to soothe Sim's tummy before eating. It was at least worth a try.

As far as the lesion in Sim's back was concerned, Dr. Crouser said he would x-ray it again to see if it had changed and would very possibly begin a long term course of antibiotics. I asked what he meant by "long course." According to the advised protocol, about six to eight weeks of the antibiotic therapy was necessary. After that, Dr. Crouser would x-ray Sim again to see how the lesion was looking.

"I just hope that Simmy can handle the antibiotic for the prescribed amount of time. Let's keep our fingers crossed that it doesn't upset his tummy to the point that he can't take it for the duration he has to," Dr. Crouser said, almost thinking out loud when he said it. I more than appreciated his concern. He got the antibiotic ready and handed me the bottle. "Let me know how things go in a couple of days."

I tried giving Sim the barium that Dr. Crouser gave me fifteen minutes before his dinner. He reacted the same way as he did with everything else. Shortly after the dose of barium was given to him, he whoopsed it up.

"Darn it, Sim. I was hoping that was going to work for you. Guess we're just going to have to figure out something else." I gave him some boiled chicken and sweet potato. Until I could find a commercial food with a protein source that Sim never had, I felt that this would be a safe meal for him. Of course, my concern was that he wasn't getting the proper vitamin supplementation in this homemade diet. He tolerated the homemade diet well and even seemed to enjoy it.

The next day, I went to the pet store and began reading dog food labels. There were only a few brands that I felt were good, so at least that limited the amount of research I had to do. I found a limited ingredient diet in a brand that I trusted. It contained sweet potato and venison. I wanted to buy the canned version, but it contained salmon oil. Remembering how allergic Sim was to fish, I had to take the dry kibble. That only had canola oil in it. I decided the best way to feed it to Sim was to soak it and then put it into the food processor to achieve the soft texture that the canned food would give me. I was trying desperately not to aggravate his tummy. He seemed to tolerate it fairly well.

I called Puritan's to let the Internal Medicine Department know how things were going. Once again, I asked for Dr. Mason, but instead another vet called me back. This was the first contact I had with him. I told him the problems I was having with any coating agent and that I had switched Sim's diet to sweet potato and venison. Sim seemed to be doing fairly well with the diet change. He said to continue what I was doing. If Sim got worse, we may have to consider giving him a low dose of Prednisone to counter the inflammation of his IBD. I told him that Dr. Crouser was handling things and we would see how everything worked out.

Sim appeared to be tolerating the antibiotic fairly well. I could tell that he was not completely comfortable but doing well enough so that we could continue the treatment. However, when I was being completely objective with myself, he was showing signs of aging. I could see that the amount of sand in the upper part of his hourglass was far less than what was on the bottom.

In spite of this, I continued to lightly train him, putting him through some of the obedience exercises he enjoyed. I would heel him a little on walks, do figure eights in our driveway around two orange cones, and have him retrieve his dumbbell. I would do the dumbbell work in the driveway, on the front or back lawn, and down the hall in the house. I would occasionally have him do a drop on recall. He seemed to like the work when he felt fairly well. It gave him a lift, and I think it helped him to forget his physical infirmities.

As the winter approached, I could see Sim's frailty increasing. It wasn't drastic, but it was enough for me to think about how he should be handled in cold and/or snowy weather. I was looking through one of the pet catalogs and saw a great-looking snowsuit. It was red with black trim and had a hood that zipped off. The pants also zipped off so that just the jacket could be used. It was made of a quilted material and looked to be nice and warm.

When I read the fit specifications, I ordered the small for him. When it came, I tried it on him. He seemed to like it. It fit well, except for around his chest. It was slightly too tight.

Frank had just had some alterations done by a young woman who made clothes as well. He said that maybe she could be of help. I called her and explained my dilemma. She said that she would make an appointment for "Mr. Sims to have a fitting." I laughed, but she remained serious. She asked if he was well behaved. I told her that he was very well trained and his behavior was exemplary. She told me what time to bring him in. She wanted him to be her last client of the day. I told Frank that I had called, and we had an appointment with Tatyana Thursday evening. We both thought it was comical, thinking of Mr. Sims having a "fitting." The only fitting that I had ever had was for my wedding gown. My wardrobe was off the rack of local department stores. Always at a discount, I might add. I envisioned Mr. Sims having his own line of doggie wear. It would be emblazoned with the logo of a fire-breathing dragon atop a pooper scooper and the words "Myassis Dragon" emblazoned on it.

We arrived at Tatyana's shop at 8:00 p.m.

She led us over to a fitting area. It had a four-way mirror and a pedestal. She told me to guide Sim up on the pedestal, and then we both would put the snowsuit on him. Sim readily complied with what we wanted him to do. Tatyana determined that she could put in an elastic panel on each side of the jacket and that would do the trick. She said it would be ready in about two weeks, and she would call us for an appointment when it was ready.

As we drove home, we talked about how Sim could go from one situation to the other without any fuss. I said to Frank that he had come such a very long way from when we first got him. "It just goes to prove what love and trust on a consistent basis can do." As I said this, I gave Sim a little hug as he rested on my lap. He sighed contently.

Tatyana called within the week to let me know that the snow-suit was ready. She wanted to make an appointment so that she could try it on Sim. I told her that he wasn't feeling particularly well and that Frank would pick it up on his way home from work. I told her that I would let her know how well it fit him. She said to give Sim her good wishes and that she would miss seeing him. Frank brought home the snowsuit, and it fit perfectly. Sim seemed to enjoy having it on now that it had been "custom made" for him.

I was in contact with Dr. Crouser on a regular basis. I did have to bring Sim in for various ailments such as a yeast infection in his ear, anal sac problems, and prepuce infections. All of these things were minor, but it still bothered me that Sim was never 100 percent healthy at any given time.

When the eight weeks of the antibiotic treatment were over, Dr. Crouser had me bring Sim in for an x-ray. This was in early November. The x-ray showed an improvement in the size of the lesion. Now it was a case of taking a "wait and see" attitude to evaluate whether Sim got better or worse or remained the same. At this appointment, I mentioned to Dr. Crouser that Sim was due for his rabies shot in February 2009. "You can put me in jail, but I will not agree to have Sim vaccinated with the rabies vaccine again. I am too afraid of what it will do to him."

Dr. Crouser smiled and told me not to worry. He agreed that it would be harmful, if not deadly, to vaccinate Sim again. However, because the rabies vaccine is required by state law, he suggested that he take some of Sim's blood and send it to be titered. He said it was an expensive test, but we would have valid results to show public health officials if the need arose. I agreed, and he took some blood to be tested. He told me it would take a while to get the results back, so we were doing it early enough to meet the February requirement.

Dr. Crouser said that depending on the results, he would write a letter for me explaining why Sim should not be vaccinated and what his immunity level to rabies was. He explained to me that if Sim had any kind of issue relating to biting someone or if he were bitten by another animal, I understood that Sim would have to be quarantined. Again, I agreed. He said he would call me when the results came back.

Within a week, Dr. Crouser called me back with the rabies titer results. "Simmy's level is more than adequate," he told me.

"What is it?" I asked.

"Well, an acceptable level ranges from 100 to 500—unless you're in Hawaii and then an acceptable level is 50. His level is 800."

Once again, a piece of news regarding Sim's health startled me.

"So it was a good thing that I was not going to allow him to be vaccinated again for rabies," I said, almost talking to myself. Dr. Crouser didn't address my musings but only said that he would prepare a letter for me explaining Sim's health history and that a rabies vaccination would be very detrimental to the dog. He also said that the Public Health people were accepting of this diagnosis, and I shouldn't have any problems getting Sim's license. If I did, they could contact him for verification.

A cold chill ran down my spine at this news. I had felt that the rabies vaccine was at the root of Sim's problems, and now it was verified. I had seen his health decline within a day of his being vaccinated in 2006. I also felt anger. It took all this time for my suspicions to be validated. Although I could not be sure, it appeared that nothing could have been done to reverse the initial damage, but I wondered if something could have been done to arrest, or at least slow the ravages that were being inflicted on Sim's immune system. I picked Sim up and held him in my lap.

"I'm so sorry, Bud. I did the best I could do for you, and yet I was unable to reverse the course that you have been put on." Tears were flowing down my cheeks. Sim licked at my tears and then tucked his head under my chin. He knew I was upset but did not know why. All he knew was that he had to comfort me.

As Sim approached his thirteenth birthday, I could see him aging more dramatically, although he still had his "agenda." He enjoyed his meals and walks on most days and even enjoyed working with me a little bit. Occasionally, he would feel good enough to play with a toy. However, he was beginning to "walk old." There wasn't the jaunty bounce in his step anymore. I had to place a small rug in front of his dishes because sometimes his back legs would begin to slide out from under him, and he would struggle to maintain his balance. The rug helped greatly, and he seemed to appreciate it.

Very often, after he finished his dinner, I would take him up in my lap and hold him. The sands in his hourglass were moving more quickly, and it was breaking my heart.

"I'm with you, Bud, for as long as you need me. I will do everything I can to keep you happy and comfortable. You are my best boy and I love you dearly, but I know our time together is limited. I promise you that your dignity will be my top priority as it always has been. I will never let it be taken from you."

Sim's response was always the same. He would snuggle his head under my chin for a while and then settle into my lap with a sigh of contentment. At least I felt that as our time together was getting shorter, our years together had formed a bond with a trust so strong nothing could break it.

Chapter 53

Old age: It's not a disease but a stage.

—Author Unknown

As 2009 arrived, Sim's health seemed relatively stable, albeit fragile. He had ups and downs with some small infections. Sometimes it might settle in his ears, urinary tract, prepuce, or a hot spot on his skin, but nothing major. However, he again began the pattern of incessant licking of his front paws, back knees, and scratching his breastbone. He was due for his annual physical in February. He had lost a little weight but nothing to be overly concerned about. Dr. Crouser felt that it could be caused by his decreasing amount of physical activity. He no longer walked his three miles a day in four different outings. So Dr. Crouser thought that his muscle tone was declining somewhat. But overall, he was pleased with Sim. He took blood and urine to analyze.

I brought to Dr. Crouser's attention Sim's problems with his eyesight. Dr. Crouser tested Sim, both with the exam room lights on and then off. He said that Sim's eyes were not responding as quickly to changes in light. He said it was part of the aging process and didn't seem to feel that this was anything unusual. We would just keep checking it to see if the problem became more advanced. I asked Dr. Crouser if he thought we should x-ray Sim's spine again to see if any change had taken place in the lesion. He agreed. He said if I would allow it, he could keep Sim for a few hours and then call me so we could go over the results.

Dr. Crouser called me at around 5:00 p.m. and said I could come in to discuss what he found in the x-ray. Frank had just come home from work, so we were able to go together. I was glad because no matter how attentive you are, you can always miss something. There would be two of us, so we should get all the information clearly.

When Dr. Crouser came into the exam room, he had Sim with him. Once again, their close relationship was very apparent. Dr. Crouser put the x-rays up on the screen. First, he showed us the original one, then the second one that showed some improvement, and finally, the one he did today. There was no change, either for better or worse. After discussing the situation, we all agreed that Sim should go on another six-week course of antibiotics and then do another x-ray to see if anything had changed. We just had to be careful that he didn't have any bad stomach upset. This was going to be quite a balancing act. However, I had to at least try this again and see if we could give Sim more relief.

The blood work and urine analysis came back within normal levels, except for his BUN rate which was slightly elevated. The BUN rate monitors kidney and liver function. It is directly related to protein intake. Dr. Crouser didn't feel that it was anything to get alarmed about but worth keeping a check on.

Sim tolerated the antibiotic fairly well until the sixth week. Then his stomach began to rebel. I called Dr. Crouser to let him know about it. He said that we should stop if it was bothering him. He also had me set up an appointment for another spinal x-ray. This time, the x-ray showed marked improvement in the lesion. Both Dr. Crouser and I were more than pleased. We had finally given Sim some relief.

In April, Sim's tummy problems began to increase again. He was having more frequent episodes of stomach upset, discomfort, and lack of appetite. I began feeding him baby food because it would be easy for him to digest. I would mix chicken or turkey baby food with sweet potato or peas baby food for a few days. That seemed to settle his tummy and increase his appetite. I would gradually add his regular dog food, which I had thoroughly soaked and pureed. My concern, once again, was that the baby food diet was not supplemented with the proper vitamins that a dog requires. Every time I thought Sim was getting better and eating more of his regular food, he would have another bout of intestinal upset.

By the beginning of May, I was in almost daily contact with Dr. Crouser. It was a difficult problem because Sim would react adversely to the usual medications that are used to soothe an upset GI tract. One evening, he was having a very rough time. He didn't want to eat his dinner, and his stool contained some mucous. Dr. Crouser had left for the evening, and I wasn't happy with the vet who was covering the ER. We decided to take Sim to another emergency/specialty facility about forty-five minutes away.

After filling out the appropriate paperwork and waiting a short while, we were ushered into an exam room. The tech came in to check Sim's vital signs and talk to us about what was going on.

I went over Sim's symptoms while she took his temperature and a quick examination.

In a few minutes, the emergency veterinarian, Dr. Miller, came in. We went over everything with her, and she felt that Sim should have an ultrasound to see how bad his inflammatory bowel disease was now. She found that he showed some discomfort when she examined his tummy. She set up an appointment for eight o'clock the next morning. She also strongly suggested that depending on what the ultrasound showed, we should make an appointment with the internist for a more thorough evaluation. She said that she would do the ultrasound in the morning and call me with the results.

When I got home at midnight, I called Dr. Crouser to leave him a voice mail, letting him know that Sim would be having the ultrasound at the other facility, and they would be faxing him the results.

Dr. Crouser called me early the next morning. Frank had already left with Sim. He asked me if I wanted him to schedule the ultrasound at Brookside Road Animal Hospital. I told him that Sim was already on his way to the other facility.

"Well, maybe that's good. Another set of eyes to check him out. Maybe I'm missing something."

"I appreciate your understanding, Dr. Crouser. Sim really didn't feel well last night so I did what I felt I had to do."

"Not a problem. I understand. Keep me posted."

"I will as soon as I hear anything,"

Later that morning, Dr. Miller called me with the results of what she found. Sim's IBD had flared, and there was a bit of inflammation. I said I would follow her instructions and make an appointment with the internist after going over everything with Dr. Crouser.

I reviewed the results with Dr. Crouser in his office. I told him that I was thinking that Sim should have a consultation with the internist at the other facility. Maybe she would have some other suggestions because Sim was so intolerant of medications. He said to go ahead and do that. "With Simmy, we can never get enough information."

"How true," I said, both of us amused as well as perplexed with all the problems Sim had.

"I'll let you know how the appointment goes. There is about a two-week wait to get an appointment with her, so I'll go ahead and make it as soon as I get home."

"Good, and I'll let you know what the internist here thinks."

"Maybe we'll get somewhere once all this information is processed. Thanks again, Dr. Crouser."

Dr. Crouser called me within a few days to tell me what his internist suggested. She thought that we should give Sim probiotics to help his stomach and intestinal tract. She also wondered if he needed vitamin B shots. I wasn't worried about the probiotics, but I questioned the vitamin B shots. "What are the side effects, if any? And is there any way we can find out if he's apt to have a reaction? We know how sensitive he is, and I don't want to cause him any problems."

Dr. Crouser agreed and said he would do some research and let me know what his opinion was. In the meantime, he had me pick up the probiotics and start them. Sim would get a very small amount of the package added to his dinner every other day and then I gradually increased the amount to see if he could handle it and if it caused him any problems or upset.

Sim's appointment with the internist at the other Emergency/ Specialty facility was in the evening.

"Doctor Nemo will be with you shortly," the vet tech said after ushering us into the exam room.

After about fifteen minutes, the internist came in. She was a middle-aged woman who seemed to have a pleasant demeanor at first. Then she looked at Sim and folded her arms across her chest. The hair on the back of my neck bristled. I had seen that attitude in physicians looking at elderly patients. Without saying a word, their body language was saying, "They're old, what do you want me to do?"

She said that because of Sim's age she just wanted to make him comfortable. "It appears that his arthritis is bothering him, and we have to be careful with the NSAIDS because of his stomach issues. I want you to give him Pepto Bismol three times a day and a dose of Metacam every twenty-four hours."

"I don't want to second guess you, Dr. Nemo, but I thought Pepto Bismol has salicylic acid, which is aspirin. Won't that upset his stomach?"

"No, he should be fine with it. I just want to keep him comfortable."

I remained silent, but I knew I would discuss this with Dr. Crouser before doing anything. I wasn't comfortable with the internist's attitude, but it was what it was. Maybe her protocol would help Sim to feel better.

We always have Pepto on hand, as well as some Metacam. I called Dr. Crouser and went over what happened at the appointment. He was surprised as well but said to try the Pepto. We could always stop it if it bothered him in the slightest. He asked me to bring Sim in for a blood test to check his cobalamin, aka vitamin B12, level.

Sim was obviously not feeling too well. Nothing acute, but I could see that something was bothering him. I asked Dr. Crouser if we had to wait for the blood test results or could we give him a shot of B12.

"I don't see anything in the shot that would bother him. It's in a saline solution, so that shouldn't cause a problem." Dr. Crouser said.

"Well, in that case I don't feel uncomfortable giving it to him. What do you think?" I asked.

"I can give it to him if you want," Dr. Crouser said.

It seemed obvious to me that we were playing verbal tennis. He didn't want to actually suggest it before taking Sim's blood, but felt it would be OK. I didn't want to overstep my bounds with Dr. Crouser medically, so we both chose our words carefully before giving Sim the B12 shot. First, Dr. Crouser drew some blood, and then he prepared to give Sim the shot. "It may sting a little Simmy, but I'll try to keep you as comfortable as possible." Dr. Crouser started to blow on the spot where he was going to insert the needle and continued to blow on the spot after he withdrew it. Sim never flinched. "Good boy, Simmy." Dr. Crouser said, giving Sim a pat. "I'll let you know what the results are as soon as I get them. If he needs the B12 therapy, he'll have to come in once a week for a few weeks and then every other week for a few weeks. After that, we'll recheck his level to see how the therapy is working."

Trying to give Sim the Pepto Bismol was torture. He didn't like the taste, so as soon as I got any in his mouth, he would shake his head and spit it out. If he swallowed any at all, it was less than a few drops.

I mentioned this to Dr. Crouser. He said, "Why don't you pick up the tablets. I'll give you some empty gel capsules. Put the proper dose in the capsule and wrap it in some cheese or peanut butter. You'll just have to figure out the corresponding dosage of the tablets to the liquid."

"Great idea," I said. "This should work well. I still wonder about giving it to him, though."

"I'll talk to you in a few days and let you know if we have to start the B12 therapy."

Frank followed Dr. Crouser's instructions and Sim took it easily.

"Whew," I said to Frank. "I'm glad that worked. Now let's see how it affects him. If we don't have any problems, you can give him another dose in the morning and then give him his Metacam." Frank was pleased that the dosing went smoothly. Maybe we finally hit upon a protocol that would give Sim some relief.

Dr. Crouser called me in a couple of days to let me know that he had gotten Sim's blood work back with his B12 level. "It is extremely low. In fact, it is so low that it is below the lowest amount that the test records. Let's get him going on the shots starting tomorrow." Dr. Crouser sounded only slightly concerned.

"Is he going to be OK?" I asked.

"Well, he definitely needs the B12 shots. We should start to see some improvement in his overall health. How is he tolerating the Pepto and Metacam?"

"So far, so good. I'm not seeing any adverse effects as of right now."

"Good," Dr. Crouser said.

As we arrived for our appointment, and I was walking Sim into the building, I noticed that he seemed to be having a problem seeing properly. I thought that possibly it was the way the sun was shining off the glass door into the lobby. I tried to guide Sim into the building so that he wouldn't bump into the door. He made it without incident but was tenuous until he was inside. When Dr. Crouser came into the exam room, I mentioned that I was concerned about Sim's sight because of the problem he had with the glass door. Dr. Crouser examined Sim's eyes and said that they appeared normal. Then he turned the lights off in the room and shined a small light into his eyes. He reiterated that probably because of Sim's advanced age, his eyes were not adjusting to light and dark as quickly as they normally should. He gave Sim his B12 shot.

"Let's see how he does with this. I'll see you in a week. If there is any problem, let me know."

"If he keeps having problems with his eyes, do you think I should make an appointment with an ophthalmologist? There is one at the facility where Sim had the appointment with the internist."

"Yes. If the problem continues, I would want to have it checked."

It didn't appear that the B12 shot caused Sim any problems. But there seemed to be more and more issues with his sight. If the sun was too bright, he picked his steps carefully as though he was feeling his way rather than seeing. And when there was a change from light to dark or dark to light, he would go into an involuntary twitching of his head, pulling away from the light. I felt it was time to make an appointment with the ophthalmologist. I was able to get an appointment for the next Friday.

When we arrived for our appointment with the ophthalmologist, her assistant came into the waiting room and led us to the nearest exam room. She reviewed Sim's chart and then asked me how long I had been noticing his eye problems. I had written some notes, so I was able to give her a fairly accurate timetable of when his problem started and how it had progressed. She said that the doctor would be right in. Sim was well behaved but appeared edgy.

When the doctor came in, I brought this to her attention and told her that he had not been feeling well for a while. I also explained that he usually was good-natured, but because of the way he was feeling, he was not as tolerant as usual. She began to examine his eyes. She asked her assistant to hold him. When she shined a very bright light in his eyes, he began to squirm. She told her assistant to restrain him more forcefully. I was beginning to see that, although her skills as an ophthalmologist might be very good, her skills at handling an infirm dog were sorely lacking. The assistant kept yelling at Sim telling him he was "a bad dog" because he was afraid and didn't like being restrained. I called an end to the exam. The ophthalmologist said that she wanted to put him on two different types of eye drops for glaucoma. She felt treatment should be started, but she was unable to test him that night to see if he really had glaucoma because of his "poor behavior." I couldn't get out of there fast enough.

That vet is quite a FOOL, I angrily thought to myself. I also refused to have the prescriptions filled and start the medications until I spoke with Dr. Crouser. "Another bad experience at this facility. I'm not planning on ever coming back or referring them, given the attitude of the internist and the ophthalmologist," I said to Frank with much agitation.

When I saw Dr. Crouser the next week, I told him how disappointed and annoyed I was with the ophthalmologist. He said that if I could possibly film Sim exhibiting this odd behavior of pulling away from light, it would be very helpful so he could see exactly what was going on. He gave him another B12 shot, and we made an appointment for the following week.

The other odd behavior I was beginning to notice was that Sim was getting more agitated at things that normally didn't bother him. I had taken him out for a walk, and he was doing well. We were on the way home, and it began to rain. I ran up our driveway, hitting the automatic garage door opener on my keys. The door opened, and I urged Sim to run so we wouldn't get wet. He began to get very pokey, moving very slowly. I encouraged him with my voice to hurry. Instead, he just moved more slowly, pulling against the leash. I was just about in the garage, and I gave him two short but gentle jerks on the leash to try to get him moving. Much to my surprise, he growled at me! In all the years I had him, he never growled at me and always showed me utmost respect. It startled me, and I raised my voice saying, "No Sim. That's bad!" Instead of getting the repentant response I expected, he growled more and showed me his teeth. Now I was really getting upset. There was no reason for him to act this way, and because I was so surprised at this behavior, I became angry. "Hurry up and get into the house!" I said to him sternly. He turned and growled again. I opened the door to the family room from the garage. I took the towel that I always used to dry him, and not only did he growl, but he also snapped at me. At the same time, he relieved his bowels on the carpet. He had *never, ever* done this. It is an action that a dog will take when it is getting ready to fight. I was in total disbelief at what I was seeing. I regained my composure, cleaned the carpet, gated Sim into the family room, and went into the kitchen to calm down. The normally loving, well-mannered dog had turned into Cujo. The phone rang, and it was Dr. Crouser. He was calling to see how things were with Sim.

I took a deep breath and told him what had happened. "I'm not proud because I lost my temper, even though it was only for a minute. I don't get it. Sim has never acted that way toward me."

Dr. Crouse chuckled because he just couldn't picture Sim in that mode. "Don't worry about it. You've been under a lot of stress trying to help him, and he may just be having an off day."

"I know, but I just don't understand what happened. Other than that, he seems to be doing all right. I have put a small piece of carpet by his food bowls because sometimes his feet slide out from under him. It's as though he can't keep himself from sliding. The carpet seems to be helping."

"Well, it sounds like you're doing all the right things. As usual, keep me posted, and I'll see you for Sim's next B12 shot."

Sim didn't seem to be getting any worse, and in fact, it appeared that the B12 shots were of some benefit to him. Most of the time, he seemed himself, but every once in a while, he seemed out of sorts, his age showing much more than usual.

Chapter 54

We've grown to be one soul—two parts;
Our lives so intertwined
That when some passion stirs in your heart,
I feel the quake in mine.

—"Hands Across the Seasons"

I had called Angie to come to groom Sim. It was a nice, mid-September day. Sim was happy to see Angie. She scooped him up in her arms to carry him to her grooming van. I told her about the change in his behavior so that she would be aware of it in case he became grumpy or grouchy with her.

"Don't worry about it. He'll be fine. He's never given me a really hard time."

"Well, I just wanted you to know so you can watch for any odd behavior."

I watched as she took Sim to her van, and then I closed the door and proceeded to go about some chores. About fifteen minutes later, I heard a dog frantically barking. *Sounds like Sim*, I thought to myself. *But it can't be. He's with Angie.*

I heard the barking again and went to the front door, opened it, and listened. The barking had stopped. I closed the door behind me.

As I began to start my chores again, the doorbell rang. It was Angie, holding Sim, who was wrapped in a towel because he was soaking wet. Angie looked concerned and Sim seemed confused, twisting his head from side to side, not seeming to know where he was. I let them in immediately.

"What happened?" I asked her as she sat down on the floor, trying to towel-dry Sim.

"I don't really know. Everything was going along fine. I bathed him and then put him on the grooming table. But when I turned on the dryer, he started to bark uncontrollably. I turned it off and he stopped. When I turned it back on again, he became frantic. That's when I thought it best to bring him in the house."

At this point, we were both sitting on the floor trying to calm Sim. "I thought I heard him barking, Angie. I don't know what to think. Let's give him a few more minutes and then unwrap him from the towel and see what he does."

Angie agreed, and after about ten minutes, when Sim seemed more relaxed, we removed the towel and watched to see what he would do now that he was free. He immediately began pacing, going from room to room, appearing not to know what to do with himself. After a few minutes of this, Angie said to me, "I'll drive, you hold Sim."

"I agree. I'm not sure if he's having a seizure because he hasn't lost any bodily fluids. But something is very wrong."

I gave Frank a quick call to tell him what had happened and that we were on the way to the vet's. I was hassled and in a hurry, so I was abrupt when Frank started to ask me questions.

"I've got to go. I'll fill you in when you get home or I'll call you once I know something."

"But what—" Frank started to say.

I cut him off sharply, saying, "I can't talk to you now," and I hung up the phone. I called Dr. Crouser's office, only to be told he wasn't in.

"Just take him through emergency," Dr. Crouser's assistant, Mary, told me. "I'll let Dr. Crouser know that you called, and he'll be in touch with you tomorrow. Good luck with Mr. Sims." I thanked her, took Sim from Angie, and we went to her van.

Sim wasn't too bad on the short ride to the vet's, but it was obvious that something was wrong. When we went into Emergency,

I asked what vet was on duty. When the receptionist told me, I said that I wanted someone else to look at Sim. They were aware that I had a less than good experience with that particular vet.

"Is Dr. Houghton in?"

"Yes, and we can check to see if he can take a look at Sim, but he's booked with his own appointments."

"OK. Thanks for checking." One of the receptionists went to Dr. Houghton's office. She came back and apologized but said that he just couldn't fit Sim in. I frowned.

"There's no way the vet that is on duty is going to treat Sim. I'm not comfortable with her."

The two receptionists gave me a knowing look. I had a good relationship with them because of renting space there for my training business on Sundays. They knew that I wasn't being unreasonable, just trying to get the best care for Mr. Sims.

"Listen, the next vet will come in for her shift at 8:00 p.m. Take Sim home now. If he gets worse, bring him back, and we'll keep an eye on him until the other vet comes in. If he stays stable for you, come back at eight."

I breathed a sigh of relief. "Thanks for your help and advice, ladies. I owe you one."

"We're more than happy to help, Peg."

Angie drove us home, and gradually, Sim seemed a bit better.

"He gave me quite a scare," Angie said. "Poor little guy. I didn't know what happened, but I could see that he was in distress."

"I know, Angie. It's a puzzle. I'll let you know what happens tonight when the vet examines him. I wouldn't let the one who was on duty now get within ten feet of him. I had one experience with her, and she just didn't know how to handle him. She was almost as bad as that ophthalmologist."

"I was really impressed how you took that stand and wouldn't back down. More people should be that adamant about how their pets are handled, even by professionals."

"Well, Angie, you've gotten to know me well enough. To the very best of my ability, nobody will mistreat Sim, either intentionally or not."

Angie smiled. "Tell me about it," she said knowingly.

When Frank came home, I filled him in on what happened. "We'll take him back a little after eight so that the other vet can examine him."

"Good thinking. I remember when that vet was on duty and how she and Sim didn't get along. She just didn't seem to know how to handle him."

"I know, and given how he was feeling so poorly earlier, I didn't want to take any chances. I still can't figure out what happened, and he's not been himself for about a month. I guess I'll have to start peeling the onion unless the vet tonight can give me some answers."

We brought Sim back that evening. The vet on duty was Dr. Shepard. She was very pleasant and was very gentle with Sim, giving him a thorough examination. I explained what happened and asked her if she thought he had a seizure. "Well, it's really hard to tell. I'm going to run some blood work to see if there is some underlying reason that might cause a seizure. I'm going to give him a very light sedative because I don't want to stress him while I'm taking the blood."

"Great. I really appreciate that. While you have him sedated, could you check the pressure in his eyes? A specialist wanted to put him on eye drops for glaucoma without testing him, and I refused. She wasn't happy with me for overriding her decision, but unless I knew that he needed them, I wasn't going to take any chances with medication."

"I'd be glad to check his eyes. I'm surprised that she wanted to start medication without testing. Once you start those drops, you can't stop them, but they can do damage if they aren't necessary. Usually the pressure in the dog's eyes is checked at least three or four times, and the meds are not started unless there are consistently high readings." She gently picked Sim up. "We'll be back shortly." Frank and I sat down on the bench in the exam room. I was exhausted and, once again, was also hoping to get some answers.

The vet came back in about a half hour. Sim was with her, looking fairly perky.

"Nothing showed up initially. I'll have all the results in a few hours, and I'll make sure that Dr. Crouser sees them. I also checked

his eyes, and his pressure is fine in each one. There is a slight difference between the pressures in each eye, but he certainly is in the normal range. I would suggest that you get that checked every so often
when he's sedated so that he doesn't become too stressed. Maybe the
next time you have his teeth cleaned, Dr. Crouser can check that for
you." I thanked her, feeling relieved but unsettled because of getting
no answers regarding this latest odd episode. Frank felt that it was a
positive sign that she didn't find anything serious. I agreed but still
wanted to know what happened and why.

I thought all weekend about why Sim had a problem. Nothing
made sense. I was doing everything the vets had told me to do. But
as I usually do, I started peeling the onion. I went over his medications and looked up side effects. He wasn't taking much, only the
Metacam, Pepto tablet, and the hydroxyzine as needed. I looked on
the Pepto box and found where it said that you should notify your
doctor if you experience ringing in the ears or hearing loss. I started
thinking about what happened with Angie that triggered Sim's episode. She said he was fine until she turned on the blow dryer. He
was OK when she turned it off, but when she restarted it, he really
became very agitated. I wondered if the sound of the dryer seemed
louder or different to him because of taking the Pepto.

I called Dr. Crouser to tell him my thoughts and ask if we
should stop the Pepto for a while to see if Sim got better. Dr. Crouser
said there would be no problem stopping it, other than he wouldn't
have coating on his stomach for the Metacam. He advised me to use
the Metacam as needed and with caution.

I went on line to research any side effects that Pepto can cause.
I was very surprised at what I found. Bismuth is a heavy metal that
can build up in the system and cause toxicity. The toxicity causes
"delirium, psychosis, and seizures and is reversible over several weeks
or months, when bismuth intake is stopped." In other words, it can
cause neurological problems. I couldn't believe my eyes. I searched
some more and found two case studies of humans who had bismuth
toxicity but appeared to have dementia or Alzheimer's disease. As I
read further, I found that once the medication is stopped, the levels
in the blood continue to rise and then begin to fall off within the

fifth week with the blood returning to normal levels in about twelve weeks.

The next day I called Dr. Crouser and left him a message as to what I had found. He called me back and was as surprised as I had been. He agreed that I should no longer give Sim any Pepto and chart if there was any difference in his behavior and physical well-being. He wanted me to keep track to see if in twelve weeks Sim showed a marked difference. I also called the vet that had prescribed the Pepto/Metacam protocol to let her know what happened and ask if she had any suggestions that might help Sim get rid of the toxicity faster than just waiting for the twelve-week period. If you remember, this was the same vet that gave me the impression that she really wasn't too interested in Sim's case because he was "old." Neither she nor her assistant ever called me back.

I now had some hope that this was what was causing Sim's current problem and that he would begin to feel better. With this change, as well as the B12 shots, maybe he would start to have a better quality of life. I fully realized that he didn't have a long life left, but at least I hoped that what he did have left would be comfortable and happy.

As the days and weeks went on, Sim appeared to be feeling a bit better. I did notice that every so often, his head would involuntarily move to the right as though someone was pulling a string. It was very subtle, and I could not find a way to trigger the response.

We continued the B12 shots, and as the protocol dictated, we went to one shot every two weeks. Sim seemed to have more energy and began to enjoy short sessions of his obedience exercises. I made them fun, and even though his obedience career was over, I wanted to keep his mind active. I started to notice that he readily ran to retrieve his dumbbell but seemed to have a slight bit of difficulty picking it up to bring it back to me. I mentioned this at one of our visits to Dr. Crouser. I wondered if Sim had any soreness in his mouth because of a tooth problem. Dr. Crouser said he would check it, but he also did a neurological exam. Sim did fairly well but seemed to be a bit confused when the room was dark. He kept moving toward the closed door where light was coming through. Other than that, he appeared to have normal responses for his age. Dr. Crouser said there was some tartar on Sim's teeth, but he said that he would take care of it at Sim's regular dental cleaning.

Chapter 55

———— ⨷⨷⨷ ————

Dogs do speak, but only to those
who know how to listen.

—Orhan Ramuk

Thanksgiving was approaching, and it had been nine weeks since I stopped giving Sim the Pepto. Although he didn't have any more episodes that could be seizures or any of the aggressive behavior, he seemed to be failing. I could see that he seemed to tire more quickly and didn't want to go very far on his walks.

We were invited to a friend's home for a visit on the Sunday after Thanksgiving. When we got home, Sim did not greet us at the door. I called him and got no response. I found him lying on his bed in our bedroom. I could see by the look in his eyes that he did not feel well at all. Frank changed his clothes and went outside to do some raking. He felt that Sim was just having one of his "off" days and I should just keep an eye on him.

I let Sim rest as I fixed his dinner and ours. When I checked on him again, I encouraged him to get off his bed. He did and started to follow me down the hall to the kitchen. When I got to the kitchen, I realized he was no longer following me. I went back to see where he was and found him in the hall circling to the right.

"What's up, Sim?" I asked, trying to sound cheerful. He slowly stopped circling and looked at me. "How about I take you out to go pee, and then I'll feed you your dinner?"

I took Sim out, and he was pokey. He was not feeling well and circled to the right every so often during the walk. I brought him back home and offered him dinner. He wasn't hungry. I knew what I had to do. I called Brookside Road Animal Hospital to see who was on call in Emergency.

The receptionist who answered the phone was one who knew me. I explained the situation and that I wanted to bring Sim in because something was wrong.

She said, "You're in luck. Dr. Murphy is on duty until midnight. He's one of the executives of corporate and is excellent. I'll be looking for you."

"Thanks, Kathy. We'll be in soon."

I went outside to tell Frank that we had to take Sim to Emergency and who was on duty. I knew he wasn't going to be happy about this because he felt that I should take a more "wait and see attitude." What I sensed and accepted that Frank didn't was that Sim was on borrowed time. I didn't feel that it was going to be very soon, but I knew that unless there was some miracle coming our way, the length of time with us was coming to a close.

Dr. Murphy came into the room and looked at Sim. Sim was on the floor circling to the right. I explained to Dr. Murphy about the Pepto Bismol and that I had stopped giving it to Sim about nine weeks ago. He looked through Sim's medical chart.

"The little guy's got quite a history," he said. He looked concerned. "I want to schedule him for an MRI right away. I think that there may be a brain tumor causing his symptoms. Let me call our office in Connecticut and see if we can get one done tonight." He left the room to make the call.

I swallowed hard and looked at Frank. "I'll be very surprised if anything is scheduled for tonight as it is Thanksgiving weekend."

Dr. Murphy came back and told us that he had scheduled Sim for an MRI at the Connecticut facility for tomorrow at 9:00 a.m.

"Don't feed him tonight because he will be given general anesthesia. The doctor that will be doing the test is one of the best in the business. If there is a benign tumor, she will be able to remove it, and he should have a good recovery. Good luck with everything, and feel free to call me if you have any questions."

He shook hands with us, and we went to the desk to pay for the visit. To my surprise, the receptionist said, "There's no charge for tonight. Here is the address of the facility that Dr. Murphy is sending you to."

"I'm surprised there is no charge. I was very pleased with Dr. Murphy, and he seemed genuinely concerned."

"Well, keep us posted on how Mr. Sims makes out. We all will be anxious to hear."

"I sure will, and I'm sure that Dr. Crouser will be sent the results as well."

The next morning, Sim seemed a little better. "Wouldn't you know it, Frank? Last night he looked like he could barely make another day, and this morning he looks markedly better. At this point, I feel more at ease leaving him, seeing that he seems a bit stronger today."

Sim sat on my lap on the ride down. He curled up and slept most of the way. When we got there, Frank walked him so that he could relieve himself. Sim seemed curious about the new surroundings and looked much healthier than the day before.

A nurse came over to us, introduced herself, and ushered us into an examination room. She took Sim's temperature and pulse and asked us some questions. She made notes while we answered her. "What a great little dog. He certainly doesn't look his age."

With that, two more doctors and what appeared to be a student came into the room. They introduced themselves and examined Sim again, asking me questions as they did. One of them also looked through the copy of his medical history that Dr. Murphy had faxed to them. This was Dr. Katherine Tooker, chief assistant to Dr. Gina Russo. Dr. Russo was the neurologist who was going to perform the MRI and spinal tap on Sim. She also was the doctor that Dr. Murphy spoke so highly of. Dr. Russo came in the room. We had been there about half an hour. She spoke to Dr. Tooker and the other staff and then spoke to us. She too looked over Sim's records.

"The little guy's been through a lot. He looks great, though, and that is a testament to the good care you've given him all these years."

"Thank you. And I've been more than glad to do it. He's done a lot for me as well." She looked at me but did not verbally respond. I could tell from the look in her eyes, however, that she could see the close bond Sim and I had.

"Let me explain to you the procedure that Mr. Sims is going to have. He'll be given the anesthesia for the MRI so that he will remain perfectly still. The MRI will show if there is a tumor or another disease going on in his brain. If the MRI shows nothing, then I will have to do a spinal tap. This means that I will remove some of his spinal fluid and analyze it to see if anything shows up there. It's sort of a good news, bad news scenario. It will be good if nothing shows up in the MRI, but it will cost more for the spinal tap." I wasn't sure if this was her attempt at humor to try to lighten the situation we were in.

"Do whatever you need to do to find out what is going on. That's the important thing here. I'll just have to find a part-time job to pay for it." We both laughed.

"Don't worry. Go home and relax. I'll call you and let you know what I've found and what time you can pick Sim up."

During the ride home, the conversation focused on Sim and all the "what ifs." What if he had a benign tumor? Would we subject him to surgery to remove it? Dr. Murphy said that Dr. Russo was the best surgeon when it came to the removal of this kind of tumor. What if the tumor was cancerous? Would we put Sim through chemotherapy or radiation? And then what would we do if she found nothing? Obviously, something was wrong with Sim, and we had to get to the bottom of the cause. I didn't express my thoughts to Frank, but I knew that Sim didn't have much time left, and I wanted to give him the best quality of life for the duration. I hated the thought of having to make the decision to end his life, but if he wasn't going to have some reasonable quality, then I had to do what was the best for him.

Just about the time we were starting to have dinner, the phone rang. It was Dr. Russo. She said that Sim was doing well. She didn't find any tumors on his brain and had performed the spinal tap. She said that the fluid from his spine would be analyzed to see if it indicated anything, particularly meningitis. She told me that Sim had a defect called hydrocephalus, which means "water on the brain." He also had a quadrigeminal cistern cyst. I swallowed hard, waiting to hear the worst. She said that he probably had been born with both conditions and there was nothing to worry about. "He's most likely had these all his life without any problems. Right now, the news is all very positive." My mind was working so fast that I couldn't remember the name of the cyst, so I didn't ask her anything about it.

"Are you prescribing any other medication to address his symptoms?"

"I want you to give him a quarter of a tablet of low-dose aspirin every other day. I'm aware of his GI problems, but I'm also concerned that he may have had a stroke. I won't be sure until I see if anything comes back in the spinal fluid analysis. The aspirin will act as a preventative against any possible future strokes. I did give him a shot of Dexamethasone. We do this routinely when a dog comes in with swelling of the brain. It usually relieves the swelling fairly quickly, and sometimes the symptoms diminish. You can take your time coming for him. He's in recovery right now and seems to be doing well. You can get him any time after eight p.m. As soon as I get the results back, I'll let you know."

"Should he be getting the Dexamethasone on a regular basis? In other words, is it something that Dr. Crouser can give him now?"

"No. It's usually a one-time thing. I will be in touch with you and Dr. Crouser with the results of the spinal fluid and see where we go from there as far as treatment for Mr. Sims. If he has meningitis, there is a course of treatment that I will explain to you."

"Well, I guess it's good news even though we don't have anything definitive yet. Thanks for your help, and I look forward to hearing from you."

Frank was watching and listening intently to my side of the conversation. "How did everything turn out?" he asked me.

"Well, I don't know whether to breathe a sigh of relief or not. So far it's inconclusive. Dr. Russo is waiting for the results of the spinal tap analysis. As of right now, nothing unusual showed up. At least there is no tumor to worry about. She said we can take our time getting there to pick Sim up. I'm glad because the longer he is there, the more the anesthesia can wear off." We ate dinner and then got ready to leave.

"He must be starving because he's had nothing to eat all day," Frank said.

"I know, but I don't dare bring a meal with me. I'll bring a few pieces of hotdog and then feed him a small meal when we get home. That is, of course, unless they tell me not to feed him at all tonight."

When we got to the hospital, an aide came along and took us to one of the exam rooms. We waited for quite a while.

"I wonder what's happening. The nurse said she would be back shortly. I hope he's OK."

"I was hoping for some more definitive answers, and a course of treatment we can follow. According to the doctor, if he has meningitis, there is a protocol on using steroids, most likely prednisone. That's a little scary because of the side effects, but if it is necessary, it's worth a shot."

With that, the nurse came in with Sim. "Sorry it took me so long, but he peed in the crate and I had to clean him up."

"Oh, poor puppy! He usually doesn't do that."

"It happens a lot here when they come out of the anesthesia. We're used to it." She then opened the folder she was carrying and went over everything that Dr. Russo told me about.

"What about feeding him when we get home?"

"I wouldn't give him his full meal. Offer him a small portion and see if he wants it. If he does, fine. If not, he'll be back to his regular eating schedule tomorrow." Sim looked a bit woozy. He was a bit clumsy walking but was not circling.

"OK, Bud," I said to Sim. "Let's get you home. We all need a good night's sleep."

I got into the car, and Frank gently put Sim on my lap. We had put his "New York Doggie Duds" coat on him because it was cold. He curled up and went to sleep.

There was a slight cold drizzle in the air as we rode home. Sim stirred occasionally but seemed content. As we got closer to home,

Sim sat up as if he knew where we were. The street lights shone into the car as we passed each one on the Mass Turnpike. He blinked and had a mild episode of the jerkiness that I had seen before. It only lasted a few seconds, and then he settled down again and was fine until we got home.

He was happy to be home and walked to his food dish and looked at me as much as to say, "I'm hungry. Where's my dinner?" It cheered me up to some degree, although I still had a nagging feeling that things were not going to get better. I made him a small portion, which he ate up happily. "I think you're like a cat, Sim. You've got nine lives." I reached down and gave him a hug. He tucked his head under my chin and seemed completely relaxed and happy.

Dr. Crouser called the next day to tell me that Dr. Russo had faxed him the results of the MRI. "That's great news," he told me. "How does Simmy seem today?"

"Actually, he seems good. He's not circling and seems a bit more perky."

"Good. Have you started the aspirin yet?"

"Yes. I gave him a quarter of a tablet this morning with his breakfast. I'm concerned because of his tummy. I guess we'll just have to keep an eye on him."

"I agree with you," Dr. Crouser said. "Normally, that low of a dose every other day should be fine, but Simmy is just so sensitive that we'll have to be careful. I know that you will notice if anything looks unusual with him. I trust your judgment. I'll be anxious to see what the spinal fluid shows, if anything. In the meantime, we'll give him the B12 shots and then test him again in February to see how his levels are."

"Thanks, Dr. Crouser. I'll see you tomorrow night."

"By the way, bring in a stool sample. I want to keep a close eye to make sure that there is no blood showing up in it because of the aspirin."

"Should I keep giving him the Metacam as needed? I'm a bit concerned that there might be a reaction with the aspirin."

"Let's try this. If Simmy looks as if he needs a dose of Metacam, don't give it to him on the day you give him the aspirin. Then give him three days of the Metacam, wait a day, then go back to the aspirin regimen. You'll have to bring in a stool sample every time you come in. This way we'll be able to catch any problem before it becomes more serious."

It was a little over a week when we got the results of the spinal tap back. Everything was "normal." There was no sign of meningitis. We continued the B12 shots, which now were given every two weeks. Sim could not tolerate the aspirin. Even though it was an extremely low dose, it upset his stomach, and a small amount of blood was showing up in his stool when Dr. Crouser tested it.

"We gave it a shot, but Simmy is just too sensitive. I know the neurologist wanted him to take the aspirin, but we just can't risk causing a serious stomach problem." After all these years of working with Dr. Crouser, I trusted him fully. He not only treated Sim as his vet but also seemed to have a genuine fondness for him. I knew that he only had Sim's best interest at heart. I did become a bit frustrated at times because Dr. Crouser always practiced the "first do no harm" rule. I had a great sense of urgency sometimes. I desperately wanted to see Sim fully healthy again, and yet I knew, when I was totally honest with myself, that wish would not be granted. He was nearing his fourteenth birthday. Considering all he had been through with physical ailments, I guess I had something to be content about.

On December 10, Sim's birthday, the saying on my daily calendar read:

All of us have equal time: 24 hours a day.
It is this raw material that we make the statement
of our lives.
Moments. Life is made up of them.

("Fully Alive")

The words gave me pause. *How true*, I thought. *It is a very fitting saying for Sim's fourteenth birthday. And I will try to make every hour he has left comfortable. He has made a statement with his life already. All that I have learned from him, going through his medical problems alone has been of great help to many of my clients' dogs.* I did the Shih Tzu swallow, trying hard to keep the tears at bay.

I was always keeping an eye out for anything that might be helpful to Sim. A new food had come out that only had two ingredients in it, plus the necessary vitamin and mineral supplements, one protein source and one carbohydrate source. I bought a can of the food and a bag of the same flavor in kibble.

I called Dr. Crouser and told him about it. He wanted to see any information that I had, and he said that it sounded good. He suggested I start Sim on the canned food first for a few days. If that went well, then I could try to add a little of the kibble each meal. Sim loved the canned food, and it seemed to agree with him. It was a very creamy-looking mixture. After about a week, I added some of the kibble, but I guess his system was too fragile at this point to be able to handle it. Again, you do what you have to do. I only fed him the canned food, and it seemed to agree nicely with him.

A couple of days before Christmas, Sim seemed to be having some stomach problems, nothing acute, but he wasn't eating with the same enjoyment as he had been. I called Dr. Crouser. I didn't want to start changing his food around. He hadn't been on this one very long, but it seemed to be doing well by him. Dr. Crouser said he thought Sim should have a course of Metronidazole. He had taken it many times before, and it always seemed to clear up any stomach problems. Because of the changes Sim was showing, Dr. Crouser said that he wanted to be very conservative with the dosage. He had me give Sim half of the usual amount.

Our friend Sue was going to come over for a Christmas visit. She had asked me about a month before if she could take some pictures of Sim. I told her "no" because of Sim's ongoing health issues. I didn't want to do anything that would violate his dignity. I guarded this like a mother bear protects her cubs. I know that she meant well and probably wanted to make some sort of collage of Sim and give it to us for Christmas. Some might say that I was overreacting, but so be it. If I were very ill and not looking or feeling my best, I certainly would not want someone taking pictures of me.

We went to Mass on Christmas Eve, as usual. When we got home, Sim greeted us at the door, which was becoming a less common event. "Maybe that's a good sign," I told Frank. "Maybe things will begin to calm down for a while."

On Christmas day, I gave Sim a special breakfast of a small bit of scrambled egg mixed in with his food and then gave him his half tablet of the Metronidazole. We were expecting company later in the afternoon. Sim seemed more quiet than usual. When I checked on him, he was lying on his mat in front of the Christmas tree.

"How are you, Bud?" I asked him. "How about some lunch?" He had a slightly dazed look. He got up to follow me to the kitchen and seemed a little unsteady on his feet. "Look at him, Frank. I think the Metronidazole is going against him. I'll see how he does for the rest of the afternoon. If he doesn't look better, I'll call Brookside Road Emergency and see what the vet on call says." With that the doorbell rang.

It was Sue, whom we had invited to spend part of Christmas with us. She had three dogs herself and was very attached to them. I would say almost too attached, if that's possible. When we visited her house, it was as though it was laid out for the dogs so that everything would be convenient for them. There were dog beds and dog water bowls in every room. I mention this because when she saw Sim, she burst into tears.

"He looks awful!" she wailed.

This was not helpful to me. I had the situation under control, and I didn't need someone overreacting. I was on a hair trigger myself. *Let everyone please take note of this:* Whether it is a person or an animal, if you know that their caretaker is very dedicated and has been diligent with their care, consider their feelings when you are interacting with them. They don't need you to fall apart and add to their stress. Even though the emotion is well meaning, it is selfish and self-serving. She composed herself, and I told her that I was keeping a close eye on Sim and was planning to call the vet after she left.

"That's all right. You can call now if you think you should."

"Maybe that's not a bad idea. Frank will visit with you while I call." I excused myself and called the hospital.

The receptionist recognized my voice and wished me a Merry Christmas. "Same to you, Kathy. I'm having an issue with Sim. He's been on a very, very low dose of Metronidazole for the last couple of days, and today he's like a drunken sailor. Could you ask the vet on duty if I have to bring him in?"

"Sure," Kathy said. "We're not busy, so I'll see if Dr. Porter can speak to you." I held on for a short time when Dr. Porter answered the phone. "Merry Christmas, Peg."

"Thank you, Dr. Porter."

"So what seems to be the problem with Sim?"

"Well, he's on a very low dose of Metronidazole because he was having some tummy problems, and he looks like he's been imbibing in the Christmas punch."

"Stop the Metro. He's having a classic toxic reaction to it."

"Really? He's only had very little of it, and he's always tolerated it well before. This is just so surprising to me."

"Well, it happens, and don't forget we're dealing with Mr. Sims. I'm here until midnight so if you need me, you know you can bring him in. I think if you just stop giving it to him, he'll be OK as it will work itself out of his system. I'll leave a note for Dr. Crouser about this, and I'm sure you two will be in touch with each other tomorrow."

Dr. Crouser called the next day and was as surprised as I was that Sim had a toxic reaction to the Metronidazole. "He just keeps becoming more and more sensitive to things," Dr. Crouser said, almost as though he was thinking out loud. "How is he doing?"

"It's the same pattern we've seen. Some good days and then some not so good. Is there anything else we can do to see what's going on?"

Dr. Crouser thought a minute and then said, "We can always do another ultrasound to see how his intestinal tract looks. But I'm thinking about testing his blood to see how his B12 levels are. He's had enough of it now so that we can get it checked. Hopefully his levels are back to where they should be."

I hung up and still had that nagging feeling. I agreed that his B12 levels should be checked now and maybe he no longer needed the shots. Sim is so sensitive that I wondered could something as benign as B12 be aggravating him. But something still didn't add up. I was seeing him trip and circle to the right every so often again.

When I brought Sim to his appointment, I expressed my doubts with Dr. Crouser. He took some blood to be sent out to see if his B12 level was "normal." I pointed out to him that when Sim was weighed, it appeared that he had lost a little bit of weight over the last couple of weeks.

Dr. Crouser checked Sim's chart. "Yes, he has. Why don't you try to feed him a little bit more each day? Add a snack or two."

"What if I feed him four times a day? Breakfast, lunch, dinner, and a snack before he goes to bed."

"Sounds good to me. Let's see if he starts gaining some weight over the next few weeks. In the meantime, I'll call you as soon as I get the results back. Let me do a neurological check right now."

Dr. Crouser had me keep Sim standing on the exam table as he shone a light into his eyes. Then he moved his index finger back and forth in front of Sim to see if Sim followed it. "I'm going to turn the lights out to do some further testing." The room became pitch black except for a sliver of light coming under the closed door to the reception room. Dr. Crouser, with Sim still on the exam table, dropped some cotton balls from each side of Sim's head to see what his reaction was. Then he put him on the floor. Sim immediately gravitated toward the light coming under the door. When he was done, he said to me, "Not bad. He's a senior now, and as I have told you several times before, I think his eyes aren't regulating as quickly to change in light. I'll check him every so often, and you can let me know if you see any more changes. I'm going to see about setting up an appointment right after the first of the year for the ultrasound. I'll be in touch as soon as I get it set up."

Chapter 56

———— ⌾⌾⌾ ————

A friend is someone who knows the song
in your heart, and can sing it back to you
when you have forgotten the words.

—C. S. Lewis

Sim's strength gradually seemed to be fading. He still enjoyed his walks, but they were becoming shorter and shorter. Not only could he no longer walk around the block as he loved to do, but he also could manage only a short way up our street or a short way down and around the bottom of our street to the next street. I would take his dumbbell and toss it down the hall and tell him to "take it." This had been one of his favorite exercises, and it still was, but I began to notice Sim exhibiting a level of confusion. I would help him find the dumbbell, and he would, but first he would try to scoop it up about two feet away from where it actually was. I always stayed upbeat around him, but my heart was heavy and aching. He was a valiant soul and was not about to give up just yet, no matter what I was thinking. *There's got to be an answer. I just can't make sense of this up-and-down demeanor. Maybe the ultrasound will show something.*

With that the phone rang. It was Dr. Crouser. He had consulted with Liz Schaler, the internist who had done an ultrasound on Sim several years ago. She felt that Sim didn't need another ultrasound of his GI tract because he had one back in May of '09, and things looked relatively unremarkable. She also had some concern that the procedure might be a bit too stressful for Sim at this point. She suggested that we continue to monitor his stool for any blood and possibly add probiotics to his food to help his digestion. Depending on how his condition progressed, she would revisit the possibility of an ultrasound at a later date.

I reminded Dr. Crouser that we had tried probiotics, and like everything else with Sim, it worked for a short time and then gave him some trouble. Dr. Crouser said to try giving him the probiotics every second day. He was hoping that this way Sim would get the benefits without having any issues from it. "Let's schedule his annual physical in a couple of weeks. He's due in February, so let's get him in sooner rather than later."

I still had that nagging feeling that something was being overlooked. "Dr. Crouser, do you think you should do a dental exam? I have been noticing that he's very reluctant to pick up his dumbbell even though he wants to. I'm also noticing that he's doing most of his chewing on the left side of his mouth. I wonder if there's something going on with the right side of his mouth. If he has pain there, maybe that's why he's circling to the right."

I heard Dr. Crouser take a deep breath. "I'm concerned about putting him under again." I heard him take another deep breath. "I suppose it's possible that something is going on with his mouth. I'll give him just the slightest bit of anesthesia so that I can examine him. I'll let you know if I find anything, and we'll take it from there.

"I just want you to know, Dr. Crouser, that I trust your judgment with Sim. I know that you want the best for him. If anything happens while he is in surgery, know that I will not hold you responsible. I am fully aware of the risk we're taking here, and ultimately, it is my decision. My hope is that something is going on with his teeth on the right side of his mouth and that's what is causing the circling due to pain."

Dr. Crouser made no comment and just gently said, "I'll connect you to the girls to set up everything for Tuesday." I could tell from his voice that he heard and appreciated what I had said. I spoke with Mary, Dr. Crouser's secretary. "We'll see you first thing Tuesday morning. Don't feed Sim anything after midnight."

When I dropped Sim off that Tuesday morning, Mary said to me, "I don't know how to write this up for billing because Dr. Crouser said he only wanted to give Sim a 'scosche' of anesthesia. He said just enough to relax Sim so that he could take a good look at his mouth and teeth."

I left with mixed emotions. I hoped that Dr. Crouser would find something that might give us an answer and some relief to Sim, but I also had a bit of uneasiness and said a prayer that Sim would come through all right. Watching him and seeing his decline, I certainly had reason to worry, but I also had the hope that I could give him some better quality of life in his waning days.

I had only been home for about an hour when I got a call from Dr. Crouser. "Well, Simmy has a deep pocket in his right lower canine tooth and a deep pocket in his right upper premolar."

"What exactly does that mean?" I asked.

"It means I'll have to sedate him more heavily and extract those two teeth. They are infected and I'm sure they have been bothering him."

"Do you think that this could be causing the circling to the right?" I held my breath, hoping for an affirmative answer.

"Could be. We'll see how he is once the procedure is done and he comes around. I'll call you and let you know how everything went sometime this afternoon."

I could feel myself wanting to be extremely hopeful on one hand and holding back my enthusiasm on the other.

Later on in the afternoon, Dr. Crouser called. As soon as I answered the phone, I could hear a dog barking frantically in the background. "He's awake and seems to be coming out of it well. Can you hear him?"

"That's Sim barking like that?"

"Yes. I gave him some morphine for pain, but I think it's making him too hyper instead of helping him to relax. There is something I can give him to reverse the effect, but I think I'll wait a little while longer to see if he calms down. I'll call you when he's ready to go home."

"OK," was all I could muster. Hearing Sim barking like that reminded me of the episode with Angie when we thought he might be having a seizure.

Once again, I didn't know what to think. *I'll just have to hold myself together a while longer*, I thought. Each episode that we would go through with no clear result grated more and more on my nerves. I kept looking for an answer, be it positive or not. The uncertainty was wearing me down.

I felt as though I had an itch that I couldn't scratch and it was getting to me. I had been fighting this battle with Sim for almost five full years. I watched Sim go from a healthy, vibrant, enthusiastic competitor to a proud, dignified dog whose life was becoming more and more limited, and all decisions were in my hands. I kept praying every day for help to make the right decision. I didn't want to "pull the trigger" on him prematurely, but I certainly didn't want Sim to suffer one day longer than he had to.

"He will let you know," a voice in my head told me.

So be it, I thought. *I'll just have to watch him closely. He's always communicated his needs to me. Now I must listen to him very, very intently.* I guess the thought process helped me to feel more settled although not resolved.

Dr. Crouser called me back at 6:30 p.m. We were just finishing dinner. "I gave him something to reverse the morphine, and he calmed right down. I'll make a note on his chart that he can't have morphine again. I gave him a little bath, and I'm brushing him right now."

"You gave him a bath?" I asked. I thought that this was above and beyond the usual exceptional care that Dr. Crouser gave Sim.

"Yes. He was a little messy on his chest and around his face from the procedure, and I wanted to clean him up. He's really enjoying the brushing."

"I appreciate the special care you give Sim, Dr. Crouser."

"Well, he's a very special guy."

"Tell me something. Is he still circling to the right, or has that stopped?"

Dr. Crouser sighed. "No, it hasn't stopped. He's still circling but not as much."

"Damn. I was hoping that we had found the source of his problem."

"Let's see how he does over the next few days. I'll want to see him in a few days to check him and see how well he's healing. I'll go over his discharge orders with you, and my nurse will go over them again when you come to pick him up. I'm headed home now. Simmy looks as though he came through everything fairly well."

"I think it's time you went home and got some rest. Thank you so much for the care and concern."

Dr. Crouser didn't comment on my compliment but instead told me that Sim would be on a course of antibiotics for a few days and should be fed a soft diet.

"How about I buy some baby food and feed him that until you see him again?"

"Perfect. That should work just fine. I'll check in with you tomorrow to see how he's doing."

The next morning, Sim ate the breakfast of baby food that I prepared for him, and I gave him a dose of Metacam for some noticeable stiffness. I'm sure he must have felt sore from the day before because of being confined most of the day.

Sim looked to be making progress over the next few days. He appeared to be tolerating the antibiotic, and the Metacam seemed to be keeping him comfortable. In fact, he gave us the impression that he was feeling well enough that Frank and I felt comfortable meeting some friends to relax and enjoy a movie. "You wait and guard the house for me," I told Sim as I always did when I left. The only difference this time was that instead of staying in the family room, Sim was more comfortable in his bed in the living room. Since his dental surgery, this was his place of choice until we went to bed at night where he slept in our room in his crate. We were gone for about three hours. On the way home, Frank and I talked about the little improvement we saw in Sim. We agreed that it wasn't much, but at least the direction he was going in was good. This gave us the confidence to leave him alone for a few hours.

When we got home, I walked through the kitchen. There is a small look-through where I could see into the living room. "Hi, Sim," I said, fully expecting to see him in his bed. Surprisingly, I didn't see him. I headed to the living room, and as I got closer, I could hear a faint cry. When I reached the slate entry, Sim was sprawled on the slates in a puddle of urine and there was a bowel movement off to his right side, a fair distance away from him. "It's OK, Sim," I said soothingly. "It looks like you didn't want to soil the rug. What a good boy." I got one of Sim's towels and wrapped him in it. "Let's get you cleaned up, Bud." My heart was breaking, and I was choking back the tears. I didn't want to upset Sim any more than he already was. I wasn't sure whether he had had a seizure or if he just was unable to control himself. *Damn*, I said to myself. *Time with him is getting shorter and shorter*. Frank came into the family room, where I was cleaning Sim with some waterless shampoo.

"What happened?" he asked me. I told him the condition I found Sim in. "We have to take him to the hospital."

Frank lost his temper with me. "It's almost midnight! He seems to be settling down. Why do you want to do that to him?" It took all I had to control myself from both getting angry and crying. I didn't want to upset Sim in any way.

"We have to take him because he may have had a seizure and may have another one. We can't take the chance. I know why you feel the way you do, but we must go now." I think Frank could sense the urgency in my voice as well as my annoyance with him. I was in no mood to be interrogated.

"OK, let's go," he said.

Dr. Danielle Munday was on duty. She was a very dedicated vet who had traveled from the Boston area to Springfield, about a ninety-mile trip, in order to work all weekend in Emergency. Although she was a petite, slender woman, she was amazingly strong-willed. She was fighting the battle of her life against cancer. Today, she no longer needed the familiar triangular scarf to cover her bald head. Her black hair had grown in and was in a cute pixie style. It had been a long, hard battle up to now, and I think her work helped her retain her emotional balance.

"What seems to be wrong with Mr. Sims tonight?" she asked me. I explained what happened.

"It's good that you brought him in. I'll examine him and do some blood work, but there really is no way to tell if he's had a seizure." She scooped him up in her arms. "I'll be back shortly." I sat down on the bench, my mind racing. I looked at Frank and said, "I don't know what the best thing for Sim is. I don't like this development at all."

Dr. Munday came back with Sim after about twenty minutes. "I'll have the results for the blood work in a few hours. Dr. Crouser will get a copy of it along with my notes. There's something neurological going on. I don't know exactly what, but throughout my exam, I kept seeing neurological issues. I'm going to give you a syringe of valium. If it appears that he is having a seizure, stick this up his butt, release it, and get him in here immediately. It will at least lessen the symptoms of the seizure." I could see the concern and frustration in her expression because there was nothing more that she could do for Sim at this point.

When I got home, I read the report Dr. Munday had written up regarding Sim's condition. It said, "Very unsteady on all four limbs. Suspected blind or partially blind with limited vision, generalized atrophy. Please call or come right back if Mr. Sims declines in any way or if he should have a seizure. Please call and discuss with Dr. Crouser."

"Damn it," I thought. *"She's really being very blunt, and I think, overstating the problem. My boy isn't blind. I know he's failing, but he's not that bad, and I still feel that something is being overlooked."*

The next day, Sim needed help to keep going on his walk and to eat his breakfast. I had my training classes that day, so Frank had to take care of Sim. He made notes so that I would know how things went. When I got home and gave Sim his dinner, he ate by himself with a little help.

"He's doing better with his meal than he did this morning. He did eat on his own at lunchtime," Frank told me.

"This is what is so frustrating to me, Frank. It's this up and down with him that is so hard to figure out. I'll call Dr. Crouser tomorrow if he doesn't call me first. Maybe he can make some sense of all of this."

Dr. Crouser's call came early the next morning. He wanted to know what I found when we got home Saturday night. I told him, "This is the first time we've left him alone in weeks, and we were only gone about three hours." My frustration was on full display. "I'm not sure if he had a seizure or not, but I felt it was important that I get him checked. Dr. Munday said that it's hard to diagnose. All I can tell you is that he was lying in his urine and couldn't get up, but the bowel movement was off to his right side about three feet away. I would think that if he had a seizure, the bowel movement would be closer to him."

"I agree with you," Dr. Crouser said. I could hear the frustration in his voice as well. "You're doing all you can. I think we should check his B12 level and see if it is where it should be. Let's see if that tells us anything. I'll see you Wednesday night. Bring a stool sample as well so I can check and see if everything is OK."

Wednesday, we took Sim into the exam room after the tech, Kelly, weighed him. He had dropped another pound. She said that she would mention it to Dr. Crouser.

"He'll be with you shortly."

As usual, I had some notes with me to go over with Dr. Crouser. I sat on the bench and put Sim next to me. He sat with me for a short time and then wanted to get down. I gently put him on the floor. As he began to walk around, I noticed that he seemed clumsier than usual, and he seemed to be folding his back toes under both feet every so often. I made a mental note to bring this to Dr. Crouser's attention. Dr. Crouser came into the room, and Sim walked over to greet him. "Hi, Simmy. How's my boy tonight?" He looked at me and could see the concern on my face. "His stool looks good. No occult blood in it."

"Good," I said. Dr. Crouser noticed the sheet of paper with my notes on it.

"Let's go over what your concerns are, and then I will examine him and take some blood to check his B12 level."

"Well, Dr. Crouser, I wasn't happy with the write-up that Dr. Munday did when I brought Sim into Emergency the other night. She made his condition sound very serious. I respect her expertise, but I want to know what your opinion is."

"Emergency doctors try to give you every possibility. She doesn't know Simmy as well as I do because I see him on a regular basis."

"I know that Sim is on borrowed time now. I don't want to have him suffer or lose his dignity, but I just don't feel that the time has come yet."

"OK, Simmy," Dr. Crouser. "Let's see how you're doing." He had me walk Sim up and down the hallway as he observed Sim's demeanor. "I see what you mean. He sort of leans to the right and then stumbles a little bit when you turn him around. Let's put him on some Metacam for a few days. It could be his arthritis that's giving him trouble." We went back into the exam room. Dr. Crouser repeated the neurological exam that he had done before. "I don't see any significant change. At least he hasn't gotten any worse. I'll take some blood from him to be tested and we'll find if his B12 level has come up. I think if you add some baby cereal to the baby food, it might help him pick up some weight. It also will add some more nutrition."

It was now February 1. Sim appeared to be on a downward spiral since the end of November. He still had a few days of the antibiotic to take. I gave him his usual dose, and within fifteen minutes, he began acting agitated and started to cough. "I guess he's had enough of the antibiotic. It seems to be going against him. I'll have to call Dr. Crouser and let him know," I told Frank. "Here we go again. I just can't seem to get a handle on what's going on with Sim or what to do for him."

I let Dr. Crouser know. He felt that Sim could not take any more of the antibiotic. "I think he's had enough for now. I don't want to get his stomach badly upset. We'll just have to play it by ear. His B12 level came back normal, so we don't have to give him any more injections."

Sim's condition varied from day to day. Some days were better than others. On good days, he had an appetite and some good energy. There was a certain pleasant look that was in his eyes that let me know he felt fairly well and was happy. Other days, he would eat very little if at all, was lethargic, and had a sad look in his eyes. It was as though he was trying to disengage himself from the discomfort he was feeling. I was in constant contact with Dr. Crouser, keeping him informed on Sim's condition and certain changes. He developed an ear infection, some inflammation in his eye, and inflammation of his prepuce. We would get one problem under control, and another would materialize. I was getting more and more concerned.

Valentine's Day arrived, and I dreaded it. For all the years that I had Sim, I always picked out a card with a cute dog on the front for Frank from him. I picked up an appropriate card for Frank, but it was bittersweet. I knew that it was probably the last Valentine's Day card from Sim to Frank that I would ever buy. I also always got a Valentine's Day–themed toy for Sim. Not this year. Instead, I decided that I would spoil him for the day, doing anything that he wanted to do that made him happy. If that meant holding him all day, I would do it. If he wanted to play, I would do that. If I fed him something and he really enjoyed it, he could have as much of it as he wanted in small portions throughout the day.

I started the day by reading the entry on my calendar. It said,

> It's not of lace and chocolate that valentines are made—
> All such things are lovely but disintegrate and fade.
> But love—when once it grows to be—
> Is richer far than jade—
> I only know—I love you!
>
> —"When Did I Start to Love You?"

The saying hit me like a ton of bricks. *How true*, I thought. *Love has a way of preparing us for the inevitable. Damn it, I'll be prepared, but I won't let go until I absolutely have to.* With that, I picked Sim up and gave him a long hug. I could feel the loss of muscle tone. "This is your day, Bud. Anything that makes you happy is what we will do today. Even if that means doing nothing, I'll be right here with you."

I gave him a kiss in that special spot on his forehead. He looked at me with soft, comfortable eyes and gave me the Shih Tzu swallow. I put him down on the floor, and he went over to his bed in the family room that was bathed in sunshine. He stayed there comfortably while I exercised. For the first time in a long while, he came over to me, brought his heart-shaped squeaky toy, and pushed it against me while I did my post-workout stretches. I laughed and hugged Sim.

"Is this what you want to do for a while?" I said as I grabbed the toy and tossed it a short distance for him. He gave me his classic sneeze as he retrieved the toy. "OK, Sim. We're not going to overdo this. I don't want to tire you out. You've got to save energy for the rest of the day." I tossed the toy again, and again he happily got it. "One more time and then I have to take my shower, Bud." I threw the toy; he brought it back to me and sat and then dropped into a down. "Guess you're telling me you've had enough for now." He got up and walked to his bed, curled up in the sun, and looked perfectly fine. I swallowed hard. As I turned to leave the room, I said to him, "It's in your paws, Bud. You keep guiding me through this journey. You've done a great job so far."

All in all, Valentine's Day was a happy one. Although the distance of Sim's walks continued to shrink more and more, he seemed perky and interested in his surroundings. His appetite was fairly good, and he enjoyed his meals. Frank commented on how good he seemed.

"I'm happy that today he seems so much better, but I'm not building any false hopes. We just have to take one day at a time."

Some of Sim's usual habits were changing. I made notes every day so that I could tell Dr. Crouser about them when I took him in for his physical. One change was that Sim would go into his crate in the bedroom when Frank went to bed. When I would come in later, I would give him a couple of "night-night" cookies, and he would sleep through the night. Now he was coming out to me about forty-five minutes after Frank had gone to bed. Sim wanted to go out again even though Frank had taken him out just before bedtime. It was cold, and there were some small patches of snow on the ground. I would bundle both of us up, grab a flashlight, and take him out. I noticed that at this time of night, he would circle to the right on the grass. Usually he would pee again, but sometimes he did nothing but circle. "It's OK, Bud," I would tell him because he seemed upset by the situation. "We're going to see Dr. Crouser soon. Let's see what he thinks." Sim just looked trustingly at me. I would then bring him back in the house and hold him to warm him up before I put him back in his crate for the night. In an odd way, he seemed to enjoy this special time together just before going to sleep for the night.

The day of Sim's physical finally arrived. I went over all my notes with Dr. Crouser. He seemed perplexed by a lot of what I was telling him. He examined Sim and didn't give me a lot of feedback as he usually did. I looked at him to see if his expression would indicate that he was sending me a message without actually saying it. I could see the sadness on his face. I broke the silence when I said, "I don't want to overreact, but I don't want Sim to suffer. That's worse than losing him as far as I am concerned."

"Let's see what the blood work shows us, and I will also send out his urine for a comprehensive test. I'm as baffled as you are because everything usually comes back within normal range."

"What do we do if everything comes back normal again? Something is wrong, and we haven't been able to figure it out yet. Should we do another ultrasound of his abdomen to see if anything is going on with his IBD or intussusception?"

"I think that's a good course of action. These tests will take a little bit longer than usual because they are so comprehensive. I'll let you know as soon as I get everything back." Once again, Dr. Crouser gave me a warm, reassuring handshake. "Take care of yourself," he told me.

I went to the desk to pay my bill. Mary looked at the charges and said, "Dr. Crouser is ordering everything from soup to nuts." She looked up at me. "You look concerned."

"I am, Mary. Dr. Crouser is doing his best to figure this out what is going on with Sim and help him, but we can't seem to get a handle on it."

It was obvious that Sim's condition was worsening. He was eating sporadically. I kept using baby food and also boiled chicken breast. Some days, he wanted a little of everything. Other days, he barely ate at all. Finally, Dr. Crouser called with the results of the blood work. Everything was within normal range other than his usual slightly elevated BUN rate. Dr. Crouser felt that it was his diet that was elevating his BUN rate and was not concerned.

"Let's schedule an ultrasound since nothing showed up in these tests," I suggested.

"OK. I'll see how Liz Schaler's schedule is and let you know. She's here on Monday. Hopefully I can get him in." I hung up the phone and looked at Sim. I could see how frail he had become. And yet he still had his agenda on good days. He would eat, take his walk, although it consisted of walking across the street to the nearest light pole to relieve himself, and occasionally play with a toy.

He also would tremble for no apparent reason, and the circling became more of a regular occurrence than an occasional one. I was realizing the sands of his hourglass of life were running out even more quickly now. But I still had no answer as to what was wrong with him and if whatever it was could be treated. All I wanted was for Sim to have some comfort and better quality of life in his last days.

Chapter 57

God can help me clear away the obstructions
and see clearly where the path is.

—"Decision Vision"

Dr. Crouser called to let me know that Sim was scheduled for the ultrasound. It was the usual procedure. I had to withhold food from midnight Sunday. This time it wasn't much of an issue as he was not eating very enthusiastically anyway.

"OK, Bud. Let's see what this ultrasound shows us, if anything. I'm doing everything I can think of to help you and I'm beginning to run out of bullets." I was holding Sim as I talked to him, and he had his head tucked under my chin. He was doing this more frequently now. It was as though being this close to me was giving him some sort of comfort.

"I love you, too, Bud. This is so hard for both of us. I can't help but think that you know what is going on." He moved his head, looked at me, and gave me the Shih Tzu swallow. "We'll work it out together. We're a good team. Maybe tomorrow we'll get some answers." Sim tucked his head under my chin again, almost as if he agreed with my assessment of the situation.

I dropped Sim off Monday morning. Dr. Crouser's tech told me he would call me with the results and let me know when I could pick Sim up. As I drove home, I kept thinking to myself, *What will I do if everything comes back normal? Something is wrong with Sim. I don't know what it could be, so where do we go from here?* I said a prayer and asked God to guide me through this one. I held Sim's life in my hands at this point. *I don't want to let him go, but if it is the best for him, I will.*

Dr. Crouser called to let know that I could come in at 8:00 p.m. to talk to him about the results of the ultrasound and to pick up Sim. He told me that he had given Sim a bath to get the gel from the ultrasound off. He commented on how much Sim seemed to enjoy it as well as the brushing he gave him. In hindsight, I realized that the brushing was a form of neurological stimulation.

When we went into the exam room to see Dr. Crouser, he had Sim's chart in front of him. It was so thick that it resembled a Congressional budget bill. He greeted us warmly, but I could tell that he was perplexed. "Everything looks good. There are no ulcers or growths. That's good news."

I looked at him and sighed.

"I guess it is, but there is something wrong with Sim, and we just haven't found it yet. When Sim had the first MRI, the report from Dr. Russo said that he had hydrocephalus. When she called me, she also told me that she gave Sim a shot of something. I don't remember the name, but it started with a *d*. She said that they give it to dogs that have had traumatic injury to the brain and it helps. I asked her if it was something that Sim should continue receiving, and she said that it was a one-time thing. Sim was noticeably improved for about ten days to two weeks after that shot."

Dr. Crouser started to flip through Sim's chart. "Was it Dexamethasone that she gave him?" he asked as he kept looking through the paperwork.

"Yes, I think that's what she told me."

"Well, there's nothing in the report about it that they sent to me."

"Yes, I know because there was nothing about it in the copy I got." I could see that Dr. Crouser was processing the information from Dr. Russo's report and continued reading through it.

"There is nothing anywhere in the report about the Dexamethasone."

"I'm sure that's what she told me when she called to tell me the results of the MRI and how Sim was doing. He definitely seemed better for a while."

"Dexamethasone is a steroid," Dr. Crouser told us. "Maybe we should start him on a low dose of Prednisone to see if that helps him. We'll try it for about a week and see what happens." I felt that doing something was better than doing nothing. Once again, I wasn't happy about the Prednisone because of the side effects, but if this would bring some relief to Sim, I was willing to try it. "Let's give it a few days and see if there is any improvement. In the meantime, I'll call the neurologist and run it by her. Maybe she'll have an idea of how we should proceed."

During the next week, Sim was up and down. His condition would wax and wane, but his "good" days were not as good as they had been. His circling to the right varied from day to day. I noticed that when Sim panted, his tongue seemed longer to me. Although I made a mental note of this symptom, I kept it to myself. At this point, other than talking to Dr. Crouser, I felt the less said the better. It was as if I spoke in a negative manner, it would hasten the inevitable.

It was a week since we had started the Prednisone. Frank and I brought Sim in for his appointment with Dr. Crouser. I had my list of observations to go over with him as well as the stool sample that he always had me bring in to check and make sure Sim's intestinal tract was not becoming upset. I told Dr. Crouser how Sim was up and down. Maybe he had some very minor improvement as far as doing less circling, but his appetite was not good. This surprised him because the Prednisone usually increases the appetite. He brought in the baby scale to weigh Sim. He was still about eighteen pounds but looked a bit frailer. His decline was becoming more and more noticeable.

"Let's increase the Pred. You did see slight improvement, and I put him on the lowest dose possible because of the possible side effects. Maybe just a little bit more will help him."

I gave Dr. Crouser the look of someone who is desperate for guidance in a difficult situation. He read it perfectly and gave me a look of deep understanding.

"Our family has been going through a similar situation with our Greyhound, Jack. I recently had to put him down. We did everything we could for him, including lots of laundry."

I nodded, knowing exactly what he was talking about.

"It was Jack's time. He no longer had any good quality of life and there were no more options to help him. We were all heartbroken, but it was right thing to do."

That night, Dr. Crouser said a lot to me without directly saying anything. I knew he would guide me in the right direction when the time was here. But for now, he still felt that we could have Sim with us for a while longer.

The increased dose of Prednisone seemed to make a difference. Although Sim was not back to perfect health, he did show improvement. The circling was less, his appetite was a bit better, and he had more energy. I didn't want to get my hopes up, but let's be honest, I did to some degree.

Once again, I ran into Dr. Munday during my Sunday training classes. She was working Emergency all weekend. She asked me how things were with Mr. Sims. I was more cheerful than usual and told her about the improvement he was showing on the Prednisone. She frowned. "I had a professor in veterinary school who performed autopsies. He told me that his patients are happy right up to the point that they meet him. Steroids make them feel good, but are not really helping. Look at me. I feel fine, and if they can just take care of the tumor on my liver, life would be good."

She took my breath away with her honesty. My raised hopes became deflated because deep down I knew she was right. And I felt bad for the condition she found herself in. She kept battling bravely, and every time she thought her life would turn around, another tumor would show up in another part of her body. As much as I may have resented my encounter with her, she gave me a good dose of reality.

A couple of days later, Sim became very agitated midmorning. He began circling vigorously again and almost looked like he was having a panic attack. Holding him seemed to soothe him a bit, but as soon as I let him go, he began circling again. I put him in his crate in the family room and called Dr. Crouser to let him know what was going on.

"I want to see you tonight. Come in at nine p.m."

Sim slept from about 10:30 until 2:30 p.m. When he woke up, I took him out for a potty walk. He seemed a bit stronger and less agitated. "How about something to eat, Bud?" Sim looked at me with brighter eyes than I had seen in a while. I dished out several different flavors of food to see which one he wanted. The way things were going with his appetite, what he ate for breakfast, he wouldn't touch for lunch, and what he ate for lunch, he didn't want for dinner. He ate some of everything. I didn't care as long as he was taking some nourishment.

At the appointment that evening, Dr. Crouser had Frank walk Sim up and down the hallway, observing Sim carefully. When we went back into the exam room, he gave him a slight physical exam but concentrated more on testing Sim's neurological responses.

"I want you to stop the Prednisone and call to make an appointment for another MRI. I spoke to the neurologist, and she wants to see if there are any changes."

I was able to get an appointment for the MRI quickly. I was to bring Sim in for it on Friday. Dr. Russo's assistant, Dr. Tooker, would be doing the MRI, but we would have to bring Sim back on Monday for Dr. Russo to do the spinal tap.

I called Dr. Crouser to let him know. He was very happy that it was going to be done that quickly.

I made some notes to take with me when I met with Dr. Tooker to let her know about the changes I was seeing. One of the biggest changes was that Sim would whimper and want to go out during the night. This was a change from when he slept through the night. Some nights after I took him out, I would sit in the antique rocking chair in our family room. I would rock him and talk to him. This seemed to help him relax.

"I know, Bud. This is hard on both of us. I don't want to let go of you, and you don't want to let go of me. Somehow we understand each other and what we need." Sim would curl up in my lap and sometimes sit up so that his head was firmly under my chin. When he seemed settled, I would take him back to our bedroom and put him in his crate. My last prayer of the night before I went to sleep was that the MRI would tell us something that would help Sim. And I would add that if this was his last day with me, let him be in my arms when he breathed his last.

We dropped Sim off for the MRI, and I went over my notes with Dr. Tooker. She was glad that I had kept such good notes. "These will be very helpful along with the information that Dr. Crouser faxed us. I'll call you when he's ready to go home. It will be sometime this evening. Unfortunately, you will have to bring him back Monday so that Dr. Russo can do the spinal tap."

We picked Sim up that evening. He seemed better than when we left him earlier. While I was paying at the desk, Frank took Sim outside so that he could relieve himself. I watched as Sim bounced alongside Frank.

Dr. Tooker greeted me. "I'll be making up my report for Dr. Russo, and I'll go over everything with you once we see the results of the spinal tap."

"That's fine. This way I'll get all the information at once. I couldn't believe how perky Sim seems."

"I gave him a shot of Dexamethasone. Keep notes at home about how he is the next few days, and let me know on Monday."

"Dr. Tooker, I've been keeping a daily chart on Mr. Sims since his reaction to the rabies shot in 2006. It's quite a pile of papers, but it comes in handy"

"Please keep doing it for him. It is very helpful to us as well if we need to know certain information for a specific time. You'd be surprised at how many owners give me a funny look when I ask them how many times the dog had a bowel movement today or what the dog ate and what time the dog ate last. I get a totally blank look. It's not that they are bad owners, but their awareness to detail is not like yours. Keep up the good work with Mr. Sims. You're doing everything you possibly can. You know you can call me anytime for any reason."

Saturday morning, Dr. Crouser called to see how Sim was doing. "They gave him a shot of Dexamethasone, and he seems stronger."

"How about the circling?" Dr. Crouser asked.

"He still is doing it, but it is much less."

"Well, I'm not quite sure what to make of it, but we'll know more once he has the spinal tap done."

We got ready early Monday morning, put Sim on the back seat, and began our trip.

As we neared the facility, Sim whimpered and extended his right front paw to me. I reached back and held it. "What's up, Bud? We're almost there. One more test and hopefully we won't have to come back. You're probably sick and tired of all the poking and prodding you've been through." He put his head back down, resting it on his favorite toy, his stuffed squirrel, and seemed to relax.

"We're here, Bud." Sim woke up and looked at me. He appeared to be the slightest bit confused. I thought it was because he had just woken up. Frank took Sim for a walk while I went in to let them know we were there.

Things were building up on me; the reality of the situation was becoming more and more clear. Although Sim had appeared a bit better since the shot on Friday, he was looking even frailer, and the recorded weight on the receipt they gave me was seventeen pounds.

Early in the afternoon Dr. Tooker called. "Mr. Sims has meningitis. We have to run tests to find out if it is bacterial or not. If it is, he will have to be on a regime of antibiotics and Prednisone. If it's not bacterial, then he'll be on a regime of Prednisone only."

"What is the prognosis, Dr. Tooker?"

"Not bad. If we can get the inflammation under control, then we manage it like diabetes. In other words, once it's under control, you may have to give him Prednisone once a week."

"What does it indicate if it's not bacterial meningitis?"

"It means that he has inflammation of his brain that is caused by his immune system overreacting."

My thoughts returned to the rabies shot Sim had in 2006 and all the health issues we had dealt with ever since. I wanted to ask the question if there was any connection, but I held my tongue. I would have to wait until the results came back.

It seemed like an eternity before the results of Sim's spinal tap came back. When it did, it showed that he did not have bacterial meningitis. He would not have to take an antibiotic. What this meant was that his immune system was in "overdrive." The amount of steroid would be raised to try to suppress his immune response. If this had been done without checking for bacterial meningitis first, suppressing his immune system would have been a grave error. Dr. Crouser consulted with Dr. Russo, and they decided on the proper amount of prednisone that would hopefully help Sim.

The higher dose of prednisone seemed to be helping, although it was day to day. Some days, even some hours, were better than others. As usual with Sim, his condition waxed and waned. The circling would diminish and then would pick up again. His eating was the same. Sometimes he could eat from his food dish with just a little help; other times, I had to hand feed him like a baby. I didn't care what I had to do, but the reality of his situation was closing in on me.

Sim's most uncomfortable time seemed to be at night. Frank would put him to bed in his crate in our bedroom. He would sleep for about twenty minutes and then come to me to take him out again. Sometimes he would have to go. Other times, he would just circle in the yard. When he didn't come out to see me, he would whimper when I came into the bedroom to go to bed and give him a pat to say "good night." I would pick him up out of his crate to take him outside. It seemed as if he wanted to be close to me during the night. I don't know if he was afraid of being alone in the dark and that by staying with him, I gave him comfort and security. After taking him outside to see if he had to relieve himself, I would sit with him in the antique rocker in the family room. If he didn't relieve himself, I would put him on his mat and either sit and sleep in the rocker or put my exercise mat on the floor, get a blanket and my pillow, and sleep on the floor next to him. I wanted to be close by in the event he had to relieve himself in a hurry.

Frank was not pleased about this. It was because he was worried about my health and not getting enough sleep. I was averaging about four hours per night. I didn't care. I cherished every moment with Sim, and it seemed as though he felt the same way.

"What do you do all night with him?" Frank asked me.

"Well, usually I sit in the rocking chair and rock Sim to soothe him. I talk to him about our years together and all the crazy things that we've been through. Sometimes I just hold him close and tell him that whatever he does, it's OK. I understand where he is at this point. And then there are the times when I sing softly to him."

"What do you sing?" Frank wanted to know.

"'You Are My Sunshine,' 'I'll Be Loving You Always,' 'Wind Beneath My Wings,' whatever comes to mind. He doesn't seem to have any preference and relaxes with all of them. And I always kiss that special spot on his forehead. I must have kissed that spot a million times in our time together." Tears were streaming down my cheeks.

Frank gave me a hug. "It's OK, Peg. You're doing all you possibly can."

"I know. I just have the feeling as though I'm on a death watch. I've been through the good times and bad times with him, and I'll miss him terribly. He's been my buddy, and without saying a word, he has always been there when I needed a laugh, someone to listen to me when I needed to vent, never questioning why, and when I needed to cry and not feel foolish, even if it was some dumb thing that had me upset. When I'm with him during the night, I almost pray that he will let go and rest in peace. But it's as though he doesn't want to put me through that. Only time will tell. If I have to stay with him and sleep in the family room on the floor every night, I will."

Frank looked at me. "I'm worried about you. You look tired and strained. This is tough duty. Do you want me to alternate nights in the family room so that one of us always with Sim?"

"I don't think so. He seems to want me, and you need your sleep because of going to work. I'll be all right. This won't last forever. In fact, I don't think it will last much longer."

I started wondering why the meningitis that we were now treating in Sim did not show up when he had the MRI in November. He certainly was showing symptoms. It kept eating at me. What if it had shown up then? We would have had more time to treat him, and he would not have gotten to the state he was in now. My emotions ran between sadness, knowing that I was going to lose him soon, and anger because I felt he was suffering needlessly.

Frank said, "What are you thinking about? I can see the sadness on your face."

I explained what was going through my mind.

"Dr. Tooker told you that this is manageable once we get it under control, right?"

"Yes, she did. But it still bothers me that Sim had to suffer all these months when he possibly could have been started on the treatment so much sooner. Why wasn't it picked up the first time?"

"Who knows, Peg? Things just happen. You did the best you could and followed the advice of the professionals."

"Sometimes, that's just not good enough. I have learned from Sim that you constantly have to peel the onion. What is on the surface is not necessarily the root of the problem. Let me go through what was going on with him when Dr. Murphy saw him and ordered the first MRI. As we know, Dr. Murphy would have bet the farm that Sim had a brain tumor."

I picked up the sizeable stack of papers that I kept on the kitchen table. It was the daily chart I began keeping since Sim's reaction to the rabies vaccine in 2006. *Time to start peeling the onion*, I thought. *The answer is in here—I just have to find it.* I started to review each page. I scoured each one, looking at each day, going over every bit of information that was written down for that day. From the time Sim got up in the morning until he went to bed at night, a notation was made as to how he was feeling, what and when he ate, how many times he peed and pooped, and if things looked normal, if he was taking any medication, when it was administered and if he was helped by it or had an adverse reaction.

If anything unusual or extraordinary happened during the day, I would take a yellow highlighter and highlight the date. This helped me when I was going to take Sim to see Dr. Crouser. I could easily pinpoint anything of importance and make a note of it.

I started anxiously going through the pages again, trying desperately to find something that could help me make sense of what was happening to Sim. "Let me go back before the Sunday after Thanksgiving when we took Sim to see Dr. Murphy. There's got to be something that will lead me to some sort of answer." I could see that Frank was interested but was not as "into it" the way I was. I was like a dog with a bone. "When I saw Dr. Murphy, I told him about the Pepto Bismol and my suspicion that Sim had bismuth poisoning." I thumbed through the pages, going back from that date.

"I think I've found the answer, Frank."

"You have? What did you come up with?"

"Well, I'm not sure, and I will call Dr. Tooker and see what she thinks about it. Remember that Sim was nine weeks past taking the Pepto Bismol, and in my research, it said that it takes twelve weeks for the system to return to normal levels in humans? I don't know if that would be the same in dogs. But he was taking the Pepto to soothe his stomach so that he could take the Metacam for his arthritis. Pepto has the equivalent of aspirin in it, and Metacam is an anti-inflammatory medication. I wonder if the combination of those two medications kept the inflammation at bay so that it didn't show up in the first MRI."

I called Dr. Tooker the next day and told her my thoughts. "That is a strong possibility. Great work figuring it all out. How did you do it?"

"I looked through the daily chart for Sim that I told you I have been keeping ever since his health began to fail in 2006. Once you told us that Sim had meningitis, it bothered me as to why it didn't show up when the first MRI and spinal tap were done. We had the tests done because he was symptomatic. So I started what I call *peeling the onion*. I went back to when his symptoms started and what, if anything, was different than now. The Pepto and Metacam got me thinking."

"Well, let's see how things go along now with the Pred. If you see anything unusual, either good or bad, feel free to call me."

On one hand, I felt that we might be making some progress, but on the other hand, I was concerned that it was going to be too little too late.

Unfortunately, Sim's accidents in the house were becoming more frequent. He was such a dignified dog that he always tried to make it to the door to let me know that he had to go out. However, in his weakened condition, he wouldn't quite make it.

I called Dr. Crouser and left him a message. I found it amusing that my messages were becoming so long that his answering machine would turn off before I finished, so I had to call back two and sometimes three times to finish my message. I would promise each time that the next time I called, I would make an effort to get all the information out on the first contact, but it was rare that it happened.

Dr. Crouser called me back late in the day. He said that he wanted me to bring Sim in on Wednesday morning to try injections of Dexamethasone. "Let's see if this works for Simmy. The Prednisone seems to be working for a shorter and shorter time. He had good results with the Dexamethasone before. The effect seemed to last for quite a while. Maybe we can get him stabilized."

"It's worth a try."

"Then I'll see you in the morning at eight-thirty."

My friend of many years, Pat, was going to come for a visit the following week. We met where we both worked as secretaries in New York City. Pat and her husband moved to Florida many years ago. Even though they had divorced, she still lived and worked there. We had made plans in March for her to come for a visit in April. I sent her an e-mail and explained what was going on with Sim. I told her that I would understand if she decided not to come. It was supposed to be a vacation for her and given Sim's condition and having to take him every twelve hours for shots, I felt that I should give her the opportunity to change her mind. She promptly sent be back an e-mail, saying that she had no problem with the situation. She would go with me each time I had to take Sim to see Dr. Crouser. "I'll drive and you hold the pooch, and we can take him for his shots. That's what friends are for!"

She had not been around Sim very much, but she was as fond of him as people who saw him every day. I was so relieved and taken by her e-mail that I wrote back to her, "Bless you, bless you, bless you. Your response brought tears to my eyes, probably because I could use a good cry to relieve the stress...no smoking to lean on anymore. Just finished cleaning up another accident, but you do whatever you have to do."

Sim seemed fairly good in the morning. It was an unusually hot early spring day. We had come out of a cold, snowy, longer-than-usual winter, which had lasted through most of March. It was now mid-April and it felt like July. I drove Sim to the appointment with Dr. Crouser. When I got there, I was a little early for the appointment, so I walked Sim to give him the chance to relieve himself. He began panting from the heat, and once again, I noticed that his tongue seemed longer than normal to me. I made a mental note of that and took him in for his appointment.

The door opened in the cubicle and Dr. Crouser came in. "Good morning, Simmy. How are you doing this morning?" Sim wagged his tail.

I picked him up and put him on the exam table. "He looks pretty good today. I want to do a brief neurological exam and then give him the shot of Dex."

I watched as Dr. Crouser tickled the bottom of Sim's paws, noting his reaction. He then took out his keys and rattled them. Sim looked at them with interest. "OK. I'm going to give him the shot."

I stood in front of Sim and talked to him as Dr. Crouser felt Sim's front leg to find a vein. "Good boy, Simmy. This may sting a little," he said as he injected Sim. He blew on the spot after he withdrew the needle. "That's my boy, Simmy. Good job." Dr. Crouser looked at me and said, "I want to see you back here in twelve hours so I can give Simmy another shot. I will be giving him a shot of the Dexamethasone every twelve hours for a week. I'm hopeful that this will help him. If not, there's nothing else I know of that I can do."

"Will you be here tonight, or will I see the ER doctor?"

"I will be here each morning and each evening to take care of Simmy."

"That's above and beyond, Dr. Crouser. I appreciate what you are doing more than you'll ever know."

Dr. Crouser smiled kindly and patted my shoulder. He gave Sim a pat and said, "I'll see you tonight, Simmy. Stay cool today."

I put Sim in the passenger seat where he always rode with me. I got in the driver's side, started the car, and put on the air-conditioning. "It'll be nice and cool for you in a couple of minutes, Sim."

He let the breeze from the vents blow at him and then lay down on the seat. I pulled out and started the drive home. With my right hand, I gave Sim a couple of strokes, Dr. Crouser's words spinning around in my head. Sim took his paw and rested it in the palm of my hand. It was as if he knew that we were quickly approaching the end of our time together and wanted to make the most of the time we had left. My eyes started to mist with tears. "OK, Bud. Enough of this nonsense. I can't drive and cry at the same time, so I'll sing to you. That should cheer up both of us." He looked up at me and gave me the Shih Tzu swallow. The song that came to my mind was "The Wind Beneath My Wings." I softly began to sing the chorus: "Did you ever know that you're my hero?" He put his head down on the seat and let out a sigh of contentment. All was well for now.

We arrived home, and I put the car into the garage. I lifted Sim out of the car and started to take him into the house. Then I had a thought.

"Let's go out and get some fresh air, Sim." Sim seemed happy to be going for a walk. He trotted around the backyard as he hadn't done in quite a while. "Do you want to go out front and see what's happening?"

He trotted to the gate and patiently waited for me to open it. He seemed to enjoy being in the front yard where he hadn't been lately. He even wanted to go to his favorite telephone pole across the street and mark it. I was so elated that I just followed him. After he relieved himself, marking the pole, he wanted to go back across the street. When we got there, he lay down in the cool grass and shade of the big maple tree. I noticed him panting and the length of his tongue again.

I was sitting on the lawn petting him when a woman walked by. She must have lived in the neighborhood, but I had never seen her before.

"What a cute dog," she said. When she got closer, she said, "Is he OK? He looks very tired."

I explained to her that he had just come home from the vet and had more energy because of the vaccine. I was elated because he had walked more than he had in quite a while. She gave me a strange look but was pleasant.

"Maybe it's getting too warm for him out here."

"I was just about to go back in the house with him when you came along."

"Well, good luck. I hope all goes well for you." She continued on her way as I picked Sim up and brought him in the house. I put him on his bed in the family room and brought him a drink of water. He drank a little and then settled down for a nap.

Frank called in the afternoon, and I told him what Dr. Crouser had said. "Dr. Crouser is going to be there every morning and every night to treat Sim for the next week? What about the weekend?" Frank asked.

"He said he wanted to be the only one to treat him. That's how devoted to Sim he is."

"That's incredible."

"I know. We'll just have to see how things work out. I've got my fingers crossed, but I don't have any false hope."

Sim woke up from his nap. I was in the kitchen, and I could hear him stirring and whining. "OK, Bud. I'll help you. Let's go out." Sim walked to the door and suddenly lost control of his bowels. I could see that Sim was not happy with what he had done. "It's OK, Bud. You tried to hold it so you could do it outside. At least you were on the tiles." I took him outside, he peed, and I brought him back in. I cleaned up the floor.

"Sim, how about some lunch? We've got quite a variety for you. Ham, peas, and sweet potato sound good to me. Let's see if it appeals to you." I took the baby food jars out of the refrigerator and warmed them up in a bowl of hot water. When the temperature of the food felt right, I put some in Sim's dish. He went to it and seemed as though he wanted to eat it but was having trouble standing to eat.

"Guess you need some special treatment, Bud." I got a small baby spoon and sat down on the rug that was on the kitchen floor near Sim's dishes so he wouldn't slip and picked up Sim's dish. He anxiously came over to me. I took small amounts of the food out of his dish with the baby spoon and offered it to him. He licked it enthusiastically. "Good job, Sim. Guess that tastes good to you."

I continued feeding him. He didn't quite finish but ate enough that I was pleased.

Frank came home and wanted me to go into detail about what Dr. Crouser had said. I filled him in over dinner. I could see the concern on his face, but Frank always tried to stay optimistic.

"How did Sim do after the shot?"

I told him, letting him know of my concerns.

"Let's just think good thoughts. As ill as Sim is, he still seems to have his own timetable."

Dr. Crouser met us at 8:30 p.m. Instead of taking us into one of the usual exam rooms, he took us into the end room, which is carpeted. "I thought it might be easier for Simmy to walk around in here. Let's see how he's doing." Once again, he tickled the bottom of Sim's paws, rattled his keys, clapped, and called him, observing him closely. "How was he today?"

I took out my notes so I could tell Dr. Crouser exactly how the day had gone.

"Sounds like there was a slight improvement today."

"I would say there was. Maybe tomorrow will be that much better."

Dr. Crouser said that he was going to get the shot ready and to bring Sim into the exam room, where he would be waiting for us. Sim walked with us but was curling his back toes under. We pointed that out to Dr. Crouser. He said, "Frank, walk Simmy down the hall so I can watch him."

Frank walked Sim up and down the hallway. Dr. Crouser crouched down to observe how Sim was walking. "Let's see how he does in the morning. I'm hoping he'll do better." He gave him the shot, being very careful and gentle with him, almost as if he was handling a fragile piece of porcelain.

As we were leaving, one of the receptionists came in and made a fuss over Sim. Sim started to walk away. "Oh, poor baby. Why is he walking like that?"

"That's why we're here, Cathy. Dr. Crouser is giving him shots of Dexamethasone every twelve hours. This was his second shot today, and it seems to be helping. I'll be back in the morning."

"Good luck with everything, Peg. I hope it all works out for you."

I could sense the dread in her by her demeanor. It shook me to my core because I wanted to deny what was so obvious to everyone else. Sim's hourglass was almost empty on the top and full on the bottom.

Chapter 58

Yesterday's gone, and tomorrow may never come,
But we have this moment today.

—"War Cry," Sept. 2, 1989

Sim woke me up in the middle of the night. He actually slept longer than he had been. I got up, took him out of his crate, and brought him outside. After quite a while, he squatted and made a large pee. I figured that the steroid was making him want to urinate more than usual. When we got inside, he was wide awake and wanted me to sit and hold him. I sat in the antique rocker and held him. He kept his head tightly under my chin. "I know, I know, Bud," I said as I gently rocked back and forth. In a few minutes, he lowered himself in my lap. Instead of curling up in his usual manner, he struck what I called a swan pose. He turned his head so that it was resting on his back, much like a swan does when it tucks its beak under its wings and sleeps. I wasn't sure why he was doing this, but he seemed comfortable and I continued to rock him. I dozed on and off during the night. Sim was sleeping peacefully, and I wasn't about to disturb him. Frank was going to get up at four-thirty because he had an early meeting at work. When he got up, I could crawl into bed and get a couple of hours' sleep. He would take care of Sim's early walk and breakfast.

I woke up to Frank, saying, "Pegs, you've got to go to bed. I'll take care of Sim." I could feel Sim stretching on my lap. I opened my eyes, and Frank was standing over us.

"I guess it's four-thirty. Will you be able to take care of him and be ready to leave in time for your meeting?"

"Sure. I'll be fine. I'll let you know when I'm leaving. Go get some rest."

I once again realized how fortunate I was to have someone like Frank who cared as much for Sim as I did. He might not completely agree with how I handled the situation, but he was always there for both of us.

Thursday was a repeat of the day before. I took Sim to see Dr. Crouser in the morning. We were brought into the carpeted exam room again. He did the same examination and seemed a bit more pleased at Sim's responses. "I'll see you tonight. Have a good day." Again, Dr. Crouser was warm and understanding. Of course, I probably looked like I felt. With only two hours' sleep, I was beginning to look like a raccoon with the dark circles under my eyes.

When I took Sim in for his shot in the evening, I mentioned to Dr. Crouser that there still was some waxing and waning of Sim's symptoms. I also mentioned about the "swan pose" and the length of his tongue. Dr. Crouser shrugged. "I don't know what to tell you about either one of those things. Only Sim knows." He repeated the exam that he had done every twelve hours since we started the process. He didn't make any comment this time other than to say that he'd see us in the morning.

Sim did not sleep as well that night. He woke me up and was more restless than the night before. He would drift off to sleep and then wake up whining, extending his front paw. As soon as I held it and talked to him, he would settle down. His appetite was not great the next morning either. The positive effects were not lasting as long. I began to wonder if every twelve hours was too much for him and if we should cut back to once a day.

Chapter 59

In evaluating a problem accurately it is helpful
To have the wise viewpoint of someone who knows us
And cares for us, yet will tell us the truth even if they know
It is something we'd rather not hear.

—"Decision Vision"

Sim was whining a lot on the way to see Dr. Crouser. I held his front paw with my right hand as I drove with my left hand on the steering wheel. This seemed to give him some comfort but not as much as it had. I started counting the traffic lights out loud for him. There were seven lights between our house and the hospital. "Five more lights to go, Sim. Four more. Now there's only three. The next one is the one we turn on to Brookside Road. This is the last one, Bud, and we're there!" I tried to sound as cheerful as possible, thinking that it might make Sim feel better.

As Dr. Crouser ushered us into the exam room, he asked how things were. "I wonder if we should cut back on the shots. Maybe he might tolerate just one shot a day. He really was more agitated through the night and didn't eat as well this morning as he had been." Dr. Crouser sat on the bench, and I was sitting on the floor with Sim.

He took a deep breath and said, "I want to continue giving him the shots every twelve hours so that he has had a complete week of treatment. As I told you, if this doesn't do it, I don't know what else we can do for him. I'm going to call the neurologist today and let her know how things are going. Maybe they can come up with something that I don't know about." He then began his exam. Sim responded to the stimuli, some better than others, so it was hard to tell if there was some improvement, no improvement, or if he had gotten worse. In the manner to which I had become so accustomed, Dr. Crouser tried to be cheerful as he said to have a good day and that he would see us tonight. "We'll just keep trying," he told me.

I left, feeling sort of hollow inside. Maybe I was being too pessimistic, but I knew Sim very well, and he didn't seem to be improving in any consistent way. It almost was like a minute here, a minute there that he would seem better, and then without warning, he would regress. Once again, on the ride home, he wanted his front paw settled in my hand. "I know, Bud. I'm here for you. Only five more lights before we get home." I swallowed hard, trying to stay calm. All of a sudden, I burst out laughing. "Wow, Sim. I just did a Shih Tzu swallow!" Sim raised his head when he heard me laugh, looked at me, and then put his head down again. *At least he's still giving me some reaction. I guess that's a positive*, I thought to myself.

I tried to make the rest of the day as comfortable and happy for Sim as possible. I had to hand-feed him in small portions. He would eat and then take a nap. When he awoke, he would "call" me with a quiet little whimper. I would pick him up and take him outside to relieve himself. We'd come back in the house, and I would feed him again. I could feel and see him becoming weaker. "Damn it, Sim, I don't want to lose you. But you let me know how I should handle this for you. If you want to let go while I'm rocking you, I will understand. I love you so much. I just want to do what is best for you. You're going to have to take the lead this time."

Sim settled down in my lap, and I rocked him. He seemed comfortable, but I could see how much the illness was taking its toll on him. Nothing was making sense. I had been told that the steroids would get the meningitis under control and then it would become manageable. "Maybe I'm expecting great results too quickly. Maybe it will take just a bit more time for the steroids to begin working," I told myself. But deep down I didn't really believe this.

Sim sat up and put his head firmly under my chin then gave me a little kiss with a fleeting flick of his tongue. He then settled down in my lap again. "I know, Bud, I know." Those words said it all.

The phone rang. I was startled because I was deep in thought. It was Donna, a neighbor of ours who sold Avon cosmetics. I had been doing business with her for many years. She had gotten to know Sim, and as with almost everyone who met him, she was very attached to him. She told me that my order was in and wanted to know if she could stop by with it. I said anytime that was convenient for her would be fine.

When she came, I greeted her at the door. I was holding Sim in my arms. Her face fell when she saw him.

She began to pet him and said to me, "He's not looking too well. He's declined quite a bit since the last time I saw him."

"I know, Donna. We're doing all we can for him, but I think time is running out."

Her eyes filled with tears. "He's been so special to me. He would always happily greet me at the door every time I came. And when I was having a tough day, he would seem to know it and give me extra attention."

"He always knew when you called to tell me you were coming with a delivery. As soon as I would hang up the phone, Sim would jump up on the antique couch by the window and watch for you. I still don't know how he knew you were coming, but somehow he did."

I paid Donna, and she turned to leave. I could see the sadness on her face.

"Take care," I told her.

"You, too," she said, her voice barely audible.

Frank and I took Sim in for his 8:30 p.m. appointment with Dr. Crouser. The tech took us right to the carpeted exam room. Dr. Crouser came in and asked how the day went. 'So, so" I said, "I wonder if you should give him a B12 shot tonight along with the steroid. His energy level seems very low."

"I'll be happy to do that. I don't see any reason why not." He began his routine of calling to Sim, jiggling his keys to see Sim's response, and tickling the bottom of Sim's paws. He seemed to feel that Sim's responses were adequate.

"I noticed that Sim seemed as though the positive effects of the shot were wearing off more quickly. It seemed like it only lasted about ten hours this time." I could see Dr. Crouser pondering what I just said. "Sim has also been striking that swan pose, as I call it."

"I know you mentioned it to me, but explain exactly what it looks like."

"He lies down and stretches his neck and head on his back so that he looks like a swan when it is sleeping. Maybe he will do it while we're here so you can see what I'm talking about."

"I called the neurologist to go over how Simmy has been doing. She agreed that I continue giving him the Dexamethasone shots every twelve hours for the next four days. There is a chance that he has something called GME. Unfortunately, there is no cure for it."

"Is there a test that can be done so that we can find out if that is what he has?"

"The only way to know would be to take tissue from the brain…" Dr. Crouser's voice began to trail off as he finished the sentence. "And I obviously can't do that."

"What is GME?" Frank asked.

"It's major inflammation of the brain."

Frank and I looked at each other and then at Dr. Crouser. I think we were all thinking the same thing. Dr. Crouser tried to sound more cheerful. "Let's see how Simmy does walking, and then I'll give him both the B12 and Dex shots."

He got up from the bench, and we followed him to an exam room. "By the way, how did Sim get his name?"

I laughed to relieve the tension. "That's easy. I love to handicap thoroughbred race horses. Most of them get their names from a combination of the names of their dam and sire. Mr. Sim's mom's name was Miss Sassy Pants, and his father was Lord of Simba. It took me about five minutes to come up with his name."

Dr. Crouser laughed. I think he was trying to relieve the tension as well. He had Frank walk Sim up and down the hallway, but this time, he only had him do it once. Usually he would have Sim walk up and down the hallway several times. Sim was knuckling under the toes on his back paws. I looked at Dr. Crouser.

"What do you think?"

"I was hoping he would be looking much better by now. Let me give him his shots, and we'll check him out in the morning. The B12 might raise his energy level." As usual, Dr. Crouser was very gentle with Sim, trying to make the process as comfortable as possible.

When we got home, I gave Sim his evening snack, which he ate up. Frank did have to help him by lightly supporting him as he ate. "I guess that's a little better. At least he's standing up to eat."

"I hope so, Frank. We'll just have to take things one day at a time."

Frank took Sim out for his last evening walk. "Should I take him with me when I go into bed?"

"No, that's OK, Frank. I'll spend some time with him before I come to bed. I'll take care of putting him in his crate." Frank gave me a kiss good night and headed for the bedroom.

I picked Sim up and sat in my chair in the living room with him on my lap. The TV was on, but I barely paid any attention to it. I hugged Sim gently. His body felt very frail in my arms, and I could feel that his bones were becoming even more prominent. I gave him a kiss on that special spot on his forehead, breathing in deeply and savoring his scent. Sim looked at me with the look of trust I had seen over and over again in the twelve-and-a-half years we had been together. It was almost as if he knew what I was struggling with and was giving me permission to obey the "Send" command that God was giving me. "I know and I think you know, Bud. Our time together is coming to a close. I just keep hoping for a miracle and that these shots will help you to feel better and give us more time. But that glimmer of hope is getting dimmer and dimmer."

Sim moved a bit in my lap and extended his paw to me, making a small whine. "We can sit here and hold hands if you want. You let me know when you're ready to go night-night." I held his paw in my hand, stroking it gently. No words were necessary now, only the closeness. As I sat there with him, I went over all the good times we had together. How he could make me laugh, how he could make me

proud, how many things he taught me, and most of all, that unconditional love he gave me without ever a question. He pulled his paw
out of my hand and sat up, pressing his head under my chin.

"What do you think, Bud? Is it time for night-night?" He gave
me the Shih Tzu swallow. I got up from the chair and took him
outside just to be sure he could relieve himself for the night. He did,
and we came back into the house. I got him one of his favorite treats.
"Do you want to walk to the bedroom, or do you want me to carry
you, Bud?" He took a few steps next me in perfect heel position and
stayed that way as we walked down the hall. I put him in his crate.
"You sleep tight now. I'll see you in the morning," I told him, mus-
tering up the most cheerful tone I could manage.

I tossed and turned for a while, wondering if the trip to
Brookside Road Animal Hospital would be a round trip for Sim or
only one way. Finally, I drifted off to sleep.

I heard Frank's alarm go off. It was about 4:45. "I'll get up, take
Sim out, feed him, and take my shower. You take a few more winks
and I'll call you so you can get ready."

Frank got out of bed and almost simultaneously I heard Frank
say, "Oh, Sim!" as a putrid smell hit my nostrils.

"What's wrong? Is Sim OK?"

"He just had an accident in his crate, and he's not trying to get
away from it." I heard Sim let out a weak whine. I started to get up.

"Stay there, Peg. I have to get him out of the crate before we can
do anything else."

"Let me know as soon as I can help." Frank carefully got Sim
out of the crate. "I'm going to have to clean him up with the waterless shampoo."

"Is he really bad?"

"No. Only a little bit."

"All right. You take care of him, and I'll clean up the crate."

"I hate to have you do that, Peg. It's really stinky."

I chuckled. "Like I didn't know that already. I'll just get a gar-
bage bag and throw away the bedding that is badly soiled. I'll see
if there is anything worth saving. Poor little guy. You know that he
would never do that unless something was very wrong."

I cleaned up the crate while Frank took Sim out. I then took my shower and got ready for our appointment with Dr. Crouser.

"How is Sim now, Frank?"

"Not great. He only ate about a quarter of his breakfast, and I had to help him. He would lick at it a little bit and then seem confused."

I made a deep sigh, resignation hitting me with its full force. "I guess it's time," I said, noting the double meaning in what I had just said.

"I'll put Sim in the car on the back seat unless you want him in your lap."

"I think he'll be more comfortable where he can stretch out."

We were about halfway to Brookside Road when Sim whined and extended his paw. I reached back to him, and he placed his paw in the palm of my hand. That seemed to reassure him, and he relaxed. He appeared to be sleeping.

"Only four more lights, Sim," I told him. Frank laughed. "I count the lights every time we come here. I don't think he understands, but it makes me feel better."

"You have such a charming way about how you handle him, Peg." I didn't answer. I could feel the tears filling my eyes.

We parked the car. Frank was going to let Sim relieve himself, and I went in to check in. I took a seat in the waiting room, and Frank and Sim came in. Frank put Sim on the floor and sat next to me. Sim circled a bit, and his back paws were knuckled under. The tears that I had been fighting started to stream down my cheeks. I heard Dr. Crouser's voice behind me say cheerfully, "Good morning."

Frank and I both mumbled a greeting, but he didn't hear us. "Good morning," Dr. Crouser said again as he came closer and could see Sim and our expressions. He gently said, "Follow me." We went into the carpeted room that I had become so familiar with and was beginning to dread.

"Sim isn't doing well this morning. He had an accident in his crate, and it was just about eight hours after his shot last night."

Dr. Crouser turned away from me and looked at Frank. "He had a lot of trouble eating this morning. I held him over his dish. He licked at it and then seemed confused. It was if he didn't know what he was supposed to do."

"How's my Simmy this morning?" Dr. Crouser asked, taking a long look at Sim. Sim did not respond to his voice. Dr. Crouser shook his keys. Sim made a very weak response to the noise. "Let me tickle his feet and see what we get," Dr. Crouser said as he touched each foot. Sim did not pull his feet away as he had done before. I could see the look of sadness on Dr. Crouser's face.

"I think we've run out of bullets, Dr. Crouser. Sim's put up a valiant fight, but I don't see even a glimmer of hope as of this morning."

I looked over at Frank. I was sitting on the floor with Sim in my lap, and Frank was sitting on a chair. The sadness in the room was so thick you could feel it in your bones. "What do you think, Frank?" I asked.

"It's up to you, pal. But I don't see where Sim is getting any better."

"Then I feel that it's time. I can't see Sim suffering just so we can have him around. That's not fair, and he shouldn't have to suffer any more."

"Have you considered what arrangements you want to make for Simmy?" Dr. Crouser asked softly.

Frank and I looked at each other and said in unison, "We want a private cremation."

"Then I'll make all the arrangements for you and will call you when Simmy comes back. The company we use is very good and very respectful. It is the one I have used for my dogs."

Dr. Crouser got up from the bench where he was sitting and said gently. "I'll go get things ready. I'll be back with some papers for you to sign." Sim sat up in my lap and pressed his head against my throat and chin.

"He looks so peaceful with you, Peg. He almost looks as if he's smiling." I could see that Frank was trying very hard to stay strong for me but was quickly losing the battle.

"I'm fine, Frank. I'm ready for this. I've been getting ready for this for quite a while now. It won't be easy, but I know it is the right thing to do for Sim. He has always trusted me, and he's trusting me right now. He doesn't know what is going to happen in a few minutes, but he knows that I have only ever done what is the best for him." With those words, Sim slid down into my lap and struck the swan pose.

Dr. Crouser walked in and handed me the papers that had to be signed. He said gently, "This just gives me permission to—" I could see he was as emotional as we were.

"Look at Sim, Dr. Crouser. There's the swan pose I've told you about." He gave Sim a pat. "I'm going to take him now." He picked Sim up and very carefully and gently cradled him in his arms. Frank and I followed him to the first exam room we came to.

Chapter 60

The weary sun cools mellow in the west
and calls to me to find a place where I can rest.
A place where they're expecting me
And I can be where I belong.

—"Hands Across the Seasons"

There was a beautiful blue blanket spread out on the exam table. It was the shade of blue that the sky turns only a couple of times a year when the air is clean and crisp. Dr. Crouser gently laid Sim on it. "Good boy, Simmy," he said. The tech asked him if he wanted her to put a catheter in Sim's front paw. "No. He doesn't need anything," Dr. Crouser said quietly.

I looked down at Sim. He looked very frail, but his gold and white coloring stood out beautifully on the blue blanket. It looked as though he was resting on a cloud in the sky with the sun lighting up his coat. Frank turned away and said, "I don't think I can do this," his voice shaking, tears in his eyes. I rubbed his back.

"That's OK. Go wait outside if you have to. I understand."

He gathered himself together and said, "I can do this. I want to be here with you and Sim." He stood on my left, and Dr. Crouser stood across the table from us. I saw him give Sim the injection. I began stroking Sim and put my forehead to his. He was in a semi-conscious state, but I felt that he knew I was there with him. *I'm here, Bud. I'm with you. You'll always be my best boy*, I thought. I was mind-melding again with him. The first time I mind-melded with

Sim had seemed so humorous, and I did it in a lighthearted way. This time it was very serious. These next few seconds or minutes would be our last. A quote flashed through my mind: "Sometimes there's nothing to be said and nothing to be done. Then, the deepest communication of all is just to be there" (Pema Chodron).

I don't know where I first heard or read it or why my mind retrieved it from seemingly out of nowhere, but it gave me focus.

This was my first time being with a dog that was being put down, and I wasn't sure what to expect. Frank had been the one to take our dogs when it was time. I always said my goodbyes at home and could take as long as I needed with them. Frank and other people who had done this told me that the dog goes very quickly. Many told me that their dog was gone before the injection was fully given.

I could feel Sim's heart beating as I stroked him. The minutes ticked by. I never raised my head. I just kept it pressed against his, trying to transfer my thoughts to him.

All of a sudden, Dr. Crouser said, "Simmy, go to the Bridge. Go see Jack." I startled as his voice broke the silence. Dr. Crouser was referring to the Rainbow Bridge and his greyhound, Jack, that had been recently put down. Sim's heart kept beating, getting a bit weaker.

"It's OK, Sim. The judge has given me the order to send you. Go guard the Bridge like a good boy. I'll meet you there when the time is right." And with that, his gallant heart stopped.

I looked up. Dr. Crouser removed the stethoscope from his ears and nodded. We all stood silent for a moment. Then I said to Dr. Crouser, "If there is anything that you need from Sim that will help other dogs, feel free to do whatever you have to do. Sim's legacy has been to teach all of us."

Dr. Crouser nodded. He knew what I meant. I remembered the conversation with him about how GME could be diagnosed. He now could take a sample of Sim's brain and have it tested if he wanted to.

He shook Frank's hand and gave me a big hug. "Simmy was very special to all of us, and he was lucky to have both of you to care so well for him. If he had been a bigger dog, it would have been much harder for you to have kept him going as well as you did for as long as you did."

"Thank you for that and all you have done for Sim and for me, Dr. Crouser."

I glanced back at Sim for the last time. He looked peaceful and relaxed. The little black rain cloud that I sometimes envisioned over head was gone. I knew I was going to miss him terribly. We had been through so much together and had built a bond so strong that even impending death was slowed down until both Sim and I had resolved ourselves to the moment.

On the drive home, Frank said that he hadn't cried that much when either his father or mother died.

"I didn't either, Frank. I think it's because we are so deeply sorrowful when someone dies that our mind makes us recall something that the person had done to offend us. It helps to ease the pain of the loss. But with an animal, especially one as special as Mr. Sims, they never do anything that we can look back at and be angry with them about. We look back at things and laugh and sometimes cry but never get angry because they never do anything deliberately hurtful."

"You know, Peg, I never thought of it that way, but it makes perfect sense to me."

Chapter 61

Life is like riding a bicycle. To keep your
balance, you must keep moving.

—Albert Einstein

When we got home, I gathered some of Sim's things up to take to Brookside Road Animal Hospital to be donated to the various local shelters. I was surprised that I was able to do it without breaking down and crying. I felt a certain special calm that comes when you know that you did the right thing, even though it may have been one of the hardest things you ever had to do in your life.

I sent out an e-mail to several of my friends to let them know about Sim. Some called rather than to send me a response to the e-mail. They all told me how badly they felt because Sim was so special. A few of them encouraged me to possibly write a book telling his story.

"When pigs fly," I would tell them.

On the following Wednesday, I got a call from Dr. Crouser. "Simmy's home now. You can come and pick him up."

"Great. Thanks, Dr. Crouser. By the way, did you take anything from Sim to be analyzed regarding the GME?"

There was a long pause. "No. I couldn't do it. I wanted to leave Simmy just as he was." I could hear the emotion in his voice.

"That's fine with me. I respect your decision. Frank and I will pick Sim up today."

We stopped at the hospital to pick up Sim's ashes and then left and headed for the airport. Pat's flight was arriving at 7:30 p.m. at Bradley International Airport. When she came walking through the airport to meet us, she gave us both big hugs. "He was just such a great little dog. I'm going to miss Mr. Sims," she said.

"Wait until we get home. You won't believe all the cards and flowers that have come since Monday. Even the neurologist called me as soon as she got the word on Monday. I thanked her, but I told her that I was convinced that the rabies shot was what caused Sim so much trouble. I also told her that one word from her about this was worth a million of mine. I'm only a trainer, but she is a neurologist at a leading veterinary hospital. She told me that they were seeing more and more of a connection between the rabies vaccine and dogs with compromised immune systems having very serious problems. She said that they were working on it. I said that if she wanted any information from me to please let me know. I would be more than glad to answer any questions she may have. She remembered the good records I kept on Sim since his problem with the rabies shot and that they might be of help at some point."

"Peg, that's great. Maybe Sim's experience will be helpful to other dogs and their owners," Pat said thoughtfully.

"I hope so, Pat."

In the next couple of weeks, more cards than I ever imagined, as well as flowers, kept arriving. The neighbors got together and purchased a "Memory Lamp" in honor of Mr. Sims. I was overwhelmed at the outpouring for him. So was Pat.

"It's like a person died," she said one morning over breakfast.

"I know. It's unbelievable."

"All I know is that because of what Mr. Sims taught me, I am a better trainer. I look at the whole dog. I ask about food, medication, physical problems, home life, and/or any lifestyle changes that have occurred in the household lately. These all contribute to the way a dog acts and responds. You can't learn these things from a text book. You learn them through experience. For instance, when a dog yawns, many times it is giving out a signal of being stressed. They're not yawning because they're sleepy."

"Really, I never knew that."

"Well, I noticed that Sim would yawn when I was trying to teach him something new. Then when I was studying to become a therapy dog evaluator, I read that yawning, among other behaviors, are indicators that a dog is stressed. That's just one of the many things Sim taught me. Patience was something else that he taught me. Patience with him, patience with other people, and patience with myself. When you are part of a team, as you are in competitive obedience, you never know when your partner may have an off day or even an off moment. You thought you had everything in order, practiced and planned out beautifully, and then something would go amiss that you never expected. Rather than get upset, Sim taught me to be patient and figure out why something didn't happen as expected. As much as I was his teacher, he was mine. I truly believe that our relationship was a once-in-a-lifetime one. I may eventually get another dog, but the relationship will be different, partly because each dog is different and partly because I am more educated through Mr. Sims and all the dogs I have trained and evaluated."

I wanted to go grocery shopping that day. I also wanted to pick up some thank-you notes to send to all the people that were so caring at this particularly difficult time. Pat came along, and we went through the store, putting things in my cart. There were some special meals that she wanted me to cook for her. I was more than happy to oblige her. As we were going along, I said to her that I was going to look at some individual thank-you notes for the girls at Brookside Road. I had picked up two boxes of candy and wanted two different thank-you cards, one for the day shift and one for the night/weekend shift. Pat decided to keep browsing around the store as I looked through the cards. I found one that was perfect. The others were OK but not exactly what I wanted.

"I've picked out two cards, but I'm not really happy with one of them."

"Come around the corner. There is a whole section of thank-you notes there," Pat told me.

I followed Pat as she turned right at the end of the aisle. There were many more cards to choose from.

"This is great, Pat. I'm sure I'll find one here."

As I looked through each card, I found one that was as good as the first one.

"I'm all set, Pat. Let me put the other one back on the rack." We both walked to the first display of cards, and I was putting back the card that I didn't want when Pat began to giggle.

"Oh my. You've got to see this. It's sooo funny!" Pat was looking at a display of gift bags near all the wrapping paper and ribbons that was on the opposite side of the aisle behind me. I turned to see what was so funny, only to have the breath knocked out of me.

Pat heard me gasp and turned to look at me. "What's wrong? Are you OK?" she asked. In the center of the display of gift bags, there was a large, shocking pink bag with orange polka dots. In the center of the bag, there was a pair of old-fashioned woman's bloomers that was raised so that it stood out. Written in large letters around the bloomers were the words "Sassy Pants."

"That was Sim's mother's name, Pat. I don't believe it. That little guy is letting me know he's here with me. I guess he approves of the cards I picked out." We both laughed and turned to go to the checkout.

I'm not sure if it was a sound that the shopping cart made or if something in it shifted, but I could swear I heard Sim give his little "I'm very pleased with myself" sneeze.

The End

Epilogue

Don't cry because it's over,
smile because it happened.

—Dr. Seuss

"And so this closes the last chapter of a twelve-and-a-half-year love affair between a dog trainer who was just starting out and had a lot to learn, and the plucky little Shih Tzu that needed a second chance, who literally became her business partner and mentor."

Every so often in our lives there are times when everything lines up perfectly, and we have an experience that leaves an ever lasting impression on us. It might be the day that you met your spouse and it was love at first sight. It might be the day that you left for a destination just a little later than you wanted to and found out that, had you left at the time you wanted, you would have been involved in some sort of serious calamity. You might have bought a scratch lottery ticket on a whim, and it was worth one thousand dollars or bet on a horse that appeared to have no chance of winning and it won the race by ten lengths, paying a bundle to win. When we think about these experiences, we say, "It was fate" or "It was meant to be."

The relationship that Mr. Sims and I shared was one of those wonderful, once-in-a-lifetime experiences when, for both of us, it was meant to be. I rescued him from a very abusive situation. He came into my life when I felt uncertain about my physical recovery and our financial stability. Other than teaching and showing him in competitive obedience, I won't try to take credit for who he was. He was born that way and just needed a loving, nurturing environment for his wonderful temperament to develop and flourish. He taught me to be a much better trainer than I would have been without the experience of working with him. As I experimented with different techniques, he taught me what would work well and what would not. If he was averse to something, he would give me a look that I learned meant, "Did you see what I said?" Dogs cannot verbalize what they are feeling, but they can communicate their feelings through their body language. Sim taught me that language. I was not the fastest learner of this new language, but he was very forgiving and patient with me. I, in turn, learned the value of patience as I taught him various skills. One of my favorite sayings was and still is, "Don't give me the labor pains, just give me the baby." When working with people and dogs who have no idea where to begin the training process, that saying could never be appropriate. I had to learn to restrain myself and become more easygoing. We became a team, working together and teaching each other as we both progressed in training.

Learning and using this very important skill helped me to have an understanding of the dogs that were brought to me for evaluation. It also strengthened my resolve of "peeling the onion" to work on getting to the heart of their problems. My job usually is to act as translator between the dog and its owner. Many times the dog is speaking very clearly, but the owner humanizes the behavior and a culture clash occurs. For instance, an owner might tell me that the dog is very finicky about eating their food and will only eat it if the owner adds table scraps. After asking the owner some questions, such as does the dog have any intestinal issues or symptoms that might indicate allergies, it more than likely turns out that the food is disagreeing with the dog. The dog can't tell us that the food makes him feel poorly after eating. When we add table scraps or something else to entice the dog to eat the offending food, it overrides the dog's natural instincts to avoid it.

Sim and I worked together as equal partners. We alternated the role of teacher and student. Many times, I would have to be his voice, especially when it involved his health issues. And many times, he would give me the silent security I needed when I found myself in a less than comfortable situation, such as my hospital stay, broken ankle, and recuperations. We shared an unbreakable bond throughout our time together. Of course, there were times when there was equal frustration when he didn't understand me and I didn't understand him. But we worked through these times, and it just made our link stronger. In any relationship, there are always conflicts, but when they are resolved, it only serves to open up a closer, more meaningful connection. And most important of all, we brought each other joy and support every day, through good times and stressful ones.

I have been surprised to learn from many people the memorable impression that he left on them. Several of my former clients have come back to me with their new puppies. Many of them will reminisce about Mr. Sims. He is mainly remembered as being the "Manners Police." They will say to me, "Do you remember when we were trying to teach my dog sit stays or down stays and when they would break the stay, Mr. Sims would look as much as to say, 'What is your problem? It's not that difficult.' Or when he would keep law and order in the group classes when a dog would become unruly?" It almost sounded as though they were talking about a favorite person.

Sim left such a strong impression on Donna that even now, when she comes to my house to deliver cosmetics, she will sometimes have tears in her eyes when I greet her at the door. She will tell me that, "It's one of those moments where I just expect to see Sim sitting at the door to greet me." And she often thinks about how Sim somehow knew when she was coming and would wait patiently for her to arrive. She has gone through some very difficult times, and Sim always seemed to sense and know when to give her some extra attention.

In writing Sim's story, it brought back many beautiful memories and the wonderful richness he brought into my life during the years that I had him. He taught me to have a discriminating eye with every dog I come in contact with. Each dog is an individual, with his or her own special style and personality. Even within the same breed of dog, each one is unique. It is up to us to learn and respect this. They say that a dog is man's best friend. I hope that this book makes this concept easier to understand and that by recognizing this, we all can develop the deep relationship with our beloved dogs that both we and they deserve.

I recently read the following poem. Although it is meant to be about a true friendship between people, it puts into perspective the deep relationship our pets offer to us. It is up to us to accept it graciously.

Friends

To offer trust in times of need,
To see misfortune through,
To feel the pain when you are cut
Because they bleed some too.
To make no judgment heedlessly,
To defend from idle talk,
To know that only you can wear
The shoes in which you walk.
To share a tear in sadness,
To be first with a hand,
To be forgiving of mistakes
Because they understand.
To only be a call away
To hear you laugh or cry,
To make your living better
And mourn you when you die.
There is no greater tribute
To which one can ascend
Than to earn the simple title—
The one that's called a friend.
(C. Tommy Hay)

About the Author

Peggy Lovelock (left) has been a professional dog trainer with over twenty years' experience with dogs of all ages, breeds, and with all kinds of challenges. She has been certified as an American Kennel Club Canine Good Citizen trainer and evaluator, a Delta Society trainer and evaluator, and a Therapy Dog trainer and evaluator after passing their testing requirements. She is also an advanced titled dog obedience exhibitor.

Her specialty is one-on-one training. She felt that this was needed in her area because there were many group classes but none that gave personal attention to both the dog and its owner without the distraction of other dogs and handlers. It was in this setting that she met Melva Michaelian (right), an English teacher and published author, and her Cairn terrier, Cappy. Melva had taken Cappy to a group class but felt that he needed the one-on-one attention that Peggy offered. After the success of her first lesson, she asked Peggy if she ever thought of writing a book about her training methods. And this conversation became the genesis of *Rescuing an Angel: Heel, Mr. Sims, Heal*. With Melva's guidance, Peggy was able to write the story of how she and Mr. Sims had taught each other about building a strong, loving partnership. Her training techniques and insights in this book should be of benefit to all dog owners.